Simone Weil and Theology

Simone Weil and Theology

A. Rebecca Rozelle-Stone
and
Lucian Stone

B L O O M S B U R Y
LONDON • NEW DELHI • NEW YORK • SYDNEY

Bloomsbury T&T Clark

An imprint of Bloomsbury Publishing Plc

50 Bedford Square
London
WC1B 3DP
UK

175 Fifth Avenue
New York
NY 10010
USA

www.bloomsbury.com

First published 2013

British Library Cataloguing-in-Publication Data
A catalogue record for this books is available from the British Library.

ISBN: HB: 978-0-5675-3724-9
PB: 978-0-5674-5383-9
PDF: 978-0-5676-0946-5
ePub: 978-0-5674-2430-3

Typeset by Newgen Imaging Systems Pvt Ltd, Chennai, India
Printed and bound in Great Britain

For
Thomas Alexander, Anthony Steinbock, and Stephen
Tyman, three exemplary teachers who embody and
inspire the love of wisdom

154
ASCENSION (not Weil's terme, but still useful v-a-v Aug. 148 159
the MORAL 136-52

CONTENTS

CF.SK: vs. "the immediate" 156→157
GOD 150
Tragedy 152 ~

* see also
The Beauty That Saves, ed., Springsted
111.8509
W 429 b
at free Library

ACKNOWLEDGMENTS

Our thinking about Simone Weil has benefited in immeasurable ways from our participation at the annual colloquies hosted by the American Weil Society. The members of the society and the participants at the annual colloquies are always patient, thoughtful, and convivial. It was during these annual meetings that many of the ideas in this present volume came to fruition, and for that we are thankful. We also want to express our appreciation and gratitude to E. Jane Doering, Larry Schmidt, and Eric O. Springsted who have been especially generous with their valuable support and considerable wisdom about Weil's life and thought. Finally, we want to thank Charles Miller who is an open and attentive interlocutor on all theological matters, offering us many inspirations as we worked through ideas presented in this book.

A. Rebecca Rozelle-Stone and Lucian Stone
Grand Forks, ND

ABBREVIATIONS

FLN   *First and Last Notebooks*, trans. Richard Rees. London: Oxford University Press, 1970.

FW   *Formative Writings 1929–1941*, trans. Dorothy Tuck McFarland and Wilhelmina van Ness. Amherst: University of Massachusetts Press, 1987.

GG   *Gravity and Grace*, trans. Emma Crawford and Mario von der Ruhr. London: Routledge, 2002.

IC   *Intimations of Christianity among the Ancient Greeks*, trans. E. C. Geissbuhler. London: Routledge, 1988.

LOP   *Lectures on Philosophy*, trans. Hugh Price. Cambridge: Cambridge University Press, 1978.

LP   *Letter to a Priest*, trans. Arthur Wills. London: Routledge, 2002.

NB   *The Notebooks of Simone Weil*, 2 vols, trans. Arthur Wills. London: Routledge & Kegan Paul, 2004.

NR   *The Need for Roots*, trans. Arthur Wills. London: Routledge, 2002.

OL   *Oppression and Liberty*, trans. Arthur Wills and John Petrie. Amherst: University of Massachusetts Press, 1973.

SL   *Seventy Letters*, trans. Richard Rees. New York: Oxford University Press, 1965.

SNL   *On Science, Necessity, and the Love of God*, trans. Richard Rees. London: Oxford University Press, 1968.

SWA   *Simone Weil: An Anthology*, ed. Siân Miles. New York: Weidenfeld and Nicolson, 1986.

SWC   *Simone Weil on Colonialism*, ed. and trans. J. P. Little. New York: Rowman and Littlefield, 2003.

SWR   *Simone Weil Reader*, ed. George A. Panichas. Wakefield, RI and London: Moyer Bell, 1977.

WG   *Waiting for God*, trans. Emma Craufurd. New York: HarperCollins, 2001.

Introduction:
On being a paradox

To think on God, to love God, is nothing else than a certain way of thinking on the world.

SIMONE WEIL

Simone Weil once wrote, "The Gospel contains a conception of human life, not a theology."[1] By this statement she did not intend a criticism. On the contrary, she was proposing a new orientation toward sacred text in which flesh and blood encounters, rather than propositions about the divine, are revealed. As philosophers, theologians, and literary critics have long understood, there are always interpretive difficulties to be faced whenever we read sacred texts, or in general, whenever we read texts that are poetic in nature. This is partly owing to the fact that a poem (whether sanctified or not) grants a glimpse of human life in a singular way that ruptures our usual systems of perceiving and knowing. Alain Badiou has helpfully described why contemporary audiences are especially handicapped in reading poetic texts:

> Poetry, alas, grows more and more distant. What commonly goes by the name of 'culture' forgets the poem. This is because poetry does not easily suffer the demand for clarity, the passive audience, the simple message. The poem is an intransigent exercise. It is devoid of mediation and hostile to the media.[2]

A poem, that is, can foster an epiphany but does not didactically disclose a set of facts; poetry "does not consist in communication," but it awaits us to be encountered as an event, and it even injects a kind of silence into the cacophonies that mask our banalities.[3] We propose that Simone Weil's approach to the Gospels is the very approach that should be taken to her own writings, poetic in mission if not in form; she does not communicate a theology but instead reveals a conception of human life, albeit in paradoxical ways.

Thinking about poetry has more to teach us, especially in preparation for encountering the writings of Simone Weil. How does a good poem come about?

Weil herself had this to say about the composition of a poem: it requires "thought without language, for the choice of words takes place without the help of words."[4] In this sense, writing a poem is akin to apophasis, a playful short-circuiting of the ordinary frameworks and discourses that structure and organize our everyday thoughts and speech. Elsewhere, she contends that writing in general is "like translating," since it consists of a "negative operation" whereby we wait, when we are composing, "for the right word to come of itself at the end of our pen, while we merely reject all inadequate words."[5] This process may sound, on the one hand, too easy to be true, or on the other, an impossible task. What kind of inspiration is this? Can this "waiting" really guarantee results? Rainer Maria Rilke (whom Weil read) understood the difficulty of writing poetry, and in *The Notebooks of Malte Laurids Brigge*,[6] he described a negative process that closely mirrored Weil's depiction. Rilke grasped that a good poem does not simply express immediate feelings, just as it does not merely recall experiences through sentimental nostalgia, or proffer conscious reflections as such. Crucially, after many, varied, and contradictory experiences in one's life, there must be a stage of forgetting that precedes what he called "blood-remembering." It is from blood-remembering that good poetry falls, like words out of the tip of a pen, or like ripe fruit from an ancient tree.[7] We quote him at length on the process by which one can write a verse of poetry:

> For the sake of a single verse, one must see many cities, men and things, one must know the animals, one must feel how the birds fly and know the gesture with which the little flowers open in the morning. One must be able to think back to roads in unknown regions, to unexpected meetings and to partings one had long seen coming; to days of childhood that are still unexplained . . . and it is not yet enough if one may think of all this. One must have memories of many nights of love, none of which was like the others, of the screams of women in labor. . . . But one must

also have been beside the dying, must have sat beside the dead in the room with the open window and the fitful noises. And still it is not yet enough to have memories. One must be able to forget them when they are many and one must have the great patience *to wait* until they come again. For it is not yet the memories themselves. Not till they have turned to blood within us, to glance and gesture, nameless and no longer to be distinguished from ourselves—not till then can it happen that in a most rare hour the first word of a verse arises in their midst and goes forth from them.[8]

A verse containing a true conception of human life, whether within poetry or sacred text, is not manufactured consciously. Given Rilke's account, the requisite elements appear to be: vulnerable and attentive engagement in the world; consent to suffer the uncertainties, contradictions, mysteries, and necessities of mortal life; formation of thoughts and memories of those experiences; and willingness to let go of those considerations in order for *an incarnation* to take place—an embodiment of the past encounters, which then seep into our movements, gazes, conversations, and, occasionally, our verses, sometimes unbeknownst to us. There is something paradoxical about detaching from our carefully constructed narratives in order for a truly inspired word to arrive, outside of our active energies. The incessant systematizing and intellectualizing of experience must at some point give way to releasing that rational control of what presented itself to our senses for it, metaphorically speaking, to "mature on the tree." In addition to this detachment, then, there must also be patience for the ripening. For as Rilke also wrote, "One ought to wait and gather sense and sweetness a whole life long, and a long life if possible, and then, quite at the end, one might perhaps be able to write ten lines that were good."[9]

Is it not to be expected that a process which requires detachment, renunciation of will, vulnerability, and patience would yield a form that harbors the "music of silence"?[10] A form that quietly folds in upon itself? Badiou tells us that "the poem is what Mallarmé called 'restrained action.'"[11] It is opposed to the language of communication, information, images, and "universal reportage," which is so predominant in our time. In this way, "the poem is a halting point," in that "it makes language halt within itself."[12] It effects a deposing of its own subject-matter through unexpected pairings

and alliances and therefore effects a similar deposing of the reader
of the poem. It disconcerts us. But this does not mean that the poem
says nothing. Poetic writing—and we contend that Simone Weil's
writings fall into this category—grants access to truths, but does
so precisely by denying the direct relation of thought to objects.
Again, Badiou puts this well: "The poem is a negative machin-
ery, which utters being, or the idea, at the very point where the
object has vanished."[13] In other words, the poem confronts us with
a certain and undeniable presence, which we are disabled from
objectifying.

If Simone Weil's writings largely do fall within the province of
poetry and what has just been said about poetry, we may be better
able to understand why, for philosophers and theologians who seek
systems and explicable objects, Weil's thought has been, as Maurice
Blanchot said of her work, "so irritating that it seems to them
scarcely a thought."[14] She is infamously not averse to employing
contradictory and paradoxical statements, such as: we must uproot
ourselves, we need to be rooted; God exists, God does not exist; we
must love that which does not exist, et cetera. Nevertheless, as with
poetry, these opposing affirmations perform an important "halting" operation that is an altogether different procedure than the
sort of mental arrest that is the product of media clichés, sophistic
political rhetoric, and cheap, grotesque, ubiquitous infotainment.
While the latter numbs and dulls our attunement to humans and
the world around us, reinforcing mental defenses and distractions
constituted by a plentitude of objectifications and easy classifica-
tions, the former, poetic way of halting thought acts instead as a
ground-clearing, opening an important and necessary space for a
fresh consideration of a phenomenon. The paradox "experienced
to the very depths of being tears us heart and soul," such that
"a kind of loosening takes place";[15] in other words, it serves as a
break from the mundane, ordinary way of viewing the world. It
challenges our assumed categories and points to truth beyond the
world of ordered and unproblematic objects. It positively creates a
silence to "speak" what has not been spoken and what *cannot* be
spoken in the language of consensus; it sets up a silence, therefore,
in order for us to hear above the din.

Patience, then, and a willingness to be deposed as sovereign subjects are requisite traits for approaching Weil's writings and the
ideas that are evoked therein. Additionally, we propose that the

very cornerstone of her thought, especially as gleaned from her notebooks and later writings, is precisely an expression of this sort of patient waiting (a vigilance that she often termed *attention*) that demanded and further enabled the subjective deposition (or what she called *decreation*). Attention and decreation together represent the crucial elements of the "conception of human life" revealed by the Gospels to Weil's mind. There is no systematic elaboration of a theology in either the Gospels or in her own writings. However, as Blanchot rightly asks, "How can one not be struck, in reading certain of her writings . . . by the tone that is hers and by the manner in which she makes her assertions: with a certitude so remote from herself, so distant from all proof and all guarantee, yet so restrained and nearly effaced that one indeed feels one cannot refuse her a hearing . . ."?[16] That is to say, Weil is a creator of fruitful silences, but she accomplishes these by means of a series of affirmations written with an air of detached certitude, many of which do profoundly contradict one another. Blanchot is correct also when he says that Weil leaves the contradictory affirmations as they are, "without seeming to renounce any of them, much less bring them into agreement. Affirming is often for Simone Weil a way of questioning or a way of testing."[17]

Therefore, if we cannot speak of a Weilienne theology in the usual way, we can perhaps describe the affirmations about spiritual matters that refuse systemization and coherence, as a theology that suspends itself, or what we would call a *reflective-negative theology* or an *atheology*. In order to consider her atheology as it relates to waiting, let us return for the moment to her statement, "The Gospel contains a conception of human life, not a theology." This claim, written in her New York notebook in 1942, is immediately followed by this analogy:

If I light an electric torch at night out of doors I don't judge its power by looking at the bulb, but by seeing how many objects it lights up. The brightness of a source of light is appreciated by the illumination it projects upon non-luminous objects. The value of a religious or, more generally, a spiritual way of life is appreciated by the amount of illumination thrown upon the things of this world. Earthly things are the criterion of spiritual things.[18]

A refusal to look away from the light bulb, according to Weil, causes a kind of blindness, in the same way that attempts to objectify and render visible experiences of the divine will necessarily distort, falsify, and indeed prevent any epiphanic arrival. In other words, Weil warns that we can only truthfully speak of and understand spiritual matters by patiently keeping our gaze on what can rightfully be *seen*—the natural phenomena we encounter on a daily basis.

Nevertheless, this prescribed attention is for Weil impersonal and detached, like the movement of Rilke's forgetting of constructed memories, and that detachment comes from the contradictory experiences and perspectives visited all along the way. The paradoxes and contradictions with which we are confronted (when we are attentive to them) prevent a greedy and facile attachment to *selective* experiences, memories, and claims—that is, dogmatism and absolutism. Instead, a commitment to regard everything that presents itself to our senses, fully and carefully, results in the sort of patience and clarity that permits the embodiment of the paradoxes. One may not be aware of the new disposition, but Weil argues that others will be able to see the manifestations of this transformation, or what Rilke would call the effects of blood-remembering.

Simone Weil's atheology is, of course, paradoxical, as we will demonstrate in Chapter 1, because the divine can only be "known" through absence and void; in fact, a particular kind of atheism may be more compatible with this approach than any orthodox theism. While Weil refrains from positing much about God or "the supernatural," her frequent references and seeming affirmations of the divine are occasioned by her ruminations on "impossible" or paradoxical situations, as well as her own well-documented mystical experiences.

But at its most, religion for Weil is simply an attentive-decreative orientation to the world. This is what she means when she says,

> It should also be publicly and officially recognized that religion is nothing else but a looking. Insofar as it claims to be anything else, it is inevitable that it should either be shut up inside churches, or that it should stifle everything in every other place where it is found.[19]

Only the world here below, including inert matter and flesh, is the universal test and filter of what is real. But this looking-at-the-world requires an apprenticeship similar to that of learning to read and write poetry. The looking that Weil calls attentiveness involves losing interested or greedy perspective, aided by the inevitable encounter of paradoxical situations and realizations.

For these reasons, this book is presented to readers as a journey of looking at different paradoxical aspects of experience, particularly those that were significant to Simone Weil, seeing how they cumulatively cast the shadow of her atheology. In the following chapters, we will explore some of the most perplexing paradoxes in Weil's thought, not to resolve their underlying tensions, but to make them more pronounced, so that they may do their work of ground-clearing. As we have described, this method, after all, appears to be Weil's own approach to the world. As Leslie Fiedler, who introduced the English translation of Weil's *Attente de Dieu* (*Waiting for God*), noted, "The outrageous (from the natural point of view) ethics of Christianity, the paradoxes on which it is based, are a scandal to common sense; but we have protected ourselves against them by turning them imperceptibly into platitudes. It is Simone Weil's method to revivify them, by recreating them in all their pristine offensiveness."[20] It is our hope that this book may evoke needed silences and fruitful spaces in contemporary theological and philosophical discourses; enduring these voids by refusing simplistic conclusions or syntheses may well be the reader's own test.

1
Atheism and mysticism

"*I will rise now and go about the city,*
in the streets and in the squares;
I will seek him whom my soul loves."
I sought him, but found him not.

SONG OF SOLOMON 3:2

You came. And you did well to come.
I was waiting for you; your fire burns
my heart, it flames.
I forgive you all the endless
hours that you were away.

SAPPHO[1]

Crises

In his discussion about the meaning of the Torah in Jewish mysticism Gershom Scholem interjects, mid-sentence, matter-of-factly that "mysticism as a historical phenomenon is a product of crises."[2] He does not go on to identify particular historical crises, describe or classify these crises, nor does he explain the causal relationship he presupposes the reader already understands and with which she concurs. He merely goes on to say:

Mystics are men [*sic*] who by their own inner experience discover new layers of meaning in their traditional religion. When their experience and speculation did not lead them to break with the traditional institutions of their religion, it was inevitable that they should come to grips with two questions: how were they to find their own experience reflected and anticipated in the sacred texts? And: how could their view of the world be brought into harmony with the view accepted by their own tradition?[3]

The figure of Simone Weil among the mystics generally speaking, and Christian mystics more specifically, both affirms and problematizes aspects of Scholem's framing of mysticism as a historical phenomenon.

To begin, contrary to Scholem's assertion that mystical visions occur to practitioners of established religious traditions—except for some contemporary mystics who dissociate from all ties to traditional religions[4]—Weil, in the strictest sense, was from the outset an outsider to religious tradition. Although her family was Jewish, they were certainly not believing and practicing Jews. In fact, they were agnostic. Weil herself attests, "I was brought up by my parents in a complete agnosticism, and I never made the slightest effort to depart from it . . ."[5] As Leslie Fiedler notes in his introduction to *Waiting for God*, "Though her ancestors had been Jewish, the faith had quite disappeared in her immediate family . . ."[6] Weil's immediate family had assimilated into secular modern French culture. Consequently, Weil's thought was more influenced by classical Greek sources than the Torah.[7]

Toward the end of her life, in a letter written to Father Joseph-Marie Perrin in May 1942—which has since come to be referred to simply as her "Spiritual Autobiography"—Weil confesses that "never at any moment" in her life did she seek for God.[8] This makes perfect sense following Scholem's logic insofar as it would be peculiar for someone raised agnostic and outside of a traditional religious community to seek after that which grounds said tradition, especially as it is expressed in its sacred literature and rites. But in her retrospective overview of her own life—as she and her family fled France due to the Vichy regime and the eventual Nazi occupation—Weil makes these surprising remarks:

I *always* adopted the Christian attitude as the only possible one. I might say *I was born, grew up, and I always remained within the Christian inspiration*. While the very name of God had no part in my thoughts, with regard to the problems of this world and this life I shared the Christian conception in an explicit and rigorous manner.[9]

In this striking passage, Weil insists that although she was not reared as a Christian within the Church—and thus, Christianity as such was not a direct influence on her thinking and social-political activities—she later came to perceive all of her thoughts and actions to have been in perfect alignment with what she deemed to be a Christian outlook. All of her thoughts and deeds, that is, were unconsciously Christian. "From my earliest childhood," she wrote in the same letter, "I *always* had . . . the Christian idea of love for one's neighbor, to which I gave the name justice—a name it bears in many passages of the Gospel and which is so beautiful."[10]

One might be struck by the fact that she perceived within herself a staggering consistency—one that spans from her early childhood until the last years of her life. And, indeed, commentators and scholars never tire of including detailed accounts of her biography as evidence of her spiritual aptitude and intellectual genius;[11] for them—and we find it impossible to avoid this perspective entirely ourselves—the truth and potency of Weil's thought is supported by her relentless embodiment of those ideals. Consequently, many have called her a "saint"[12] and her biography reads almost like hagiography—for example, at the age of five, in a show of compassion for the French troops at the front in World War I cut off from rations of sugar, "she refused to eat sugar."[13] Her life is filled with such self-sacrificial decisions—often simpatico with those who suffer at the hands of injustice and affliction—until and perhaps including her untimely death.

For our purposes, it is important to remember that these gestures were only latently determined to be "Christian" by Weil, who, prior to making this declaration, had three mystical experiences (to which we will turn at the end of this chapter). Technically, then, there was no causal relationship between Christianity as such and her thoughts and actions antecedent to her mystical encounters—the first of which occurred in 1935, when she was 26 years old. That is to say, temporally speaking, these thoughts and actions could not have been *consciously* informed by participation in Christian sacraments, adherence to Christian doctrine, rooted in Christian belief, committed to Christian principles, et cetera.

That being said, her insistence that she was always a Christian evinces a trend in mysticism observed by Scholem, namely, after their mystical encounter(s) mystics seek "to find their own experience reflected and anticipated in the sacred texts." But Weil extends this reading of the sacred text not only to explain her latter mystical experiences but also to reflect her prior conduct as being Christian. Thus, in the Gospels Weil finds what she previously held to be "justice" in its articulation of love of neighbor. In this way she roots herself *within* the Christian tradition. So much so, in fact, that she writes: "Of course I knew quite well that my conception of life was Christian. That is why it never occurred to me that I could enter the Christian community. *I had the idea that I was born inside*."[14]

It is this last point that brings us to Weil's sense of the crises of her times and to which, perhaps, her mysticism, as Scholem hypothesized, was a direct though unintentional response. As has been mentioned, even as a child she paid uncanny attention to the social and political ills in French society such as poverty, hunger, poor working conditions, and, of course, war. As she matured, her awareness and involvement with these and related issues intensified. This development coincided with the growing disparities between the rich and the poor, the tensions between the workers and the bourgeoisie, the proliferation of bureaucratic corruptions and abuses of power, nihilism, capitalism, the rise of fascism, and, most significantly, the emergence of Hitlerism.[15] Crucially, Weil's explicit turn to religious thinking was not, as many might cynically presuppose, a desperate attempt to find consolation from fear and frustration caused by these worldly affairs. To her reckoning, Christianity is not—or at least properly speaking ought not to be misconstrued as—a transcendental refuge from the hardships of lived experience. Instead, Weil's seizure by Christianity paradoxically rooted her more firmly *in* the world. She writes,

> Our neighbor, our friends, our religious ceremonies, and the beauty of the world do not fall to the level of unrealities after the soul has had direct contact with God. On the contrary, it is only then that these things become real. Previously they were half dreams. Previously they had no reality.[16]

Thus, Weil's religious awakening resulted in two radical conclusions. First, Christianity—or rather, Christ—is exemplary of the unflinching attention necessary for addressing the problems in this world. Second, attention not only led her to acknowledge the spiritual crisis afflicting the world at large (a commonplace observation for religious devotees) but also that which contaminated religious institutions such as the Church. In this manner—and in agreement with Scholem's observation—it can be said that Weil's entire outlook was a direct and unflinching confrontation with the crises at hand, which included: social-political injustice, intellectual and spiritual nihilism, and the corruption of religion, especially the Catholic Church. And Weil experienced each of these personally.

In the sections to follow, we examine the development of Weil's diagnosis of these crises ("Idolatry," "The Great Beast," and "Religious and political anathema,"), as well as her prescribed responses: "Atheism as a form of purification," and "Mysticism."

Idolatry

Weil's thought was principally motivated by the perennial philosophical pursuit of truth. More specifically, she fixated on the problem of discerning reality (truth) from appearance (opinion). Certainly, her attentiveness to the ills of the world gave urgency to this philosophical problem, for as she saw it, until this epistemological dilemma is resolved all varieties of injustices will be perpetuated and inflicted upon the world under the guises of "truth" or "reality," and by extension "justice," "goodness," and "beauty"— and all substrate value fields that traditionally fit within these categories.

As we have explained above, Weil personally felt the crises she diagnosed as afflicting human society. This epistemological-ethical issue came to a head when Weil struggled with the question of whether or not she should be baptized.[17] She had a strong affinity for the holy sacraments. "The sacraments," she wrote, "have a specific value, which constitutes a mystery in so far as they involve a certain kind of contact with God, a contact mysterious but real."[18] In order to properly partake in sacraments such as the Eucharist, however, she would have had to be baptized—that is, to formally join the institution of the Catholic Church.[19] But whereas she recognized the possibility of a *real* contact with God through the sacraments and other religious rituals, to her mind there is too much evidence that the Church, ironically, has a distorting effect upon the sacraments as they are institutionalized and thereby experienced by most practitioners. Consequently, she writes, "I think that most believers . . . approach the sacraments only as symbols and ceremonies."[20] This, she forcefully argued, is symptomatic of the very nature of the Church as a social institution and, as consequence, instead of drawing adherents away from selfish relativity toward real contact with God, only satisfies their baseness.

It is in this satisfying-function of the Church that we find clues to Weil's notion of idolatry, which was ultimately shaped by her reading of Plato.[21] Not surprisingly, then, she returns frequently to Plato's famous allegory of the cave, especially when demonstrating the gulf between the appearance of religiosity and true religiosity.[22] "There is a distinction between those who remain inside the cave, shutting their eyes and imagining the journey, and those who really take it."[23] Most, she observed, either unbeknownst to themselves or despite their conscious protestations to the contrary, do not bear the mark of having truly made the journey to God (or, Platonically speaking, truth). In short, people are inattentive. Attentiveness—as we will discuss in Chapter 4—is what is required to arrive at both epistemic truth and ethical practice. Weil's written work as well as her activism are best seen as attempts to reorient our gaze toward immanent and transcendent truth—or necessity/suffering and God respectively.

Simply put, according to Weil there is an incongruity between the individual and God born of metaphysical necessity. The very assertion of God—who for her is good before being powerful—is simultaneously the recognition of humankind's derivative status. As such, every individual self, or ego, is seen in relief of God. The Christian model for humanity, which we will explore in more detail in Chapter 2, is of course Jesus, especially as witnessed during the crucifixion. For our purposes at this time, what is most important to note is the strict dichotomy—metaphysically, epistemologically, and morally—between humans and God. (But Weil's acknowledgement of this bifurcation in no way should be interpreted as an excuse for human apathy, to not seek "the impossible" or to act as Jesus did.)

The ego—manifest through its earthly desires—seeks to be the center and therefore is inattentive to all else except insofar as those others or other things are mere means to the ego's end. Its natural perspective is, in other words, narrow and consumptive.

Theologically, this narrow perspective takes the form of forcing God (the impossible-to-conceive and the impersonal truth) to fit human demands and frameworks (what is conceived of as logically possible and personally gratifying). But Weil cautioned: "We must be careful about the level on which we place the infinite. If we place it on the level which is only suitable for the finite it will matter very little what name we give it."[24] If, then, there is an expressly theological concern for Weil, it entails the confusion of symbols and modes of religious hermeneutics and how they may or may not misappropriate (whether intentionally or unintentionally) God for their own purposes. She recognized how religious symbols too frequently and conveniently correspond to human aspirations, in contrast to the impossible demands of Christ's exemplarity.

> God and the supernatural are hidden and formless in the universe. It is well that they should be hidden and nameless in the soul. Otherwise there would be a risk of having something imaginary under the name of God (those who fed and clothed Christ did not know that it was Christ). . . . *Christianity (Catholic and Protestant) speaks too much about holy things.*[25]

Christ, in other words, is fetishized through self-fashioned and self-serving symbolic orders. "Man always devotes himself to an *order*. Only, unless there is supernatural illumination, this order has as its center either himself or some particular being or thing . . . with which he has identified himself. . . . It is a perspective order."[26] In fact, she attributes this fundamental theological error as the primary cause of all of the crises we listed above. As she writes, "The errors of our time come from Christianity without the supernatural,"[27] the absolutizing of the relative or the relativizing of the absolute.

Much of what has come under the guise of "religion" or "Christianity" is only so by name and in appearance. Rather than being authentically oriented away from the self/ego toward God, theological narratives, dogmas, doctrines, and their corresponding rites more often than not are purely self-serving. Even in matters expressly religious, subjectively, the pull of the ego proves far more resilient than the impossible and impersonal nature of God (truth/reality). Thus, Weil observed that the reality of Christ's example is eclipsed by the increasingly opaque symbols and linguistic

structures devised, paradoxically, for the purpose of discoursing
about and, one supposes, being drawn to God. Somewhat tragically, this confusion plagues the Church. As she writes, "If one asks
several priests whether such-and-such a thing is strictly an article of
faith, one obtains different, often dubitative, answers. That creates
an impossible situation . . ."[28] Ultimately, Weil argued, theology
necessarily fails at ensuring communion with God. Human language cannot capture God. The hermeneutic systems and symbols
theologians create become idols—that is, mistaken for God (or, in
a more strict sense, the theologians' and their adherents' self/ego
stands in God's place)—and religion (the graven image of the self)
is made into an idol. God is created in man's image[29] and not vice
versa as the case is otherwise theologically stated to be.

"Idolatry is," evoking the Platonic allegory yet again, "a vital
necessity in the cave" because it inevitably sets "narrow limits for
mind and heart."[30] Rather than being transparent symbols that
function by allusion, theological symbols are an ersatz of God. The
theological God acts like a Rorschach test. The viewer's perception
and/or construction of the theological blot on the page, metaphorically speaking, is far more self-disclosive than it is disclosive of
the supernatural. Nevertheless, theological authority asserts that
its symbolic order is in fact an, or rather, *the* accurate measure of
God. Socially and politically, in fact, it does come to function as
such because predictably, Weil contends, its theology appeases the
individual and collective ego, giving people firm ideas and concepts
they can latch onto and oftentimes use to explain and appease their
suffering.[31] The collective body of the Church reifies this symbolic
order; that is, the supposed sacrality of the symbols and rites is
mistaken as the very object of worship; appearance is taken as reality, the means are taken as the end.

Weil never tired of pointing out that what passes for religiosity
is frequently nothing more than hubris. In practice, obedience is
given to values derived from the self (e.g., greed, pride, etc.) and the
collective (e.g., nationalism, capitalism, etc.) and not those found
in the example of Christ (e.g., humility, charity, and love). In other
words, falsehood is the order of the day, and thus is the root of the
crises and the outright obliviousness to our own roles in creating
them.

[F]alsehood is an armour by means of which man often enables
what is unfit in him to survive events which, were it not for

such armour, would destroy it (thus pride manages to survive humiliations), and this armour is as it were secreted by what is unfit in order to ward off danger (in humiliation, pride makes thicker the inner falsehood which covers it). There is as it were a phagocytosis in the soul: everything which is threatened by time secretes falsehood in order not to die, and in proportion to the danger it is in of dying. That is why there is not any love of truth without an unconditional acceptance of death.[32]

Truth, in the Platonic sense, is transcendent and, therefore, universal and eternal. Philosophy, insofar as it is leading an examined life out of love of truth/wisdom, is the practice for dying and death.[33] It requires, in other words, a commitment to let go of false beliefs when they fail to stand up to the scrutiny of the intellect despite appeals to tradition, authority, or even the consequential suffering the self must endure in relinquishing otherwise self-serving positions. This is the meaning of self-sacrifice. Only those ideas and practices that stand up to the impersonal standards of being universally and eternally true should remain. The ego/self is not of this category according to Weil. In her metaphysics the self is a product of creation and thus is susceptible to temporality and mortality—though it disavows itself of this recognition. As Weil observed in the quotation above, those things that are most severely self-centered (false) and, hence, fated to die (e.g., authoritarianism, totalitarianism, etc.) resist the inevitable most vehemently—usually by force and violence.

The theological implications of this logic were clear to Weil. Returning to the question of baptism, she had to answer honestly what it would mean for her to join the Church (the collective). Would she then be forced to compromise the application of her intellect, for instance, and thus philosophical inquiry? Would she be an accomplice to the injustices and untruths shrouded by a false sense of religiosity?

Reflecting further upon her frustration from getting inconsistent and even contradictory answers to questions that she posed to a variety of priests, she concludes: "It does not seem that the Church can be infallible; for, in fact, it is continually evolving."[34] Unless one willingly turns a blind eye toward Church history, it is undeniable that the Church itself has demonstrated the fluctuations characteristic of the world of appearances. Its proclamations at any given point in time are opinions (*doxa*), not understanding (*noesis*), in the Platonic usage of those terms. Thus they change. Just as there is an inherent incongruity between man and God, then, there persists an incongruity between the Church and God. Weil argues that this basic distinction is lost in the aura of religiosity that is commonplace among the collective. As far as the Church goes, in fact, she contends that there is a mistaken belief that the Church, as the "mystical Body" is God incarnate—not Jesus. "But," she counters, "there is a slight difference, which is that Christ was perfect, whereas the Church is sullied by a host of crimes."[35]

The Great Beast

In her assessment of the Church, Weil was sympathetic to its susceptibility to corruption. It should not be forgotten, after all, that she was genuinely struggling with her decision to forego baptism. It was not an insincere pretense to critique the Church. So what was it that made the Church as such so vulnerable to distractions away from the divine?

As we have seen above, Weil argues that the root cause of our crises, spiritual or otherwise, is attachment to ego and the striving for self-satisfaction and self-preservation (immortality) at the expense of truth and justice. Somewhat paradoxically, we pursue our most egotistic desires, caprices, and delusions of grandeur more zealously within a collective. The collective—wherein a consensus is arrived, which panders to our basest desires, "the lowest common denominator"—provides us with a specious claim to legitimacy.

> There are two goods of the same denomination but radically different from each other: one which is the opposite of evil and the one which is absolute. The absolute has no opposite. The relative is not the opposite of the absolute; it is derived from it through a relationship which is not commutative. That which we want is the absolute good. That which is within our reach is the good which is correlated to evil. We betake ourselves to it by mistake. . . . It is the social which throws the color of the absolute over the relative. . . . Society is the cave. The way out is solitude.[36]

The above passage reiterates Weil's framework. Her conceptualization of Christianity is Platonic in the sense that the individual is the site of what we might call an existential schizophrenia: a material existence (the body) that is drawn toward the world and a spiritual existence (the soul) that, though tethered to the body, is drawn toward truth. What we *really* want—that is, in the soul—is absolute good (God). However, due to our bodily presence, gravity pulls us to the earth. The earth's horizon is limited by the ego's presence. Left unto herself, however, the individual stands a better chance for seeing her own limits and recognizing her errors. Immersed within the social, she is further deluded in her self-referential logic. For Weil, of course, the only answer to dualism is to surrender the ego pulled by gravity in the service of truth, goodness, justice, and beauty.

The call to surrender one's self/ego to God/the Good is predictably met with great resistance. It requires, after all, "an unconditional acceptance of death."[37] Sacrifice. An individual's existence seems more real than God experientially—especially when we factor in Weil's premise that we must love a God who is absent. *Common sense* dictates that one should and, indeed, only *can* love that which is present. Who we are—our identities—seem far more real in our lived experience than an invisible, impersonal God. But as we have seen, it is precisely this tension that is at the root of Christianity according to Weil. Following the basic Platonic structure, the fact that relative "goods" participate in the absolute Good is more problematic than if we were called upon to distinguish between the latter and an equivalent absolute Evil. Since relative goods imitate the Good they thus *appear* to be absolutely Good to an inattentive audience. Because the ego/self is not absolute but is itself a derivative of God through creation, attachment to these relative goods appears to have more veracity and is certainly more pragmatic.

The collective, or as Weil called it after Plato, the Great Beast,[38] seizes upon the selfish inclination born in human nature, exacerbating it by making it seem as if the collective's directives are in the interest of each individual. Although truth is not democratic, to recall Plato's contentions, the Great Beast makes it seem so by manipulating the ego's capacity to deceive itself (so as not to endure any discomfort). Individuals in the collective independently believe that "*I* am 'good' and 'just' in *my* present form." Life as presently lived goes unexamined. Even when crises are at hand, fault always lies at another's feet, is due to chance, "destiny," or, even, is

understood to be part of a larger Perfection. The Great Beast succeeds insofar as it sustains the illusion that it does not contradict
each individual's self-interests and that it, in fact, *furthers* each
individual's narrow desires. To the degree that it maintains this
appearance, the Great Beast functions as an ersatz divinity idolized
by the populace.

Here Weil takes recourse in philosophy. But as Plato presci-
ently noted, "[T]he majority cannot be philosophic."[39] The Great
Beast, like the Sophists to whom the ancient Greek philosophers
objected, does nothing other than teach (or preach as the case may
be) "the convictions that the majority express when they are gath-
ered together." The expressed "truth" of the collective is at best the
least common denominator. Plato continues in *Republic*:

> It's as if someone were learning the moods and appetites of a
> huge, *strong beast* that he's rearing—how to approach and
> handle it, when it is most difficult to deal with or most gentle
> and what makes it so, what sounds it utters in either condition,
> and what sounds soothe and anger it. Having learned all this
> through tending the beast over a period of time, he calls this
> knack wisdom, gathers his information together as if it were a
> craft, and starts to teach it. In truth, he knows nothing about
> which of these convictions is fine or shameful, good or bad, just
> or unjust, but he applies all these names in accordance with how
> the beast reacts—calling what it enjoys good and what angers it
> bad. He has no other account to give of these terms.[40]

Instead of climbing out of the allegorical cave, or in Weil's
Christian terms, standing before the impersonal and impossible
God, the individual finds solace in the warm embrace of the collective whose message conveniently matches the individual's base
tendencies. Moreover, the individual is easily managed—manip-
ulated—by the collective.[41] Rather than remaining steadfast in
search of truth, goodness, beauty, and justice, "[c]onscience," Weil
writes, "is deceived by the social."[42] This brings to mind another
Socratically inspired Christian philosopher, Søren Kierkegaard,
who quipped, "A crowd is . . . untruth."[43] Truth and, by extension
for Weil, ethicality—true religiosity—are too often abandoned in
favor of the Great Beast.

"The collective is the object of all idolatry . . ."[44] Selfish individuals happily join organizations and put their full faith in them insofar as they shield them from having to face the reality of who they really are as reflected in the stark contrast between the ego and divine truth. They avoid having to think themselves otherwise than being. Attention is absent; distracted by the ego/self, all energies are directed at the collective. The framework for openness to the ethical (truth) is overcome by the societal revelry of the spectacle (appearance).

Anathema sit—Political theology

In light of the two previous sections, we now turn more directly to Weil's view of the Church and by extension the political. Her refusal of baptism is grounded in her understanding of the Church as a social entity. "What frightens me," she writes, "is the Church as a social structure. Not only on account of its blemishes, but from the very fact that it is something social."[45] For, as she says elsewhere, "the social feeling is so much like the religious as to be mistaken for it."[46] The experiential similarities between religious experience and the self-satisfied elation felt from immersion in the collective are too subtle to discern except by the most attentive. The confusion of the collective spirit with that of authentic religiosity creates a dangerous, even deadly, situation. Thus, in the same sense Weil was skeptical about the social in general, she was prima facie dubious about an institution that in name and mission is in service of the sacred, but which in fact is a social entity like all others. But with an added twist:

> A society like the Church which claims to be divine is perhaps more dangerous on account of the *ersatz* good which it contains than on account of the evil which sullies it. Something of the social labeled divine: an intoxicating mixture which carries with it every sort of license.[47]

To summarize her logic thus far, then, Weil traced the root of corruption to the ego/self. It is primarily driven by desire (which by nature is infinite) for material pleasures (which by nature are finite). The draw toward worldly "goods" expands outward, from individual to collective (where the promise of infinite pleasures is articulated and reified). The collective, now the idol, is empowered to pursue its unquenchable thirst for material goods, instantiating an ersatz divinity.

> [P]ower must not seem to be arbitrarily allocated, because it will not then be recognized as power. Therefore prestige, which is illusion, is of the very essence of power. All power is based, in fact, upon the interrelation of human activities; but in order to be stable it must appear as something absolute and sacrosanct, both to those who wield and those who submit to it and also to other external powers.[48]

In essence there exists a political-theology, the emphasis being placed on the *political* as preceding the ersatz religiosity.

Interpreting the devil's words to Christ in the Gospel of Matthew, "All this power will I give thee and the glory of it, for that is delivered unto me and whomsoever I will give it,"[49] Weil writes, "It follows from this that the social is irremediably the domain of the devil. The flesh impels us to say *me* and the devil impels us to say *us*. . . . And, in conformity with this particular mission, the devil manufactures a false imitation of what is divine, an *ersatz* divinity."[50] There remains, and always will remain, an insoluble tension between the collective religion or its corresponding theologies and what Weil understood to be true religiosity—which is only possible in the site of the individual. Since the Church is by nature social, and the social is inherently "the domain of the devil" offering in place of God an ersatz divinity, joining and consequently serving the Church (as a duty) would be to abandon conscience and intelligence.

Weil did not cease her scrutiny of the Church here as if the *only* point of her query was for personal reasons. Instead, she extends it into a full-blown critique as one instance among many tragically misguided collectives. As the adage goes, power is intoxicating, especially the type nourished by feelings of social security. Religious—and political—homogeneity is more readily accomplished when the goals and consequences are pleasurable, as opposed to those that might result in suffering, or even demand self-sacrifice (e.g., charity). Religion as such is merely a populist movement. One need only consider the emphasis placed on the numbers of congregants as a measure of the validity of the message of a particular Christian church or denomination—more so, even, than systematic theology. Furthermore, the increase in contemporary worship services and other such liturgical innovations—not to mention the rapidly increasing number of nondenominational churches geared toward attracting as many worshippers as possible by appealing to pop culture, feel-good theologies, and so on—are all designed to reassure and appease (following the trend of modern self-help[51]) rather than to challenge Christians in their ways of thinking and acting in the world.

Evidently, the sense of belonging has more value than the truth of the message. "The power of the social element. Agreement between several men brings with it a feeling of reality. It brings with it also a sense of duty. Divergence, where this agreement is concerned, appears as sin."[52] The ability to speak truth to power in the style of Jesus is rendered impotent because only the dominant discourses can be heard. "Truth" is defined by the majority. Consensus requires compromise.[53] But for Weil, Jesus' message of love and charity was uncompromising. Once the "us" of consensus is established, all that is "other" is deemed "evil,"[54] anathema. The us is obliged—it has a mission—to exclude those others and defend itself against those who are perceived to be hostile to itself or as possible contagion to its "pure" mission while expanding its realm of influence as much as possible. The larger the collective, the more power and authority it harnesses.

It should be readily apparent at this point that the collective turns Christianity as Weil understood it on its head. She argued that the Church, to put it simply, gets it wrong. "Christianity is catholic by right but not in fact."[55] As a case in point, proving to Weil the sheer power of the Great Beast to corrupt even the most spiritually devout, she cites those Catholic saints who seemed to her to relinquish their commitment to Christ's epistemic-ethical calling and endorsed the infliction of violence upon others.

> There were some saints who approved of the Crusades or the Inquisition. I cannot help thinking that they were in the wrong. I cannot go against the light of conscience . . . [T]hey were blinded by something very powerful. This something was the Church seen as a social structure.[56]

The Church, with all of its systematic theology, symbols, and sacred rites, failed to prevent the weakening of the saints' consciences *because* as a social construct it is yet another manifestation of the Great Beast embellished by the appearance of having *religious* authority.

Although up to this point we have been analyzing the spiritual crisis as a result of the social dimension of organized religion, we ought not forget that this line of thinking was simultaneously applicable to the growing social-political crisis that preoccupied Weil as the tide of Hitlerism loomed ominously over all of Europe.[57] These were not unrelated phenomena to Weil's mind. Indeed, the slope bridging these two spheres is so slippery as to be a foregone conclusion that the two would elide into an unholy alliance with devastating consequences. The spiritual crisis and the social-political crises plaguing modern society were directly related. In Weil's assessment, the Church, after Rome, was a prototype of the political-theology to come.

> After the fall of the Roman Empire, which had been totalitarian, it was the Church that was the first to establish a rough sort of totalitarianism in Europe in the thirteenth century. . . . And the motive power of this totalitarianism was the use of those two little words: *anathema sit*.[58]

As E. Jane Doering comments,

> The pope's thirteenth-century support of the Inquisition and the genocidal crusade against the Albigensians had nurtured the growth of totalitarianism already present in the institution of the Church. In Weil's opinion, the formula for excommunication, *Anathema sit*, which denied any possibility of truth and its incarnation outside the Church, was proof of the Church's excessive authority. Over the many centuries, the Catholic hierarchy had supported the Inquisitions' methods of using fear and physical torture to ferret out heresies against Christianity. The Albigensian or Cathar Crusade (1209–29), sanctioned by the Church, had employed extreme violence, even by medieval standards, against the Cathars of Languedoc, accused by the Roman Catholic hierarchy of having abandoned their religious faith. The annihilation of the Cathar civilization of Oc in southern

France provoked a poignant sorrow in Weil, for she felt that the Albigenses had formed a rare society inspired by true love of neighbor.[59]

As a social construct, the Church cannot tolerate too much diversity. It demands orthodoxy—homogeneity. Heterodoxies and heresies are by definition impermissible. The logic of excommunication, Weil contended, contradicts Jesus' radical wisdom to love one's neighbors and enemies alike. Unfortunately, as we have seen, identitarian logic is more forceful in the wider populace. For example, consider the fanaticism of sports enthusiasts' unconditional loyalty to a team, or the zeal of affiliates within a secular political party or nation-state. These are only a few examples of the ersatz religiosity that Weil feared would too readily lend itself to the purely political.

Hitler's nationalism fabricated a religious aura around itself—a simulacrum of religious experience. The love of self was transmuted into the love of the social (the Great Beast), which was further reified and transmuted into the love of country or nationalism.[60] And Hitlerism too, tragically, decided that entire groups of people were anathema ("them") to its social-political vision ("us") and sought to systematically eliminate them from the face of the earth.[61] For Weil, the true Christian orientation would necessarily refute such claims and would in fact move in the opposite direction toward nonidentitarianism or, even, anti-identitariansim. This universalism is the true meaning of catholicism. Identity is necessarily ego-centered and, therefore, un-catholic. Identifying with any collective—whether a religion, nation, economic philosophy, et cetera—is tantamount to self-love writ large and is essentially idolatrous in that it demands uncompromising, unconditional allegiance to said identity. Patriotism (when indistinct from nationalism)[62] is the most pernicious social identity. Thus, Weil writes, "We must not have any love other than charity [which is necessarily selfless]. A nation cannot be an object of charity."[63] Nevertheless, in an especially candid moment in a letter she wrote to Father Perrin, she confesses,

I am aware of very strong gregarious tendencies in myself. My natural disposition is to be very easily influenced, too influenced, and above all by anything collective. I know that if at this moment I had before me a group of twenty young Germans singing Nazi songs in chorus, a part of my soul would instantly become Nazi.[64]

Lost in the mass hysteria created by amphibolous words and symbols—which Weil called "words with capital letters"[65]—and the faux religious experience in group-belonging, is sincere care for truth, justice, goodness, and beauty. Terms like "Democracy," "Communism," "Freedom," and "Terrorism," and even words such as "Christianity" as publicly conceived, lack clear definition. Nevertheless, countless human beings have killed or have been killed in service to them. "If we grasp one of these words," she writes, "all swollen with blood and tears, and squeeze it, we find it is empty. . . . [W]hen empty words are given capital letters, then, on the slightest pretext, we will begin shedding blood for them and piling up ruin in their name, without effectively grasping anything to which they refer, for the simple reason that they mean nothing."[66] The capitalization of such terms is for effect only. That is to say, the words are given an inflated sense of significance—in the double sense of the term—by mere affectation. It is not that the words actually *do* signify something real and are therefore capitalized such that men are willing to act violently on their behalf, but they merely will them to have more meaning than they actually do or resist defining them so as to avoid the limits a definition would impose. Weil's radical remedy is philosophic:

> [W]hen a word is properly defined it loses its capital letter and can no longer serve either as a banner or a hostile slogan; it simply becomes a sign, helping us to grasp some concrete reality or concrete objective, or method of activity. *To clarify thought, to discredit the intrinsically meaningless words, and to define the use of others by precise analysis—to do this, strange though it may appear, might be a way of saving human lives.*[67]

This holds equally true for "Hitlerism" as it does for "Christianity."

Another philosopher who was concerned with, studied, and analyzed totalitarianism, Hannah Arendt, through a very different route, came to conclusions that are complementary to Weil's diagnoses. Writing after World War II, Arendt observed, "Where all are guilty, no one is; confessions of collective guilt are the best possible safeguard against the discovery of culprits, and the very magnitude of the crime the best excuse for doing nothing."[68] In other words, among the anonymity of the collective, the individual escapes all sense of culpability—privately and publicly—whether s/he directly participated in mass crimes against humanity or remained hidden in the shadows. Weil would fully agree with Arendt's point here. And she would reiterate her explanation that the root causes are the ego's unwillingness to suffer, even for the sake of truth and justice, in combination with the allure of the collective prestige that corrupts conscience. All of this is packaged and sold—reified and idolized—in words with capital letters.

Weil offers two seemingly contradictory methods for reorienting ourselves to respond properly to these crises: atheism and mysticism.

Atheism as purification

"We must," Weil insists, "prefer real hell to an imaginary paradise."[69] Properly understood, religion ought never to be a form of escapism. Theologies that emphasize teleological, messianic, paradisiacal, or apocalyptic visions misguide our orientation toward the world. True religion is not a guaranteed source of solace, for Weil, for properly speaking religion is not a *tool* for us. Primarily it functions in quite an opposite manner. The incongruity between the world as is and the hierophany (the world as it ought to be) is a constant source of anguish. Hence, for Weil, "Religion in so far as it is a source of consolation is a hindrance to true faith . . ." She continues, "[I]n this sense atheism is a purification. I have to be atheistic with the part of myself which is not made for God. Among those men in whom the supernatural part has not been awakened, the atheists are right and the believers wrong."[70]

As we have seen above, collective representations of divinity are in essence idolatrous. It follows that the necessary first step is to bracket inherited presuppositions about God. It would become wildly confusing to maintain fidelity to a theological system and try to root out only the mistaken bits, as it were. In a fashion reminiscent of Descartes' method of doubt, Weil suggests that atheism "is a purification of the notion of God."[71] In other words, apologist philosophers of religion and theologians alike are necessarily confined by preexisting frameworks for understanding and representing God. Their efforts at best amount to word games because the words they have either inherited or created themselves in response to the preexisting narratives are always distanced from actual divinity as well as the world itself. Atheism affords a clean break from this circular reasoning.

One might object that atheism necessarily closes off the possibility of a transcendent reality such as one finds in religious traditions like Christianity, or even philosophical systems such as Platonism. But Weil was merely suggesting that atheism clears the ground for the possibility of being truly open to the experience of what appears to transcend "natural" encounters in contradistinction to merely thinking about, conceptualizing, and intellectually capturing "God." Thus in this fashion Weil has more in common with contemporary phenomenologists such as Jean-Luc Marion[72] and Anthony Steinbock[73] than she does with atheist philosophers seeking to refute the existence of God. In its most basic form, she saw atheism as a means to root out all of the implicit problems within traditional theological frameworks and philosophies of religion. She did not intend by this statement to imply that atheists are in possession of certain knowledge as such, especially with respect to the existence or nonexistence of God. If the latter is held, it replicates the error of traditional theologies—it lacks epistemological humility and openness—and, therefore, is another form of idolatry (e.g., as is found in capitalism, scientism, et cetera). Simply put, then, Weil reckoned that insofar as atheism is not bewildered by the trappings of theology and religious philosophy, or socially constructed visions of God, it is preferable and even an advisable starting point.

Previously we described her stance as a reflective negative theology, or atheology. These terms convey the sort of renunciation at the base of a purified religious stance that is void of affirmations about the divine but where "religiosity" can be observed only in individuals' orientations to the world. Collectively bargained theologies in particular are a threat because, as we have seen already, once formulated and reified, they are no longer completely open to intellectual inquiry. There is to be no questioning of what are taken

to be fundamental theological truths such as the existence of God.
It is straightforward dogmatism. Weil counters by writing,

> In so far as 'God exists' is an intellectual proposition—but *only*
> to that extent—it can be denied without committing any sin at
> all either against charity or against faith. (And, indeed, such a
> negation, formulated on a provisional basis, is a necessary stage
> in philosophical investigation.)
>   Christianity has, in fact, since the very beginning, or nearly so,
> suffered from an intellectual malaise. This malaise is due to the
> way in which the Church has conceived its power of jurisdiction
> and especially the use of the formula *anathema sit*. Wherever
> there is an intellectual malaise, we find the individual is oppressed
> by the social factor, which tends to become totalitarian.[74]

The confluence of the political and the theological, then, is *causa sui*
anti-philosophical. The enforcement of homogeneity, theologically
and socially, is prohibitive of philosophical investigation. Weil, to
the contrary, was fully committed to the spirit of philosophy.

> Complete liberty within its own sphere is essential to the
> intelligence. The intelligence must either exercise itself with
> complete liberty, or else keep silent. Within the sphere of the
> intelligence, the Church has no right of jurisdiction whatsoever;
> consequently, and more particularly, all "definitions" where it is
> a question of *proofs* are unlawful ones.[75]

With respect to classical issues raised in theology and philosophy
of religion—especially about the existence of God, God's nature,
the problem of evil, God's relationship to the world and humans, et
cetera—Weil's approach is a form of negative theology that begins
with her *experience* in the world. Consequently, it is never a question of proving or affirming God's existence. Rather, she writes,

> I saw the problem of God as a problem of the data of which
> could not be obtained here below, and I decided . . . to leave it
> alone. . . . I neither affirmed nor denied anything. It seemed to
> me useless to solve the problem, for I thought that, being in this
> world, our business was to adopt the best attitude with regard to
> the problems of this world . . .[76]

The last line of this passage seems to indicate that Weil's method—if it does not completely close us off from a transcendent
God—leaves us suspended in the immanent world. And this is true
to a certain extent, since, as we shall see in later chapters, grace is
supernatural and, thus, is not in our power. At this time, however,
the important distinction to be made is that Weil's appeal to atheism as a form of purification shifts the question of whether or not
God exists to *how* we should attend to the world—or, *how* we
should experience.

A clue to this answer is found yet again in Plato who, after Weil's
own mystical encounters, she came "to feel . . . was a mystic."[77]
Weil understood philosophy—and by extension true religiosity or
mysticism—as the practice of dying. "This is why in the ancient
mysteries, in Platonic philosophy, in Sanskrit texts, in the Christian
religion, and probably everywhere and always, detachment has ever
been compared to death, and the initiation to wisdom regarded as
a kind of passage through death. This idea is found in the most
ancient texts we possess concerning human thought . . . and it is as
ancient as is humanity itself. So every search for wisdom is oriented
toward death."[78] According to her, the only means of resistance to
the base inclination to idolatry is that highest capacity of detachment that "we do not [naturally] possess," that is, "the power of
supernatural attention," which furthermore, "we have not the
patience to allow . . . to develop."[79] Insofar as we are naturally
inattentive, then, what hope is there for emerging from the social,
political, and religious caves in which we normally reside?

Mysticism

The first stage of the art of dying—mysticism—is renouncing collective identities. Until the very end of her life—depending on
whether one believes that Simone Deitz baptized her or not[80]—Weil
resisted baptism primarily on the bases outlined above. She definitively declared: "There is a Catholic circle ready to give an eager
welcome to whoever enters it. Well, I do not want to be adopted
into a circle, to live among people who say 'we' and to be part of
an 'us,' to find I am 'at home' in any human *milieu* whatever it may
be."[81] Liberation from the collective requires intellectual independence. Although Weil did not advocate monasticism as such—which

certainly played an important part in the historical development of Christian mysticism[82]—it was in moments of quiet solitude that she eventually had experiences that she later came to identify as mystical encounters.

Weil noted that "almost since the beginning, the individual has been ill at ease in Christianity."[83] There is, in other words, an inherent tension between the individual and the collective in religion which is identifiable in the varying manners Christ spoke depending on whether he was "speaking before an assembly such as a council," or with a "well-beloved friend."[84] The "language of the marketplace,"[85] as Weil called collective language, lends itself to the phenomena described above: the Great Beast and idolatry. The faculty of the intellect with its inherited linguistic frameworks deals squarely with these problems, but then it too must be abandoned in favor of the possibility of actual encounters and the language of intimacy. Thinking *about* always requires a distancing—perspective is gained from a distance between the thinker and the object of inquiry. Love, on the contrary, is the experience of wanting to close the gap between the subject and the object, but it is simultaneously a sign of that distance, too. Intellectualizing is not loving. And theorizing about loving is a further perversion of the orientation that Weil understood Jesus to have embodied. Thus, Weil says that only the "language of the nuptial chamber"[86] can be used with respect to the "word of God," which "is the secret word."[87]

At stake in this discussion of language, then, are the registers of intimacy. How do we experience phenomena other than how they are normally construed within our existing linguistic and logical structures? Our self-created communicative tools preclude the most intimate encounters with others or with God by rejecting a priori certain modes of evidence gathering or simply by forcing such experiences into collectively determined generalizations—the language of the marketplace. Anthony Steinbock notes the prevailing prejudice against a plurality of modes of such intimate experiencing thusly:

> The prejudice is this: All matters, especially those that concern the Holy, have to conform to *one* type of givenness in order to be given and hence to be experienced. If they do not conform, they are said to remain essentially on the limit of experience and are subject only to theory, speculation, or mere personal belief.[88]

If an experience is not immediately identifiable through a preexisting linguistic or logical construct, then it automatically is reduced
to pure subjectivity or abstract speculation. In other words, static
categories and stabilizing concepts render only specified experiences as "intelligible," meaningful, and even *real*.

These constrictions apply as much for secular frameworks as
they do for theological ones such as the political-theology of the
Church discussed previously.[89] "Sensitivity to vertical givenness is
not accomplished by constructing a metaphysics or by applying
either theological convictions or ethical belief systems to the experiences," argues Steinbock, "but by . . . evaluating what is actually *given in human experience*, thereby expanding our notion of
evidence."[90] True disinterestedness, paradoxically, requires a radical sensitivity and openness. The self is dis-posed of in order that
the experiencer is open "to being struck *in which ever way* the
given gives itself."[91] Hence the importance of Weil's statement that
she "never at any moment in [her] life . . . 'sought for God.'"[92] To
go looking for God would entail a purposeful search. This interested approach is suspect for producing the results one intends,
or seeing what one wants to see, and thus all resulting evidential
claims are dismissed as prejudicial. One of Steinbock's contentions,
which aligns with Weil's own, is that the adherence to preexisting
modes of knowing is itself such a (self-)interested project. Equally
important along these lines, before providing an account of Weil's
mystical experiences, is her sense of relief due to the fact that she
had not read other mystical writings before she had her own mystical experiences, "so that it should be evident to me that I had not
invented this absolutely unexpected contact."[93]

Weil's mysticism was the result of intellectual honesty and constant philosophical analysis and critique, that is, not a flimsy, shod-
dily constructed, self-interested spirituality intentionally wrapped
in vague language. At the same time, she understood that genuine
philosophical reflection is problematized by assumed linguistic
frameworks. She wrote, for instance, "Language is not made for
expressing philosophical reflection."[94] Her constant self-critique
had the effect of decentering her "self."[95] As such, she was vulnerable to being struck by un(pre)determined experiences, whether
of the ordinary (e.g., human pain and suffering) or extraordinary
(e.g., religious) variety. Many of these experiences were, in fact,
decidedly not in her self-interest.[96]

From April to August 1934, Weil endured her first stint working in the dehumanizing conditions of factories. Although her family had the financial means to support her, or at the very least to take good care of her during off hours with proper food, clothing, and other daily necessities, Weil insisted that she live exactly as her coworkers who were forced to subsist on the meager wages they earned. Consequently, she often went hungry, and her general appearance was unkempt. In the end, she described herself as being "in pieces, soul and body. . . . That contact with affliction had killed my youth. . . . As I worked . . . the affliction of others entered into my flesh and my soul."[97] The effects of the unbearable working and living conditions—which so many of the world's population have no choice but to endure—were exacerbated by the fact that Weil suffered from severe migraine headaches her entire life. Emotionally exhausted and in wretched physical condition, she said that the experience turned her into a "slave."

Later in 1934, Weil traveled with her parents to a small fishing village in Portugal. During a celebration of the town's patron saint, Weil witnessed a procession of women "making a tour of all the ships, carrying candles and singing what must have been very ancient hymns of a heart-rending sadness."[98] The experience was beyond words. Suddenly, she writes, "the conviction was borne in upon me that Christianity is pre-eminently the religion of slaves, that slaves cannot help belonging to it, and I among others."[99] This was the first of her three mystical experiences. The second came in 1937 in Assisi in the chapel of Santa Maria degli Angeli, "where St. Francis often used to pray."[100] There she describes an event in which "something stronger than [her] . . . compelled [her] for the first time in [her] life to go down on [her] knees."[101] Her first prostration of prayer, then, was not a supplication stirred by selfish desire, nor the fulfillment of ritual obligation as deemed by religious authority, but was a response to her sense of a supernatural love. The last of her reported mystical experiences occurred when she was reciting George Herbert's poem, "Love." In 1938 she attended the Easter celebration at the Benedictine Abbey Solesmes. Suffering from migraines as she frequently did, she sat in the cathedral where the monks were singing Gregorian chants. In their chanting she found "a pure and perfect joy,"[102] which provided her relief from the distracting headaches and offered her a glimpse of "the possibility of loving divine love in the midst of affliction."[103] On the recommendation of an English Catholic she met at Solesmes, she read, memorized, and regularly recited Herbert's poem, often "at the culminating point of a violent headache. . . . It was during one of these recitations that . . . Christ himself came down and took possession of [her]."[104]

This final mystical experience is the culmination—not the contradiction—of all of Weil's philosophical thinking. Mysticism is not the opposite of philosophy, but the consequence of philosophical investigation. As it is commonly bound by language, philosophy is limited, but it can bring us to a state wherein we are more open to those experiences and truths that surpass what has been produced as "intelligible." "In my arguments about the insolubility of the problem of God," she reflects, "I had never foreseen the possibility of that, of a real contact, person to person, here below, between human being and God."[105] For all of their logical literacy, nobody has accused philosophers of being too loving or philosophy for promoting loving and intimate encounters with others. The commonplace idea is that love is the province of poetry—not philosophy (despite philosophy's literal meaning, "love of wisdom"). Philosophy has been assumed, especially recently, illiterate in love's expression, possibly because the role of philosophy has been narrowly defined as "construct[ing] systems to eliminate contradictions."[106] However, Weil's own life is a testament to the fact that there can be no divorce between genuine philosophical rigor and the kind of vulnerable and attentive sensitivity to the world that draws love and with it, divine inspiration. We should not forget Plato's contention that philosophy, like poetic inspiration, is a kind of madness: "[the philosopher] stands outside human concerns and draws close to the divine: ordinary people think he is disturbed and rebuke him for this, unaware that he is possessed by god."[107] In her own encounter with the supernatural, however, Weil "only felt in the midst of [her] suffering the presence of a love, like that which one can read in the smile on a beloved face."[108]

After this final mystical experience, Weil never again "wondered whether Jesus was or was not the Incarnation of God; but in fact [she] was incapable of thinking of him without thinking of him as God."[109] Jesus as the incarnation of truth, as we will see in the next chapter, is of central importance to Weil's thought.

2

Christology and religious pluralism

"Let us do evil that good may come?"
Their condemnation is deserved!

ROMANS 3:8

Extended, the lines of relationships intersect
in the eternal You.

MARTIN BUBER[1]

Letter to a priest

In 1942 while living with her family in exile in New York, at the urging of the Catholic philosopher Jacques Maritain, Weil wrote a letter to the Dominican priest Marie-Alain Couturier (1897–1954). This letter contains her most explicit and complete set of philosophical-theological questions, systematically presented for his consideration in 35 discrete sections. She opens the letter by saying,

> When I read the catechism of the Council of Trent, it seems as though I had nothing in common with the religion there set forth. When I read the New Testament, the mystics, the liturgy, when I watch the celebration of the mass, I feel with a sort of conviction that this faith is mine or, to be more precise, would

be mine without the distance placed between it and me by my imperfection. This results in a painful spiritual state. I would like to make it, not less painful, only clearer. Any pain whatsoever is acceptable where there is clarity.[2]

Thus, she continues by requesting from him unequivocal answers to her concerns:

> I am going to enumerate for you a certain number of thoughts which have dwelt in me for years (some of them at least) and which form a barrier between me and the Church. I do not ask you to discuss their basis. I should be happy for there to be such a discussion, but later on, in the second place.
>
> I ask for you to give me a definite answer—leaving out such expressions as 'I think that,' etc.—regarding the compatibility or incompatibility of each of these opinions with membership of the Church. If there is incompatibility, I should like you to say straight out: I would refuse baptism (or absolution) to anybody claiming to hold the opinions expressed under such headings numbered so-and-so. I do not ask for a quick answer. There is no hurry. All I ask for is a categorical answer.[3]

We have already dealt with the question of Weil's internal struggle over baptism, and although it is on this very pretense that she wrote this letter to Father Couturier, what is of significance in this letter for our purposes is that it contains many of Weil's near final thoughts about theological issues before her untimely death. In particular, the questions she poses to the Dominican friar express her ideas about the centrality of Christ (especially the incarnation and his crucifixion) as well as the issue that has come to be known as religious pluralism.

Weil's Christology and her religious pluralism will be analyzed at length in this chapter. An honest engagement with these subjects, however, also necessitates addressing Weil's estranged relationship with her family's ethnic Jewish identity, and, more importantly, her controversial statements condemning the Jewish faith. Many have praised Weil's inclusive stance with respect to non-Christian religious traditions while excluding (or, at least minimizing) the evidence of her animosity toward Judaism (and additionally Islam, as we shall see). Just as many critics, it must be admitted, have cited her vitriolic critique of Judaism as sufficient justification for dismissing her entire oeuvre and all of her contributions to religious philosophy and social activism without even considering the arguments underpinning her denouncements. We aim to avoid both of these errors in this chapter and instead take this occasion to discuss directly and extensively the complex and controversial theological-philosophical-ethical questions raised by Weil's treatment of these subject matters—many of which are still of central importance in contemporary theological, political, and ethical debates.

Christology

Weil's philosophy is unapologetically a Christian philosophy. This means, of course, that her entire worldview is shaped by her understanding of the figure of Jesus, who she most commonly refers to as Christ, and emphasizes his role as a mediator between the divine and the human. But unlike some other Christologies, Weil's analysis of Jesus' words and deeds does not single out his resurrection as proof of his divinity and establishment of the Christian mission. Instead, Weil argues that it is Christ's suffering on the cross that is exemplary. As we will explain, Weil's Christology—and therefore her metaphysics and ethics—stands in contrast to other interpretations of Jesus that spread the good news of his triumphant holiness as witnessed through the resurrection and advise Christians, in Panglossian fashion, to rest assured.

In her letter to Father Couturier Weil writes, "And if the Gospel omitted all mention of Christ's resurrection, faith would be easier for me. The Cross by itself suffices me."[4] Theologies focusing on the event of the resurrection, to her mind, miss the mark. At the very least, they privilege a certain temporal hierarchy; that is, these theologies tend to be forward looking—eschatological—instead of attentive to the present. Consequently, the present (*what is*) is framed entirely by an imagined future (*what may/will come*). But the "future," she exclaims, "is a filler of void places. . . . [T]he future hinder[s] the wholesome effect of affliction by providing an unlimited field for imaginary elevation."[5] To put it differently, all futural orientations are the products of and only serve to affirm the imagination and pertain little, if at all, to objective reality.

NB

Weil insisted that truth is bound with necessity. Psychologically and intellectually, and thereby ethically, dwelling upon the (unlimited) future is detrimental to the present in all of its particularities, which are necessarily limited. In situations that present themselves as painful because there is a sense of disequilibrium, injustice, or resistance to our selfish desires, rather than facing the facts, the imagination turns toward the indefinite and pliable future. This maneuver frees the imagination from necessity in order that it might construct a sense of equilibrium. Because the lever can be extended to whatever length the imagination desires, it can "balance" out even the most horrific and anguishing present conditions. For example, faced with terminal illness, one can readily imagine a "purpose" or providential reason for having been afflicted thusly, or a happy ending in some eternal paradise, thereby relieving oneself from the burden of carrying the full weight of the reality of the situation. The indefinite future diminishes and, therefore, distorts our perception of the present reality. Furthermore, theological beliefs and practices framed thusly have the additional effect of reducing the present (including persons) to mere means serving an ulterior, later end. Therefore, Weil contends, the futural gaze of the unbound imagination always misrepresents reality and poses grave ethical consequences.

Freely imagining in this way amounts to placing oneself on par with God. Rather than acknowledging and accepting the truth of creation as it is/has been given, one imaginatively "creates" (i.e., fictionalizes) the world in a manner she prefers it to be/have been given. "It is much easier to imagine ourselves in the place of God the creator," writes Weil, "than in the place of Christ crucified."[6] Hence, humans are naturally inclined to construct theologies that express how the world would be if the author(s) were God rather than theologies that are disinterested accounts of reality. (As we explained in the previous chapter, the Christ of popular theology is an ersatz divinity—a creation of humankind rather than a response to the present reality of creation itself.) Returning to a familiar motif, Weil likens imaginative and therefore futural thinking to projecting and predicting shadows on the wall of Plato's allegorical cave. She then concludes, "To come out of the cave, to be detached, means to cease to make the future our objective."[7] By remaining fully present, or "innocent" in her words, we relinquish all expectations or claims to equilibrium. "To be innocent is to bear the weight of the entire universe. It is to throw away the counterweight."[8]

For Weil, the event of the crucifixion awakens us to the present. The literal suffering and eventual death of Christ ought to evoke compassion (a suffering with Christ on the cross), and in no way should it be diluted, falsified, misrepresented, or erased by the imagination. The crucifixion stands as an impregnable testament to the reality of an order that is not man-made but is the result of God's withdrawal from the world and Jesus' perfect response to the necessarily asymmetrical relation between the creator and the created.[9] The crucifix represents the tension within creation.

Truth is laid bare on the cross. "The Passion is the existence of perfect justice without any admixture of appearance."[10] A Christology inferred from the resurrection as proof of Christ's divinity would logically stress hope in the ultimate victory of goodness over injustice in the same miraculous manner in which Christ defeated death. The result of Weil's Christology, however, is her designation of Christianity as the religion of slaves, not of victors and therefore masters. She stands the theological paradigm intuited in popular imagination on its head.

> Christ healing the sick, raising the dead, etc.—that is the humble, human, almost low part of the mission. The supernatural part is the sweat of blood, the unsatisfied longing for human consolation, the supplication that he might be spared, the sense of being abandoned by God.[11]

For Weil, then, to be Christian is not to believe in the God of miracles, is no guarantee that all prayers will be answered, and it is not to be on the winning team, especially one that is rigged so that the outcome always falls in the Christian's favor. The supernatural truth of Christ is evident in his affliction—the paradoxical intersection between the two furthest points: horizontally oriented humankind on one hand, and God's verticality on the other. Christ's suffering and humiliation on the cross is not merely the reconciliation between God and humanity redeeming original sin, according to Weil; rather, it is Christ's *loving* consent to the distance between God and his creation.

The cross, therefore, serves as the ultimate theological (and ethical) symbol in that it provides the true measure of the disequilibrium between God and humanity. "The cross is infinitely more than mar-tyrdom. It is the most purely bitter suffering—penal suffering. This is the guarantee of its authenticity."[12] Jesus' anguish was real and therefore should not be curtailed theologically by interpreting it as having been predestined or as a means for a greater, more purpose-ful end. To the contrary, its reality renders all human expectations and claims to anything more than what has been given illegiti-mate, hubristic, and idolatrous. God abandoned Jesus on the cross. Hence, Christ's plea, "My God, my God, why has thou forsaken me?" is understood by Weil to be "the real proof that Christianity is something divine."[13] That Jesus was not granted reprieve on the cross and remained there suffering unto death is, unexpectedly, proof of God's love, to Weil. "The abandonment at the supreme moment of the crucifixion, what an abyss of love on both sides!"[14] During this event neither God nor Jesus filled the void.

Intellectual honesty and fidelity to the cross, then, prohibits the construction of compensatory theologies.[15] In his teachings, Jesus emphasized his Father's love and compassion. He described it as unconditional love—the greatest form of love. "So that the love may be as great as possible," writes Weil, "the distance is as great as possible."[16] God created this abyss through his withdrawal in creation, and this gulf is inscribed in the event of the crucifixion, symbolizing God's refusal to command everywhere he has the power to do so.

> God wears himself out through the infinite thickness of time and space in order to reach the soul and to captivate it. If it allows a pure and utter consent (though brief as a lightning flash) to be torn from it, then God conquers the soul. And when it has become entirely his he abandons it. He leaves it completely alone and it has in its turn, but gropingly, to cross the infinite thickness of time and space in search of him whom it loves. It is thus that the soul, starting from the opposite end, makes the same journey that God made towards it. And that is the cross.[17]

The possibility of expressing infinite love requires there to exist an infinite gulf between the lover and the beloved. God's act of uncon-ditional love is evident in his refusal to intervene and console his son crying out in agony, thereby sustaining the very possibility of Jesus' willing consent. (We will also see, in the next chapter, how

God's love also manifests as creation itself.) Christ, for his part, loved his Father despite his incarnation and the wretched conditions of his death.

Weil's argument follows that the love Jesus exhibited—in both word and deed, but especially on the cross—was infinite and unconditional like his Father's. As such, he is the Mediator, and therefore, exemplary. Weil takes this point quite literally. In her religious philosophy, Christ is not an inimitable deity, but a model for human religious/ethical behavior. She is highly critical of theologies that give lip service to Christ, but never genuinely advise being Christ-like. "In order that *the imitation of God should not be a mere matter of words*, it is necessary that there should be a just man to imitate . . ."[18] Christ crucified, in other words, amounts to an ethical imperative. Jesus mirrored God's love; Christians are commanded to love just as Jesus loved in the void. "I have to be like God, but like God crucified. Like God almighty in so far as he is bound by necessity," she writes.[19]

In Christ on the cross, Weil sees the incarnation of the perfect love—loving in God's absence/abandonment and with acceptance of necessity—in proportion to the love received from God.[20] Christ is mediator and therefore calls to our attention humanity's true relation with God. This is why she writes, "The function of mediation in itself implies a tearing asunder."[21] In other words, the crucifixion serves to tear us from our attachments to selfish thinking and self-oriented action. The natural attitude is devoid of, or at least forgetful of, vertical relationality. Weil finds evidence of theological perversions of this essential point even in translations of sacred scriptures:

> The very fact that *Logos* has been translated by *verbum* shows that something has been lost, for λόγος means above all *relation*, and is a synonym for ἀριθμός, number, with Plato and the Pythagoreans. Relation, that is to say proportion. Proportion, that is to say harmony. Harmony, that is to say mediation. I would translate as follows: In the beginning was Mediation.[22]

Errant proportions distort the proper relationship between humankind and God. Whereas Jesus embodied the zero-point—egolessness resulting from emptying the void through love—such that God literally became flesh (incarnation), in Weil's understanding,

humanity continues to tilt the scales toward individual and collective desires, seeking to be omnipotent and ever-expansive. For Weil,
however, Christ's death on the cross is a calling for all humanity
to respond in kind. Looking at the symbol of the crucifix ought
to recall the one time in Christian history where there was *actual*
equilibrium and recognize fully what it entailed.

Intimations of religious pluralism

As the title of this section suggests, we will be arguing that the
religious pluralism often favorably attributed to Weil is, properly
speaking, at best a qualified one. Whereas she does demonstrate
a great deal of openness to and even reverence for other religious
traditions—going so far as to suggest that Christianity does not
hold the sole claim to truth and, in fact, has much wisdom to learn
from non-Christian religions—there are two principal concerns
that significantly diminish, if not outrightly disqualify any claims
of religious inclusiveness in her philosophy: first, Weil ultimately
interprets and values non-Christian religious traditions in purely
Christian terms (especially incarnationism), and, second, Weil's
religious pluralism is contested by her categorical exclusion of
Judaism and Islam.

A recurrent concern throughout her letter to Father Couturier
is the Church's position on and relationship with non-Christian
religious traditions. In particular, Weil finds a great deal of value
in her studies of other religious traditions and sacred literatures,
and she is concerned that showing any sympathy toward these traditions would be grounds for exclusion from the Church. (Recall
her criticisms of *anathema sit* outlined in the previous chapter.)
Repeatedly, she insists that Father Couturier answer directly
whether or not someone who found truth in these other religions
would be admitted into the Church and be able to partake in the
holy sacraments.

Weil has many good reasons to be suspicious of the Church's
position with respect to non-Christian religions. The most obvious reason of all was the fact that Christian missionaries had been
and continued to be the handmaidens of empire, if not its principal architects.[23] Colonial expansion was aided and abetted by
Christians desiring to convert native populations, and thus, it was

often the case that missionaries were the first to arrive in the so-called new territories. As Weil makes clear, however, "Missionary zeal has not Christianized Africa, Asia and Oceania," rather it "has brought these territories under the cold, cruel and destructive domination of the white race, which has trodden down everything." She continues,

> It would be strange, indeed, that the word of Christ should have produced such results if it had been properly understood.
>
> Christ said: "Go ye, and teach all nations and baptize those who believe," that is to say, those who believe in Him. *He never said*: "Compel them to renounce all that their ancestors have looked upon as sacred, and to adopt as a holy book the history of a small nation unknown to them."[24]

As we discussed in the previous chapter, in Weil's analysis political-theology is the contradictory admixture of the collective will (the Great Beast) and Christ's exemplarity, which always results in significantly contorting the latter (the religious) for the sake of the former (the social-political). It is predicated on a mistaken interpretation of Jesus' mission; that is, he did not exhibit or mandate to his followers an imperialist imperative to homogenize—by coercion and domination—all humanity under a single theological order. Ultimately, Weil thinks that Jesus "commanded his apostles to bring glad tidings, *not a theology* . . . But the command was misunderstood."[25] He commanded, in her view, that Christians accept their neighbors and enemies without expectations or reducing them to the same. In fact, in most cases, as we will explain in further detail below, she thinks that changing religions is harmful.

The Church perverts Christ's teachings when it condones, is complicit with, and actively participates in deception, exploitation, and the brutal use of force in colonialist expansion. These historical facts were a grave source of consternation for Weil, both as a French citizen and as someone who earnestly tried to model her behavior on Christ's exemplarity.

> But . . . as to whether a Hindu, a Buddhist, a Muslim, or one of those termed pagan has not in his own tradition a path toward that spirituality which the Christian churches offer him, in any

case Christ never said that warships should accompany, even at a distance, those who bring the good news. *Their presence changes the nature of the message.* It is difficult to retain the supernatural virtues attributed to the blood of the martyrs when it is avenged by force of arms. *You are asking for more trumps in your hand than is allowed when you want at one and the same time Caesar and the Cross.*[26]

Human violence belongs to the social and political domains. And this violence cannot be reconciled with Christianity because it corrupts the image of Christ in the same way as the Great Beast disavows true religiosity. Even when Weil reluctantly gave up being a pacifist in order to maintain logical consistency, she admitted that to take up arms is to acknowledge the justice of all harm that might come to all willing participants, including herself, as a result. In no uncertain terms, Weil affirms that all forms of violence are blatant contradictions of Jesus' example, and therefore, those who rationalize the implementation of physical threat or force, are decidedly *not* acting in a Christ-like manner. "Whoever takes up the sword shall perish by the sword. And whoever does not take up the sword (or lets it go) shall perish on the cross."[27] To be Christian is to bear the cross.

Weil's position against Christian missionaries is far more than a political condemnation of violence and colonialism, however. She constructed philosophical-religious arguments against this practice. She witnessed the damaging effects of what she calls "uprootedness"—when people are forced (i.e., they do not freely give their consent) to abandon their land, their language, their cultural traditions and literatures, and especially their religion.[28] This type of being "torn asunder" is not the same as the one she positively described with respect to the cross. The former consists in the deprivation of others' ability to renounce their egos and consent to the void; the latter is the effect of experiencing God's love and consenting to loving him in return. They produce opposite results. Uprootedness strips life of any sense of meaning and order. This is why she writes in her letter to Father Couturier, "I think that for any man a change of religion is as dangerous a thing as a change of language is for a writer. It may turn out a success, but it can also have disastrous consequences."[29] By definition, conversion to a different faith under duress is not consensual and, thus, not born out of love. There lingers a reasonable doubt regarding the authenticity of the act. Moreover, conversion is not merely a question of changing systems of belief. Missionaries' pretensions to the possibility of humans convincing other humans that their present religious tradition is inferior to Christianity, and thus should be relinquished in favor of "accepting Jesus Christ as lord and savior," is grossly arrogant in her view. It is hubristic in the same way as is the use of political force and potentially equally damaging to its intended targets. Religious truth is not arrived at in winning a theological disputation or through appeals to emotion, fear, pride, et cetera. Hence, Weil emphatically condemns all missionary practices: "It is, therefore, useless to send out missions to prevail upon the peoples of Asia, Africa or Oceania to enter the Church."[30]

The basis for her defense of other religious traditions goes well beyond her critique of Christian missionaries' role in colonialism or its own internal theological and ethical contradictions, however. Weil was very learned about other religions and cultures. She expended a significant amount of time and effort learning languages, such as ancient Greek and Sanskrit, in order to study other traditions' sacred literature. During the course of her studies, she found a great deal of inspiration and truth in their teachings and practices. She went so far as to affirm the truth claims made by other religious traditions.

> Every time a man has, with a pure heart, called upon Osiris, Dionysus, Krishna, Buddha, the Tao, etc., the Son of God has answered him by sending the Holy Spirit. And the Holy Spirit has acted upon his soul, *not by inciting him to abandon his religious tradition*, but by bestowing upon him light—and in the best of cases the fullness of light—*in the heart of that same religious tradition*.[31]

From this passage it is clear that Weil does not view non-Christian religions as competing with Christianity in the marketplace of ideas, where the religion or denomination with the highest numbers wins, or where one tradition will be declared the sole victor on the epistemic battlefield. Theologians that think in such combative terms tend to focus on the differences between their orthodox set of beliefs, doctrines, and rites and those of other religious traditions. This is especially true of Christians with an evangelical mission. The process leading up to the Christians' inevitable self-declared victory includes not only a systematic theological account of their own tradition, but also by extension translating other religious traditions into Christian theological terms so as to demonstrate on what bases Christian belief is incompatible and, ultimately, they presuppose, superior to those non-Christian religions. This is why, for example, it has become quite natural for uneducated and unsympathetic Western commentators to desire a (Protestant type) reformation in Islam (with the hopes of finding the Muslim "Martin Luther"[32]), as if Islam is simply on a parallel trajectory, only lagging hundreds of years behind Christianity and littered with mistaken premises. At the same time, these commentaries betray the arrogant assumption that Christianity (or the so-called West) in its present form is obviously superior to Islam in its traditional and present forms. Or take as another illustration of this point, the professor teaching a course on World Religions, World Humanities, or other non-Christian based worldviews who must frequently contend with students' questions or comments situating whatever concept or practice being discussed vis-à-vis Christianity: "X is like/unlike Christianity in the following way(s) . . ." As well intentioned as the students' efforts may be, they nevertheless skew the subject matter by forcing everything into Christian theological terms.

Although, as we will see shortly, Weil, too, errs on the side of assimilationism, at this stage we want to demonstrate her ecumenical leanings. Rather than compatibility/incompatibility being the basis of critical analysis in order to determine once and for all which, if any, of these traditions has legitimate claims to truth, Weil takes the stance that most religious traditions are equally true. She writes,

> The story of the creation and of original sin in Genesis is true. But other stories about the creation and original sin in other traditions are also true and also contain incomparably precious truths. They are different reflections of a unique truth untranslatable into human words. One can divine this truth through one of these reflections. One can divine it still better through several of them.[33]

If we recall that Weil maintains that the intellect is limited and, therefore, no single (i.e., limited) vantage can fully grasp and articulate the divine, then her stance on non-Christian religions is consistent. Hence, she advises that Christians can learn a great deal of truth and obtain wisdom from intense study of all religious traditions (with a few exceptions). However, she also understands that the "comparison of religions is only possible, in some measure, through the miraculous virtue of sympathy."[34] Clearly, antagonistic theological outlooks—that is, those looking for and emphasizing differences between religious traditions for the sake of self-assurance—preclude the possibility of such sympathy. But Weil approaches the encounter between faith traditions very seriously and, at least initially, she does so openly and offers important insights relevant to contemporary ecumenical dialogues and comparative approaches to the study of religion. We quote her at length:

> We can know men to a certain extent if at the same time as we observe them from outside we manage by sympathy to transport our own soul into theirs for a time. In the same way the study of different religions does not lead to a real knowledge of them unless we transport ourselves for a time by faith to the very center of whichever one we are studying. Here, moreover, this word *faith* is used in its strongest sense.
>
> This scarcely ever happens, for some have no faith, and the others have faith exclusively in one religion and only bestow upon the others the sort of attention we give to strangely shaped shells. There are others again who think they are capable of impartiality because they have only a vague religiosity which they can turn indifferently in any direction, whereas, on the contrary, we must have given all our attention, all our faith, all our love to a particular religion in order to think of any other religion with the high degree of attention, faith, and love that is proper to it. In the same way, only those who are capable of friendship can take a real heartfelt interest in the fate of an utter stranger.[35]

Defensive postures are just as prohibitive to learning as aggressive ones in comparative religious studies. Being guarded renders the encounter disingenuous in a very real sense, according to Weil and probably *prevents* the encounter altogether. Take for example an actress. A good actress *becomes* the character she is portraying on stage. Her dialect, bodily gestures, facial expressions, et cetera

must be—not just appear—natural. To the degree that she accomplishes this transformation through an essential vulnerability to
the narrative she brings the performance to life. If the audience
can perceive that she is "acting," it is because she is perceptibly
someone other than the character she is portraying. The most common source of the inability of the actress to step outside of herself
and into character is that she is too self-conscious. Stage fright is
the result of being hyper self-aware and neurotic. Failed actors, in
other words, are those who are always consciously not the characters they portray. In the same way, all approaches to other religions
fail when the participants remain self-consciously and guardedly
at a distance. Catholics, Weil reminds Father Couturier, admit as
much while defending or promulgating their faith.

> The Catholic religion contains explicitly truths which other
> religions contain implicitly. But, conversely, other religions
> contain explicitly truths which are only implicit in Christianity.
> The most well-informed Christian can still learn a great deal
> concerning divine matters from other religious traditions;
> although inward spiritual light can also cause him to apprehend
> everything through the medium of his own tradition. All the
> same, were these other traditions to disappear from the face of
> the earth, it would be an irreparable loss. The missionaries have
> already made far too many of them disappear as it is.
>
> St. John of the Cross compares faith to reflections of silver,
> truth being gold. The various authentic religious traditions are
> different reflections of the same truth, and perhaps equally
> precious. But we do not realize this, because each of us lives only
> one of these traditions and sees the others from outside. But as
> Catholics are for ever repeating—and rightly—to unbelievers, a
> religion can only be known from the inside.[36]

What Weil thinks is necessary for the study of other religions is
actual sympathy, and this is only possible when the possibility
exists for genuine friendship. (In the next section we will examine
the complications created by the dictum "Love thy enemies" in
Christian theology with respect to Judaism and Islam and how it
manifests itself in Weil's most controversial writings.) Friendship,
however, is equally rare as it entails openness, vulnerability, and
the "consent to preserve an autonomy within ourselves and in

others."[37] In other words, there ought to be no ulterior motives in the study of other religions; that is, there can be no desire to transform or to convert them, even, or especially, for the sake of self-preservation or self-enlargement.

The list of religious and ancient cultural traditions Weil admires is as long as it is diverse: Hinduism,[38] the ancient Greeks[39] and Egyptians,[40] Taoism, Buddhism, European mythology and folklore,[41] among others. And, we must not forget, she even holds atheism in high regard. The consequence of her openness to other ways of (religious) thinking hints to a sort of flattening out of distinctions, however. One can only imagine, for instance, Father Couturier's initial reaction when he read Weil's account of the parallelism between Christian theism and atheism: "So likewise an atheist or an 'infidel,' capable of pure compassion, are as close to God as is a Christian, and consequently know Him equally well, although their knowledge is expressed in other words, or remains unspoken."[42]

Comparative approaches to religion and philosophy, even with the best intentions, are prone to conflating all traditions to a single universal truth. The argument goes that each tradition remains distinct in its outward (exoteric) manifestations (i.e., orthodox sets of beliefs, sacred literatures, and rites), but also, at the same time, each expresses the same transcendent truth (i.e., the Divine).[43] Inspiration for this type of thinking is most commonly found among the mystics (esotericism). Weil, in fact, evinces a similar conclusion when she writes,

> In practice, mystics belonging to nearly all the religious traditions coincide to the extent that they can hardly be distinguished. They represent the truth of each of these traditions.
>
> The contemplation practiced in India, Greece, China, etc., is just as supernatural as that of the Christian mystics. More particularly, there exists a very close affinity between Plato and, for example, St. John of the Cross. Also between Hindu Upanishads and St. John of the Cross. Taoism too is very close to Christian mysticism.
>
> The Orphic and Pythagorean mysteries were authentic mystical traditions. Likewise the Eleusinian.[44]

But if we look carefully at the wording of this otherwise innocuous passage, we see signs of assimilationism. Granted, this passage appears in the context of a letter written to a Catholic friar for the purpose of posing to him Weil's specifically Christian theological questions, but in each comparative citation, the benchmark is a *Christian* mystic. She does not demonstrate her point by offering a comparison between Taoism and the Hindu Upanishads, for instance. This tendency to simultaneously uphold the legitimacy of non-Christian religions by their relation to Christianity occurs repeatedly in her letter (and other writings). As another case in point, she writes, "There have *perhaps* been among various peoples (India, Egypt, China, Greece) sacred Scriptures revealed *in the same manner as* the Jewish-Christian Scriptures."[45]

Up until this point we have seen that Weil insists that we "consent to preserve an autonomy . . . in others." Yet, in the instances cited above and in many others as well, she departs from this position and adopts a more typical attempt to value non-Christian religions on the basis of their intimations of Christianity.[46] In particular, she finds (rather hypocritically we must add) these other religious traditions agreeable insofar as she can detect in them acceptance of incarnationism, actual incarnations, or even a foreshadowing of *the incarnation in the body of Christ*. Hence, in the passage quoted earlier, she identifies the Holy Spirit as that which bestowed light on the prophets of the non-Christian religions included in her assemblage.[47] In some of these traditions, such as the ancient Eleusinian mysteries, the Holy Spirit manifested itself in the sacred rites, which, according to Weil, "were real sacraments, possessing the same virtue as baptism or the eucharist." This is true, however, only insofar as they presage "Christ's Passion" which was "then to come. Today it is past. Past and future are symmetrical,"[48] she informs Father Couturier. With respect to some religions, Weil takes the radical position—especially for a Christian—that some of those prophets may have been, not merely human messengers of God, but actual divine incarnations. "At all events," Weil writes to the Dominican priest, "we do not know for certain that there have not been incarnations previous to that of Jesus, and that Osiris in Egypt, Krishna in India were not of that number."[49]

The takeaway from all of this is that Weil's Christian conviction, in the end, does color her perception of other religions. Although she views *many* religions in a favorable light—because after all, according to her, they all reflect the light of the Holy Spirit sent by the Son of God—there are others, as we will see in the next section, that are distinguished and excluded from her positive assessment. In fact, she is outright antagonistic toward them primarily on the basis of their denial of the Christian theological doctrine of the incarnation.

Love's implicit enemies—The Jew, the Muslim

Relatively little of what Weil wrote was ever published during her lifetime. The majority of her writings, from which scholars have since pieced together her philosophical-religious views, were published posthumously and mainly consist of letters and her reflections recorded in her *cahiers* (notebooks). Weil never intended, of course, for her personal correspondences and scattered notes to be made public. She left her notebooks with her friend and confidante Gustave Thibon for safekeeping before she left for America with her family in 1942.[50] She died the next year.

In 1947 Thibon published a collection of passages from her notebooks under the title, *La pésanteur et la grâce* (translated into English as *Gravity and Grace*).[51] The publication of this collection nearly coincided with the Zionist formation of the state of Israel in 1948, and as Thomas Nevin has observed, "More than any other volume bearing her name, with the possible exception of *Attente de Dieu* [*Waiting for God*], published three years later, *La pésanteur et la grâce* shaped Weil's image and reputation for her first generation of readers."[52] This work is especially important for the impact it made and continues to make upon Weil's English language audience, including the present authors. Anticipating a negative backlash to the selections Thibon collated under the heading "Israel," especially in the aftermath of World War II, the editors of the first translation into English published by Routledge in 1952 omitted this section. The omission has just recently been rectified when, according to Lawrence Schmidt, "Under pressure from [Palle] Yourgrau, Routledge had the chapter translated by Mario von der Ruhr and finally included in the 'First Complete English language edition' published in 2002."[53] What exactly did Weil write in these passages that the editors feared would prove detrimental to her reception in the English-speaking world?

Before we answer that question, it does bear noting that their suspicions have been justified, even if their decision to censor the material has not. Few commentators have resisted taking Weil—and her admirers—to task for "her narrow, willful, and ignorant reading of Judaism."[54] The list of prominent scholars and public intellectuals who criticize her for "rejecting" or even "hating her Jewish identity" includes: George Steiner, Robert Coles, Anna Freud, Alfred Kazin, Rachel Brenner, Witold Rabi, and Jeffrey Mehlman.[55] Emmanuel Levinas—perhaps her most eminent critic (and admirer)—goes so far as to declare that, "Simone Weil *hates* the Bible [i.e., the Old Testament, or Torah]."[56] Perhaps Levinas' curt summation of Weil's position on Judaism is correct. But given Weil's otherwise consistent appeal to reason and compassion, it bears examining how she arrived at what others perceive as obviously mistaken and prejudicial positions, ones that run contrary to the entirety of her religious philosophy.

Despite countless analyses and cautions about the dangers inherent in the union of theology and politics (see Weil's own warnings as discussed above and in Chapter 1), religious intellectuals continue to construct apologia while denouncing what they deem fundamental misunderstandings and misappropriations of religious ethical-social-political values. In fact, it is often argued that it is precisely within religious discourse that the kernels of universal justice (and human rights) are to be found. Weil is one of those figures frequently cited and praised as a fecund source of religio-political inspiration—as someone who embodies and articulates a *true* Christian ethos, rooted in the unconditional love of God, and who advocates universal justice against the tyrannies of relativism, capitalism, bureaucracy, and totalitarianism.

That being said, in the section on Israel (Judaism) published in *Gravity and Grace*, in addition to other comments found throughout her *cahiers* and personal correspondences, one finds severe and unforgiving criticisms of Judaism—and Islam—that lack the intellectual sensitivity with which she otherwise has come to be associated. Take for example the following passage, in which she writes,

> Evil is to be purified—or life is not possible. God alone can do that. This is the idea of the Gita. It is also the idea of Moses, of Mahomet, of Hitlerism . . . But Jehovah, Allah, Hitler are earthly Gods. The purification they bring about is imaginary.[57]

Jehovah (the God of the Jews), Allah (the God of the Muslims), and Hitler (the God of the Nazis) are grouped together in her purview, and stand diametrically opposed to the nonimaginary purifications she contends are offered by the God of the Christian and the Hindu, and intimated by the ancient Greeks, among others. This supposition demands serious investigation if thinking about Weil's religious philosophy is to remain relevant and responsible.

The first sign of the estrangement of Judaism and Islam in Weil's philosophy is their conspicuous absence from the catalog of religions that she held in high regard.[58] When either of the religions that share the Abrahamic heritage with Christianity is mentioned in the same passage as the non-Christian traditions she favored, it is usually for the purpose of serving as the foil in her argument. As Levinas observes about Weil's treatment of Judaism in his jeremiad, "Only Greek, Chaldean, Egyptian and Hindu writings contain an unsullied generosity. Jews possess only a God for armies—how horrible!"[59]

The basis of her caustic criticisms of Judaism and Islam is twofold: both religions, she claims, are motivated by a will to power, and they both reject the incarnation. As we have seen, these are not unrelated issues in Weil's philosophy.

Building her case for the former accusation, she writes, "The veritable idolatry is covetousness . . . and the Jewish nation, in its thirst for carnal good, was guilty of this in the very moments even when it was worshipping its God. The Hebrews took for their idol, not something made of metal or wood, but a race, a nation, something just as earthly. Their religion is essentially inseparable from such idolatry, because of the notion of the 'chosen people.'"[60] To put this slightly differently, according to Weil's reading of the Old Testament,[61] instead of truly renouncing idolatry as was commanded—"You shall not make for yourself an idol, whether in the form of anything that is in heaven above, or that is on the earth beneath . . ." (Exodus 20:4)—and worshipping the invisible and self-renouncing God, the Hebrews desired other nations' earthly wealth and power. To acquire it, Weil contends that they constructed a theology—one with a remarkably complicit God—that hypocritically denounces idol worship while simultaneously erecting itself as the new idol—the nation of Israel.

Following this line of reasoning, Weil concludes that Judaism is in essence an "[e]xclusively collective religion."[62] As such, its aspirations are purely temporal and of this world, and the means it employs to attain those ambitions are of the same kind.[63] The God of the Jews not only committed violent acts, as recorded in the Old Testament, but He also commanded—thereby providing a supposedly divine justification for—Jews to commit mass atrocities in order to achieve their own self-serving ends with a great cost for their neighbors. Weil finds this ethically reproachable, and logically inconsistent with the God she knows via Christ.

The language she uses in her critical retellings should sound quite familiar, as it is the very language she employs against idolatrous ersatz religions formed and perpetuated by the Great Beast (see Chapter 1):

> The Hebrews call their own collective soul God; they pretended, and convinced themselves, that it was the creator and ruler of heaven and earth. This was not always easy to believe . . . Nevertheless, it seems that it must have given them an extra strength. As for the neighboring peoples, they had to be conquered before they could be convinced of it. Their neighbors were unwilling to associate with them except on terms which obliged them to practice idolatry, because their claim to possess God as a national fetish and to possess him exclusively implied a terrifyingly imperialist outlook. With a people which was still weak and very unmilitary, and which had been broken by slavery, such an attitude could hardly succeed.[64]

She adds, "With the Moslems it [i.e., theologically motivated conquest] succeeded much better."[65] For, according to Weil, Muslims, too, "aspired to temporal domination in the name of religion,"[66] and, she writes elsewhere in her *cahiers*, "They made converts, not without a certain amount of violence."[67] Drawing a direct connection between Judaism and what she has previously called the Great Beast, she declares, "What we call idolatry is to a large extent an invention of Jewish fanaticism." And then she goes on to speculate in her letter to Father Couturier, "If some Hebrews of classical Jewry were to return to life and were to be provided with arms, they would exterminate the lot of us—men, women and children, for the crime of idolatry. They would reproach us for worshipping Baal and Astarte, taking Christ for Baal and the Virgin for Astarte."[68] In summation, Weil concludes that both Judaism and

Islam are essentially idolatrous, fundamentally violent, and purely politically minded ersatz religions.

In addition, theologically they exclude the possibility of the one pure means to resolve the problem of the will to power. The real crux of the matter, or at least the most deep-seated basis of her anti-Jewish and anti-Islamic point of view, rests on the centrality of the incarnation in her thought. As we demonstrated in the previous section, Weil's positive assessment of some non-Christian traditions comes at the expense of those religions in and of themselves, on their own terms, as she values them only insofar as they corroborate the Christian belief in the incarnation. The same cannot be said of Judaism and Islam. "In reality the process by which Simone Weil establishes this perfidy of the Jews is at the very least original," writes Levinas, who then adds, "It consists first of all in crediting every nation on earth, with the exception of Israel, with a prefiguration of the Passion."[69] In her own words, Weil posits as irrevocable truth:

> There can be no *personal* contact between man and God except through the person of the Mediator. Without the latter, God can only be present to man collectively, nationally. Israel chose the national God and simultaneously rejected the Mediator; it may, at one time or another, have moved towards true monotheism, but it always fell back on, and was unable not to fall back on, the God of the tribe.[70]

The theologies of both Judaism and Islam deny this theological claim. "The prophet," according to the Jewish theologian Abraham Joshua Heschel, "is a person. . . . The prophet's task is to convey a divine view, yet as a person he *is* a point of view."[71] The prophet does not lose his particularity (personhood) and is not, in other words, identifiable as being God incarnate; he always maintains a certain distance from God. Theologically, Judaism and Islam have more in common than either independently has with Christianity on this very basis. But Christian political theology has succeeded in dividing them from one another (the habitual refrain "Judeo-Christian" has the effect of theologically disavowing Islam from its Abrahamic heritage), perhaps for the purposes of conquering both.

In his book, *The Jew, the Arab: A History of the Enemy*, Gil Anidjar has convincingly argued that the Jew and the Arab (i.e.,

Muslim) are prefigured as the implicit enemies of Christianity (and by extension, of Europe and the West).[72] As it says in the Gospel of Matthew, "one's foes will be members of one's own household."[73] Upon a certain reading, then, Christianity's foes, in other words, are its Abrahamic companion religions, Judaism and Islam.

First, they are made identical with one another: non-Christian. But, the commandment is to "love thy enem*ies*" thereby necessitating there to be not a single enemy but numerous enemies within the "household." Second, Judaism and Islam must be separated from one another to account for this plurality. Following the generation of Augustine's and Aquinas' just war theories, Anidjar explains how Christianity's enemies came to be distinguished from one another, first by spatial metaphor, "near" (Judaism) and "far" (Islam), and subsequently, on theological and political grounds:

> Aquinas [in *Summa contra Gentiles*] distinguishes and separates the Jew from the Arab, the Jew from the Muslim, by affirming that a theological struggle, a religious disputation, is possible only on the basis of a prior agreement, a consensus and common ground, a common text. Such theological common ground is available only with the Jews, not the Muslims. [Aquinas writes,] "The Mohammedans and the pagans do not agree with us in accepting authority of any scripture. . . . Thus, against the Jews we are able to argue by means of the Old Testament, while against heretics we are able to argue by means of the New Testament. But the Mohammedans and the pagans accept neither the one nor the other."[74]

Judaism is cast, therefore, as the internal theological enemy of Christianity. Despite there being theological differences, in part there remains a shared scriptural tradition. Perceiving no theological common ground with Islam, then, Aquinas locates Islam on the other end of the spectrum and reduces it to being the external political enemy of Christianity. Anidjar goes on to enumerate a litany of casualties of this line of thinking.

Because the pinnacle of Weil's religious philosophy is incarnationism—a theological contention—she does *not* maintain the distinction between Judaism and Islam as explained above; they are both theological *and* political enemies. Precisely due to their theological denial of the incarnation, they are deemed by her to be motivated by political desires. It is *only* through the incarnation that a (non-imaginary) just balance can be established. Christ (or Krishna, etc.) is the lynchpin. As she says to Father Couturier, "*[T]here is no purity without participating in the divine incarnation . . .*"[75] What remains is an either/or decision on the incarnation. All religions, therefore, that refuse or even refute the incarnation, are impure (i.e., have made the wrong decision and, therefore, willfully perpetuate an unjust balance) in her view.

"It is Platonic clarity which haunts Simone Weil,"[76] writes Emmanuel Levinas. Ironically, her exacting analyses of the crises facing humanity, and her equally precise and tightly woven solutions to those crises, arrive at a single absolute principle from which she cannot waver, no matter what the consequences. As we have already discussed, Weil "found unacceptable and repugnant the Church's refusal to disavow or to be contrite over past actions that had destroyed vulnerable human lives."[77] In fact, as E. Jane Doering has noted, Weil intended to write an essay summarizing "her thoughts on the need to redirect the course of Christianity, purge it of influences that glorified force, power, and prestige, and *eliminate the idea of exclusivity.*"[78] But because of her utter reliance on the incarnation to solve perennial philosophical, religious, *and,* by extension, social and political dilemmas, she ultimately sides with religion as being in sole possession of *political* authority. So-called religions that do not at the very least intimate Christianity, such as Islam and Judaism, "the Great Beast[s] of religion," are "not likable," for, as she says, "[t]he Great Beast is always repulsive."[79] As Doering explains further, "Weil had come to the firm conviction that *the Christian spirituality of love, charity, and faith had to permeate any civilization that wished to counter the force of gravity in human nature that pulled human beings toward the exploitation of their fellow beings.*"[80] This point is made abundantly clear when Weil concludes, "There can be no legitimacy without religion,"[81] which she has narrowly defined to the exclusion of the Jew and the Muslim. The practical implications of this line of thinking are frightfully clear.

Weil ends up where she began, but, unfortunately, this time on the other side of the proverbial coin. What at first was the subject of her philosophical-religious critique, Weil now forcefully advocates during what amounts to the construction of her own political-theology. She reminds us that Christ did not "prescribe

the abolition of penal justice."[82] Then, she adds, the "legal character of a punishment has no true significance if it does not give it
some kind of religious meaning . . . and therefore *all penal offices,
from that of the judge to that of the executioner and the prison
guard, should in some sort share in the priestly office."*[83] The inter-
locking of the political apparatus and the supernatural sounds sus-
piciously familiar to the unholy union she identified at the root of
the Church's abuses, and, which, she originally sought to expose
and challenge.

Then, in a move so flagrantly contradictory to her prior criticisms of the Church to be almost unthinkable, at one point Weil
condones *anathema sit.* In the fourteenth question that she poses
to Father Couturier, she says,

> To keep in line with St. John, [*the Church*] *should never have
> excommunicated any except the Docetae, those who deny the
> Incarnation.* The definition of faith according to the catechism
> of the Council of Trent (firm belief in everything taught by the
> Church) is very far removed from that of St. John, for whom faith
> was purely and simply belief in the Incarnation of the Son of God
> in the person of Jesus. . . . According to St. John, the Church has
> never had the right to excommunicate any one who truly believed
> Christ to be the Son of God come down to earth in the flesh.[84]

We might concede that this makes sense internally to Christianity;
that is, only those who accept the incarnation are properly
"Christian." But Weil has already made clear that identity in a collective is in itself problematic for the universalist message revealed
in Christ—hence, her own resistance to baptism. As if the contra-
riety of her position is not confounding enough, in the very next
question to the friar—numbered fifteen—she returns to her usual
habit of admonishing the Church for, among other things, not having "learned from [the] parable [of the Good Samaritan] never to
excommunicate any who practices love of his neighbor."[85]

Weil would have been aware of the original Greek usage of the
term *anathema*, especially in the biblical context, where it denotes
"the object of a curse."[86] All who do not accept the truth of incarnation, or intimate it, are cursed and are rightfully banished according to Weil who cites St. John as precedent, else the host society
risk contagion. They are enemies.

Consequently, Weil's critique of Judaism turns into blame.[87] First, because Judaism is an earthly religion, in her account, and Jesus' message inverts that perspective in favor of the truly transcendent because loving God,[88] she holds the Jews (in connection with the Romans) responsible for Jesus' crucifixion, saying that they are, "[a] people chosen for blindness, chosen to be Christ's executioner."[89] Accusing Jews of the persecution and eventual murder of Jesus is certainly not original, and historically it has accompanied sinister intentions resulting in abhorrent and bloody consequences.

This brings to mind the second and most sweeping and bewildering charge she levels against Judaism. Namely, Weil blames Judaism for corrupting Christendom.

> . . . To speak of an 'educational God' in connection with this people [Jews] is a cruel joke. It is not astonishing that there should be so much evil in a civilization—ours [i.e., Christian European]—contaminated to the core, in its very inspiration, by this terrible lie. The curse of Israel rests on Christendom. Israel meant atrocities, the Inquisition, the extermination of heretics and infidels. Israel meant (and to a certain extent still does . . .) capitalism. Israel means totalitarianism, especially with regard to its worst enemies.[90]

What *is* astonishing to us, alongside countless other critics, is that, given her own sensitivity to the rise of Nazism, she intimates their anti-Semitic rhetoric. After all, Nazi propaganda, likewise, framed European Jewry as a contagion. And this language, as it was designed to do, incited violence and genocidal behavior.

But as Weil sees it, Judaism is a spiritual saboteur of Christianity and European civilization. "The Jews, that handful of uprooted people, have caused the uprootedness of the whole terrestrial globe," she writes, continuing,

> Their involvement in Christianity has made of Christendom, in regard to its own past, something uprooted. The orientation of the Enlightenment, 1789, secularism, etc. have infinitely increased this uprooting, through the lie of progress. And uprooted Europe has uprooted the rest of the world, by colonial conquest. Capitalism, totalitarianism, have a share in this progressive uprootedness . . .[91]

Her claim, as absurd and obscene as it sounds, is that Judaism set off a domino effect resulting in every major crisis in the classical and modern worlds, including and especially the spiritual crisis in Christianity and all the sins it has perpetrated falsely in the name of Christ.[92]

These remarks must be read in conjunction with an important biographical note, lest they result in the mistaken impression that Weil was (self-)hateful of the Jewish race. In August 1940 Weil applied for a teaching post, hoping to be assigned to one of the French colonies as a means to get out of France. After not having received a reply, she inferred that she had been denied an appointment due to the racist policies of the Vichy government as outlined in the statute concerning Jews that was issued on October 3, 1940. According to her friend and biographer Simone Pétrement, who ascertained the following based on documents she obtained while compiling research for her book, Weil had actually been "appointed a professor at the girls' lycée in Constantine on October 1, 1940," but, "for some reason the information never reached her."[93] Unaware of her appointment, in November Weil composed a sardonic reply to the Minister of Education.

Similar to the letter she sent to Father Couturier, in this letter Weil poses a series of questions to the unsuspecting Minister of Education. This letter, unlike the one written in earnest to the Dominican priest, however, is dripping with sarcasm and is intended to lay bare the racist ideology at the heart of Nazism and their Vichy collaborators. She opens the letter stating her intentions. "I want to know to whom this Statute applies, so that I may be enlightened as to my own standing. I do not know the definition of the word 'Jew'; that subject was not included in my education."[94] Citing the statute's exact wording, which stated that a "Jew" is "a person who has three or more Jewish grandparents,"[95] Weil proceeds by constantly referring to herself as the case in point, forcing the Minister, should he respond, to provide her with a clear definition of the term as well as to explain how his office determined that she fit the definition.

Does the term "Jew" denote someone of the Jewish faith, or does it denote someone of the Jewish race, she queries? If it designates the former, she informs him that she has "never been in a synagogue, and [has] never witnessed a Jewish religious ceremony."[96] Then, in a mordacious tone, she writes, "On the other hand, I know definitely that both my maternal grandparents were free-thinkers."[97] "But perhaps," she continues, "the word designates a race?" To which Weil explains that, according to the historian Josephus, Titus succeeded in exterminating this race, and so "it seems highly unlikely that they left many descendents."[98] So, how exactly did the Vichy government verify that she was of the Jewish race, she asks, to which, in the same manner that Socrates answered his own questions in the *Apology*, Weil surmises that it would "be quite difficult to get reliable information on this point."[99] Weil closes the letter asking once again, "But I should like to be officially enlightened on this point, since I myself have no criterion by which I may resolve the question."[100] Not surprisingly, Weil "never received a reply."[101]

Pétrement soberly summarizes the gist of this letter as follows:

> Obviously this letter did not mean that Simone was not in solidarity with other Jews. The arguments she raises in regard to race were valuable for all Jews. On the contrary, she was mocking the "Statutory Regulations on Jews" and the confused ideas on which all anti-Semitic racism rests.[102]

Although for some the temptation to claim otherwise has proven too much to resist, in this light it is clear that Weil was not racist. Even if she did not use such derogatory language in the exact same manner employed by the Nazis, however, it is inexcusable for a thinker with such intellectual acuity, and one so morally minded, to be as callous and unjust in her treatment of Judaism and, we would add, Islam. "Simone Weil's anti-biblical passion," Levinas cautioned, "could wound and trouble Jews."[103] Her remarks about Judaism and Islam cannot be passed over or uncritically accepted as being benign. What are we, then, to make of them?

To begin, we follow Levinas and other critics who have exposed Weil's ignorance of Judaism. Weil never took the time to study Hebrew, or Arabic for that matter, not to forget her nonchalant condemnations of Islam. She admits as much throughout her writings when she confidently corrects translations of ancient Greek, without any reference to their Hebrew equivalents when it would be appropriate. Her demand for accuracy in representing religious symbols and religious language seems not to matter so much to her with respect to the Jewish and Islamic traditions.

One could go so far as to say that her approach to Jewish and Islamic literature is dilettantish. As a result, her readings of each are reductive and, at times, childishly naïve. As Levinas writes in his rejoinder to Weil's interpretation of Judaism,

> We cannot reproach Simone Weil's culture for being ignorant of the fact that notions like goodness are not simple, and that they can call up and encapsulate notions which seem opposed to them. And while the dialectic of Christian experience excites her, she is content to remain on the level of immediate notions whenever it involves referring to the Old Testament. Here she casually repeats Voltaire's argument that "Abraham began by prostituting his wife."[104]

Furthermore, her biased reading of the Old Testament—and near nonexistent reading of the Qu'ran or other Islamic literature—lacks nuance and sophistication. It also lacks humility. It is difficult to fathom that the author of these commentaries on the Old Testament is the same astute reader of ancient Greek texts, such as *Iliad* or *Antigone*, or the *Bhagavad Gita*. But, as Levinas rightly notes, Weil misses a fundamental yet obvious point about the stories in the Old Testament.

> Israel is not a model people, but a free people. It is of course, like any people, filled with lust and tempted by carnal delights. The Bible tells us of this lust in order to denounce it, but also knows that it is not enough to deny. It seeks to elevate matters by introducing the notion of justice.[105]

Weil interprets most of the stories in the Old Testament as mythical affirmations of the collective desire of the Jewish people. Somehow she managed to gloss over much of the inherent complexity that exists within Judaism and Islam and their sacred literatures. But Weil presumes that a true religious text must provide people with an exact model of goodness, one that uniformly solves all dilemmas in the same manner as the Passion of Christ in the New Testament. In the end, we are justified in being suspicious of the conclusions she draws.

To carry forward a metaphor we previously used, in her treatment of Judaism and Islam, we can see plainly that she is acting.

She never succeeds in having true *sympathy* with them. Recall that she said to be in a position to claim knowledge of another religion is to "transport ourselves for a time by faith to the very center of whichever [religion] we are studying." What is required, in other words, is to "have given all our attention, all our faith, all our love . . . that is proper to it."[106] By her own standards, Weil's readings of Judaism and Islam are clearly done in bad faith. Like a failed actress, she never loses herself in the role of being a Jew or a Muslim; she remains self-conscious—that is, consciously Christian—and, therefore, at a critical distance from these religions. Her own personality intrudes upon the scene. Thus, she never consents to their autonomy which is necessary—again according to her own philosophy—for friendship. In this way she affirms our suspicion that Judaism and Islam are the implicit, if not explicit, enemies of Weil's Christian love.

In retrospect, Weil's treatment of Judaism and Islam backs her into a corner, and the best possible explanation is that she is guilty of not practicing her own philosophy. On one hand, she champions the disenfranchised, the downtrodden, the outcasts, the afflicted, and, generally speaking, the most vulnerable among us. Weil questions the social, political, and religious boundaries created by self-interested will to power. She challenges the Church and its complicity with values and practices contrary to Christ's exemplarity. She even seeks wisdom within a plurality of religious and cultural traditions and denounces Christian missionaries and the colonization of indigenous peoples. On the other hand, because she staunchly opposes relativism, and following the Platonic model, thinks justice can only be had through a universalizable truth, her system hinges on an abiding belief in an absolute, unchanging, transcendent ideal—God. As Levinas observes of her philosophy, "Good [is turned] into an absolutely pure idea [by Weil], excluding all contamination or violence."[107] This ideal, this goodness, was most clearly embodied in Christ. As consequence, other religions are valued insofar as they either have within them possible events of incarnationism or admit of the possibility of the incarnation of God in Christ. Otherwise, her system does not hold together—to the detriment of Jews and Muslims above all.

Another way of framing the tensions in Weil's thought about Judaism in particular, especially given her letter to the Minister of Education, is to place her within the long line of Jewish intellectuals who struggle with the question of what it means to be Jewish. And it is here that Weil's criticisms can at least serve as an occasion to consider some important religious, ethical, and political concerns specifically pertaining to Judaism, and where, unpredictably, her philosophy parallels other Jewish thinkers in some fascinating and potentially incisive ways.

On October 22, 2009, New York University's Institute for Public Knowledge, the Social Science Research Council, and Stony Brook University convened four of the most prominent living philosophers—Judith Butler, Jürgen Habermas, Charles Taylor, and Cornel West—for a colloquy on religion in the public sphere.[108] Butler's presentation was titled, "Is Judaism Zionism?"[109] As promised by the title, in her lecture she dared ask the question that Weil posed to the Minister of Education: "What is a Jew?" It goes without saying that the answer to this question has taken on special importance since the rise of anti-Semitism, Nazism, and the Holocaust. But now it is also recast in light of the formation of the state of Israel on the basis of a Zionist philosophy. For many Jews and non-Jews, Zionism has come to be synonymous with Judaism. But for many others, again both Jewish and non-Jewish alike, Zionism and Judaism are not identical. There is a sense of urgency surrounding this question due to the ongoing occupations of the West Bank and Gaza, and the human rights abuses suffered by Palestinians, and even non-Jewish immigrants in Israel.[110]

Butler's essay summons Weil's contemporary Hannah Arendt, another Jewish philosopher who "made clear in her early writings, Jewishness is not always the same as Judaism. And, as she made clear in her evolving political position on the state of Israel, neither Judaism nor Jewishness necessarily leads to the embrace of Zionism."[111] Unsurprisingly, her position on Zionism led to harsh criticisms and even ad hominem attacks from her fellow Jewish community members; as Butler notes, Gershom Scholem went so far as to question Arendt's Jewishness.[112] Ironically, it is this very gesture—taking it upon oneself to *choose* who is and is not to count or live among us—that Arendt observed at the trial of Adolf Eichmann and toward which she directed her philosophical critiques. "According to Arendt," Butler writes, "Eichmann thought that he and his superiors *might choose* with whom to cohabit the earth and failed to realize that the heterogeneity of the earth's population is an irreversible condition of social and political life itself."[113]

The Nazis decided that Jews, homosexuals, gypsies, and others did not fit within their idealized society and eugenic aspirations and, hence, set out to exclude (*anathema sit*) them once and for all. Judaism, Butler argues, provides a direct yet paradoxical response to such exclusivist enterprises, including, she adds, Zionism.

Judaic ethics require the suspension of the principle of identity, according to Butler. As she explains, "[W]ithin several ethical frameworks, Jewishness is itself an anti-identitarian project insofar as we might even say that being a Jew implies taking up an ethical relation to the non-Jew."[114] The ethical imperative is cohabitation. To face the other is to give full consent to the other's alterity. An equivalent to this ethical imperative is found in Weil's understanding of friendship. Or, as Levinas writes, "To love one's neighbor can mean already to glimpse his mastery over us, and the dignity he has as someone who is associated with God and has rights over us."[115] Accepting the other *as other* displaces self-privilege, or egoistic desire. As Butler writes,

. . . we must actively preserve the nonchosen character of inclusive and plural cohabitation: we not only live with those we never chose, and to whom we may feel no social sense of belonging, but we are also obligated to preserve those lives and the plurality of which they form a part. . . . To cohabit the earth is prior to any possible community or nation or neighborhood. We might choose where to live, and who to live by, but we cannot choose with whom to cohabit the earth.[116]

No person or group warrants special preference over and above others, yet alone at the expense of others.

The paradox of the principle of Jewish identity being anti-identitarian as expounded by Butler coincides with Weil's ethics. As such, we propose that Butler's paradox is a corrective to the internal contradictions within Weil's oeuvre, as evidenced by her selective advocacy of *anathema sit*, as well as her outright caustic remarks about Judaism and Islam. It functions as such by evoking and then emphasizing the most prescient ideas in Weil's thought—albeit Butler arrives at the problems from a different direction—to a degree that prohibits the transgression of the paradox itself.

To begin, Weil likewise acknowledges necessity (or, our external limits), whereas in Butler's terms as stated above, it is "to realize that the heterogeneity of the earth's population is an irreversible condition of social and political life itself." On these very grounds, Weil rebuked the Church and European colonialism for attempting to and at times succeeding in eradicating non-Christian, non-European cultures.

Weil, as we will describe in the next chapter, singles out selfish desire and the imagination as the root of evil. Self-identity and by extension collective-identity reify our imagined selves, motivating a will to power. Rather than recognizing our inherent vulnerability, we tend to superimpose our imagined selves over and against the world and others—the euphemistic collateral damage of our selfish desires. In her mystical philosophy, Weil argues that we ought to be porous. As we explained in the first chapter, both philosophy and mysticism are the preparations for death (of ego). The preparation means refraining from exercising our will to power. This, in turn, ultimately entails remaining detached, and renouncing our individual and collective identities. In short, Weil's ethics are anti-identitarian.

We think it fitting to set ourselves and Weil aside and leave the last words on this topic to Butler:

> We are outside ourselves, before ourselves, and only in such a mode is there a chance of being for another. We are, to be sure, already in the hands of the other before we make any decision about with whom we choose to live. This way of being bound to one another is precisely *not* a social bond that is entered into through volition and deliberation; it precedes contract, is mired in dependency, and is often effaced by those forms of social contract that depend on an ontology of volitional individuality. Thus it is, even from the start, to the stranger that we are bound, the one, or the ones, we never knew and never chose. If we accept this sort of ontological condition, then to destroy the other is to destroy my life, that sense of my life that is invariably social life.[117]

3
Human nature and decreation

The Pharisee, standing by himself, was praying thus, "God,
I thank you that I am not like other people: thieves, rogues,
adulterers, or even like this tax collector. I fast twice a
week; I give a tenth of all my income." But the tax collector,
standing far off, would not even look up to heaven, but was
beating his breast and saying, "God, be merciful to me, a
sinner!" I tell you, this man went down to his home justified
rather than the other; for all who exalt themselves will be
humbled, but all who humble themselves will be exalted.

LUKE 18:11–14

Few speak humbly of humility, chastely of chastity, dubious-
ly of skepticism. We are nothing but lies, duplicity, contra-
diction, and we hide and disguise ourselves from ourselves.

BLAISE PASCAL[1]

In the beginning—Creation

The previous two chapters have explored the paradoxes of Simone
Weil's explicitly religious thought. Underlying her atheology with
its Christian interpretations is a set of assumptions about human

nature. Although she never systematically outlines a metaphysics of humanity, it is possible to find consistency in her descriptions of human proclivities and constitutions scattered throughout her *Notebooks*. These natural dispositions are one part and inevitable result of the act of creation, which consists of supernatural self-withdrawal to permit something else to exist; creation is both the act of divine renunciation *and* the name for this other existence that includes human beings. At the same time, Weil contends that we are to give up the conceits, privileges, and illusions of self-sufficiency that accompany our created status. That is, she sets forth religio-ethical prescriptions that directly challenge our natural tendencies; we are to return the nature that attends our creation by a process she calls *decreation*. In what follows, we detail the contours of Weil's concepts of creation, the resultant human nature, the related source of evil, and, finally, redemption by decreation. In view of these discussions, we hope to shed light on the inherent paradox that characterizes an individual's struggle for ethical innocence in a world governed by forces of moral gravity.

As we have seen, there are aspects of Simone Weil's religious thought that appear more like a systematic theology than a mystery-laden atheology. Her writings on the creation of the universe arguably fall under the former category or at least suggest a more formal cosmological view than would be expected from a negative theologian and mystic. It is also by way of these descriptions that we find a particular *quality* of the divine emerging; for Weil, in these accounts, what defines "the true God" is God's love or the refusal to exercise power everywhere.[2] God's creation, she writes, "is an act of love and it is perpetual. At each moment our existence is God's love for us."[3] In creating us, however, God renounced being everything and forewent commanding everywhere he had the power to do so. That is, God consented to withdrawing from being *all* to permit existence independent of him. For Weil, this consent to and recognition of the independent existence of another is nothing other than the meaning of love. She described creation as an act of love in this way:

> On God's part creation is not an act of self-expansion but of restraint and renunciation. God and all his creatures are less than God alone. God accepted this diminution. He emptied a part of his being from himself . . . God permitted the existence of things

distinct from himself and worth infinitely less than himself. By this creative act he denied himself, as Christ has told us to deny ourselves. God denied himself for our sakes in order to give us the possibility of denying ourselves for him. This response, this echo, which it is in our power to refuse, is the only possible justification for the folly of love of the creative act.[4]

While our "echo" to God's creation will be discussed at length in the last section of this chapter, for the present, it is imperative to grasp the Christian interpretation at hand in Weil's remarks above. God's self-denial has at least two facets: the act of creation and Christ's kenotic existence, wherein divine omnipotence is surrendered for the sake of experiencing human *pathos*. But God's self-emptying is not restricted to two discrete events in time; as Weil notes, our continued existence is proof that creation, as love, is "perpetual." Our freedom to exist outside of God's will and power is, paradoxi- cally, due to God's ongoing generosity.

In the love of creation, God withdrew, and this act provided us not only with our very existence, but also gave us the ability to love him in return, according to Weil. However, by virtue of God's withdrawal, God is not present here below as a direct object of our love. In her *Notebooks* we find: "The drawing closer together of God and man is prohibited by the very nature of creation, by the gulf separating being from appearance."[5] This distance is also required for love. As she explains elsewhere,

For if we were exposed to the direct radiance of his love, without the protection of space, of time, and of matter, we should be evaporated like water in the sun; there would not be enough "I" in us to make it possible to surrender the "I" for love's sake.[6]

Such consent to God's own absence, or to a distance, is the essence of the purest love possible for a human, according to Weil. The sign of this love would be an insatiable yearning for the super-natural (the good), a hungering that is not falsely sated by relative or natu- ral goods such as political solutions, relationships, or material pos- sessions. Thus, this love would have no *object*, as such, for it would be directed toward an elemental absence—a void.

In addition, our love must imitate the love of God, by being constituted by self-renunciation for the sake of the free existence of

others. This is why love is also understood as "belief in the existence of other human beings as such."[7] When we love something
purely, we desire only that it should exist and be part of creation;
we do not wish to change or modify a beloved, for instance, nor
do we wish to assume power over or possess a beloved by eradicating the distance between distinct beings. It is in the same way that
God's creation was an act of love, pure consent to distance, pure
consent to our existence.

And yet Weil recognizes that the act of creation also entails a
cruel irony: the withdrawal of God means license in human willing, but this freedom is qualified and conditioned by natural forces
that result from the vacuum left by God. Weil writes, "Thus the
existence of evil here below, far from disproving the reality of God,
is the very thing that reveals him in his truth."[8] Our existence, in
other words, is of necessity plagued by the absence of pure goodness; what we humans can accomplish by our own powers, desires,
and wills can only be *relatively* good, as the source of real goodness is not in us, but external to us. Thus, our plane of existence is
essentially constituted by emptiness of the good, and consequently,
as we have mentioned, a yearning for that good, which we lack.
On an individual level, too, we are constituted by this void of perfection and goodness; to be created means to be empty and to be
hungry for union with God, or with truth, goodness, and beauty.
But our necessary distance from God permits a forgetfulness of
this essential void and a tendency to seek any sort of palliative for
this hunger.

Human nature—The void

We need to take a step back here to grasp the crucial notion of
"the void" (*le vide*) in Weil's thought. According to Weil, "void" is
constitutive of our true nature and is experienced as asymmetry,
insatiable hunger, lack of equilibrium, or vacuum, but we continually attempt to escape that experience by positing or appropriat-
ing various fillers. She continually reminds us that "man's misery
consists in the fact that he is not God. He is continually forgetting
this."[9] This forgetfulness is not just the result of a poor memory,
however. Our created state characterized by incompletion, mortality, and privation of real good is practically unbearable without

not easy;
see Caputo book on exist.!

compensatory thoughts, at the very least. Since unpleasant situations tend to recall to us this unbalanced nature, the faculty of the imagination is always at work, building up a false sense of stability, and with it, a false ego. For instance, Weil tells us, "Like a gas, the soul tends to fill the entire space *which is given it*," but "not to exercise all the power at one's disposal is to endure the [given] void. This is contrary to all the laws of nature."[10] We should note Weil's articulation of the *given* emptiness of the human soul and the soul's own natural proclivity (through the imagination) to fill in that space. To leave the emptiness intact by renouncing the workings of the imagination, or to maintain the hunger, feels and *is* unnatural. But in Weil's religio-ethical thought, this maintenance of the void is precisely what is required, for attempts to fill the void are nothing other than the roots of evil.

Psychology tells us that experiences of emotional imbalance, mental suffering, depression, and in general, those states that Weil would classify as the natural effects of our created status, are to be addressed and resolved for the sake of mental "health." Psychical equilibrium is the goal. We hear this message not only from the practices of psychology and psychoanalysis, but also from our contemporary Western self-help culture that has superficially appropriated many of the findings from these disciplines.[11] Not surprisingly, Weil herself was very critical of Sigmund Freud, especially of his contention that universal or religious love is simply aim-inhibited and sublimated erotic libido, but she did agree with Freud that "any object whatsoever . . . can become an object of desire."[12] For instance, what Freud demonstrated by his theories of the pleasure principle, and more importantly, through its deferral by the reality principle, is the phenomenon by which the human psyche strives for what he called "constancy," or a plateau of regulated stimulation. In his theory, our drives—that is, our libidinal and aggressive drives—seek external and internal satisfaction that is characterized by conservatism. In other words, according to Freud, our perpetual searches for satisfaction have more to do with avoiding tension and the displeasure of excessive stimulation than they do with chasing novel and positive pleasures. Due to this conservative tendency, he argued, the libido tends to be narcissistic, returning to the ego, as if by a strong gravitational pull. For this reason, the ego, eager to appease its drives and to reduce the stimulation it receives from the external world, seeks to appropriate its love-objects as part of its identity. However, if they show resistance to such identification, the ego becomes either sadistic toward those objects, or masochistic toward itself as an object.[13]

In any case, Freud presents us with an image of a psyche that will not withstand the displeasure of tension; energy that must be displaced from one (forbidden or unavailable) object to another (more convenient) object is "desexualized libido," or "sublimated energy."[14] Such a process occurs to avoid real frustration that issues from an encounter with the external world and explains, in his view, phenomena like appreciation of art and religious devotion. But in Freud's metapsychology, the drives that are constitutive of the human are never permanently satisfied; human existence is marred by a never-ending process of managing these energies in negotiations with the external world. He describes our essential situation in *Civilization and Its Discontents*:

> Life, as we find it, is too hard for us; it brings us too many pains, disappointments, and impossible tasks. In order to bear it we cannot dispense with palliative measures . . . There are perhaps three such measures: powerful deflections, which cause us to make light of our misery; substitutive satisfactions, which diminish it; and intoxicating substances, which make us insensitive to it. Something of the kind is indispensable.[15]

To put his assessment in Weil's terminology: humans require void-fillers. It would be absurd (and neurotic) to forego the consolations afforded by fantasies and distractions, which, after all, make civilization possible. Moreover, we yearn for constancy and equilibrium, an ultimately "inorganic state" that Freud also interprets as the *origin* of those drives and that evidences our essential "need to restore an earlier state of things."[16]

For Weil, however, the inevitable tension and lack of equilibrium that characterizes human life is *itself* due to an earlier state of things. As we have said, insofar as our existence is the result of the withdrawal of pure goodness, we have necessarily inherited that vacuum, which manifests itself as a longing or desire for the good. Aristophanes' account of the origin of desire, as it appears in Plato's *Symposium*, may serve as a helpful illustration here. According to the myth, originally we were spherical beings with two heads, four arms, four legs, and so on, who became so hubristic that we rolled right up Mount Olympus in a challenge to the gods. As a result, Zeus decided to cut us in two, which caused these now-partial beings to roam the earth, looking and yearning for their other half.[17] This splitting appears to explain the origin of desire (or the "void") and, hence, human nature.

However, there is something telling in the original challenge to the gods that is often taken for granted. As Anne Carson points out,

> Aristophanes' judgment ([that] "no lover could want anything else" [than eternal oneness]) is belied by the anthropology of his own myth. Was it the case that the round beings of his fantasy remained perfectly content rolling about the world in prelapsarian oneness? No. They got big ideas and started rolling toward Olympus to make an attempt on the gods (190b–c). They began reaching for something else. So much for oneness.[18]

In this significant interpretation, even the "earlier state of things" as original unity does not preclude a longing for *something else*. Indeed, Weil's cosmology does not suggest any primeval wholeness that was ours. But our very beings are partial, finite, and therefore constituted by desire *because* we are created; that is, we are the products of love and are destined to love—in the sense of the Greek *eros*, which denotes lack and a reaching for what we do not have. Thus, Weil affirms Diotima's correction of Aristophanes:

> Now there is a certain story . . . according to which lovers are those people who seek their other halves. But according to my story, a lover does not seek the half or the whole, unless, my friend, it turns out to be *good* as well . . . That's because what everyone loves is really nothing other than *the good*.[19]

So the original desire for the good, in order to remain vital, entails endurance of the void that carries with it a feeling of imbalance or asymmetry and necessarily involves suffering—a prescription *contrary* to those "pragmatic" recommendations of psychology and psychiatry. Indeed, as Iris Murdoch, a scholar and admirer of Weil, described, the void is "the anguished experience of lack of balance. We have been unjustly treated, insulted, humiliated: we want to get our own back, to get even, if need be to hurt innocent people as we

have been hurt."[20] But that lack of balance is essential because it is
what makes us conscious of our disposition with relation to reality,
namely, that we are not God (or the good). In a statement that captures this fact via her unique atheology, Weil writes, "We can only
know one thing about God: that he is what we are not. Our misery
alone is the image of this. The more we contemplate it, the more
we contemplate Him."[21] This is why loving truth means enduring the void and refusing the deflections, substitutive satisfactions,
and intoxications Freud described. To gravitate toward and make
use of those compensations as a means to establish equilibrium for
oneself is, as Weil put it, "bad because it is imaginary."[22]

Because in Weil's understanding, humans are constituted by
void and are continually "hungry," we grasp for consolations that
will provide the illusion of being "full" and complete. Not surprisingly, then, we frequently lose consciousness of our void altogether (and thereby our proper position in relation to the universe),
and this negligence is further reinforced by earthly successes and
privileges. (It is thus harder for those more prosperous to recall
their true nature as finite, created beings than for the materially
poor and afflicted.) Mere complacency, negligence, and forgetfulness may sometimes be the culprits for our turn toward baseness, but more often than not, rewards are greedily sought out and
accepted, burdens are displaced on others, suffering is intentionally deflected, revenge is enacted, grudges are clung to, and distractions are welcomed—in short, the void is actively covered over and
disguised. In all such cases and numerous others, we have negation
of void—a-voidance—and the hasty workings of what Weil called
l'imagination combleuse, the filling imagination, the source of
all evil.

Comfortable illusions—Evil

In her letter to an injured soldier, Joë Bousquet, in May 1942, Weil
confessed,

> I believe that the root of evil, in everybody perhaps, but certainly
> in those whom affliction has touched and above all if the
> affliction is biological, is day-dreaming. It is the sole consolation,
> the unique resource of the afflicted; the one solace to help them

bear the fearful burden of time; and a very innocent one, besides being indispensable. So how could it be possible to renounce it? It has only one disadvantage, which is that it is unreal.[23]

It is perhaps astounding that an activity as seemingly innocuous as reverie should be called "the root of evil." Even Weil acknowledged—paradoxically—that it is an "innocent" consolation for the afflicted, who are desperate for any reprieve whatsoever from their overwhelming and excruciating suffering. However, as she also indicates, the problem with daydreaming is that it is "unreal," escapist. More generally, *l'imagination combleuse*, for her, is not only inherently distracting, but it is also destructive and a "liar" because it flattens phenomena into two dimensions and conveniently conceals the relations between events.[24] This is the sort of imagination that is more closely associated with fantasy than with inspired and creative thinking about real problems.

We know that Weil was influenced by Blaise Pascal in this regard, and it is likely that in his discussion of "diversion," we find the germ of what was to become her notion of *l'imagination combleuse*. For instance, in the *Pensées*, he writes:

> Being unable to cure death, wretchedness and ignorance, men have decided, in order to be happy, not to think about such things . . . The only good thing for men therefore is to be diverted from thinking of what they are, either by some occupation which takes their mind off it, or by some novel and agreeable passion which keeps them busy, like gambling, hunting, some absorbing show, in short by what is called diversion.[25]

Such a description has much in common with her statement that "the thought of death calls for a counterweight, and this counterweight—apart from grace—cannot be anything but a lie," wherein this counterweight is a reference to the imagination, the "filler of the void."[26] As a mental faculty, the imagination accurately captures most of our waking life so that we may *a-void*, that is, negate the feeling of emptiness that inevitably manifests itself in our being.

Thus, we are masters of a-voiding (reality) by imaginarily "filling" the emptiness that constitutes our true being as finite creatures. But Weil describes this movement as a mechanical process, analogous to the laws of physical gravity (*la pesanteur*), such that we are naturally prone to and pulled toward distractedness and fantasy. But this fact does not relieve us from a moral responsibility to resist that gravity. In the same way that many Christian theologians have argued that we must overcome our "original sin," Weil thinks we must not give in to the moral baseness that characterizes the force of gravity. She writes, "Obedience to the force of gravity. The greatest sin."[27] It is, however, natural that the likelihood of a-voidance is at its highest when one is reminded (through suffering) of one's inherent finitude or disequilibrium, and in particular, after one has gotten accustomed to those comforts and luxuries that have negated the sense of void.

Recall that according to Weil, when we suffer, we almost always attempt to establish "equilibrium" by deflecting the suffering back onto the world. Sometimes these deflections take the form of revenge; sometimes they take the form of an imaginary reward for the suffering. In all cases, these deflective consolations are anesthetic distractions that constitute evil. Weil herself confesses, "I must not forget that at certain times when my headaches were raging I had an intense longing to make another human being suffer by hitting him in exactly the same part of his forehead."[28] We are reminded, too, of Rilke's verses:

Defiance. The child bent becomes the bender,   ~~spanking~~
inflicts on others what he once went through.
Loved, feared, rescuer, wrestler, victor,
he takes his vengeance, blow by blow.[29]

Weil expands upon her statement: "The search for equilibrium is bad because it is imaginary" by warning us about the temptation of vengeance. "Revenge. Even if in fact we kill or torture our enemy it is, in a sense, imaginary."[30] Needless to say, it is not the destruction in such violence that is imaginary, but rather, the sense that equilibrium has been truly established is fictional. As Iris Murdoch has written, "We console ourselves with fantasies of 'bouncing back,'" but "we must hold on to what has really happened and not cover it with imagining how we are to unhappen it. Void makes loss a reality."[31] The loss exists, is real, and cannot be dissipated by whatever form of repayment or revenge. Moreover, given that the void is the essence of human nature, our sufferings may be viewed as signs pointing to our necessary status as created beings. This is what Weil means when she writes, "We do not have to acquire humility. There is humility in us—only we humiliate ourselves before false gods."[32] The "false gods" in question here include social power, prestige, individual pride, and collective approbation.

Our struggles, our sufferings, and especially affliction (*malheur*), when experienced, reveal our inherent mediocrity, incompleteness, and humility (not as a virtue, but as the essence of our being). Predictably, this constitution is susceptible to a continuous stream of distractions that are either sought out or created. Pascal understood this:

> That is why men are so fond of hustle and bustle; that is why prison is such a fearful punishment; that is why the pleasures of solitude are so incomprehensible. That, in fact, is the main joy of being a king, because people are continually trying to divert him and procure him every kind of pleasure. A king is surrounded by people whose only thought is to divert him and stop him thinking about himself, because, king though he is, he becomes unhappy as soon as he thinks about himself . . . Thus men who are naturally conscious of *what they are* shun nothing so much as rest; they would do anything to be disturbed.[33]

Hence, even, and *especially*, a king contends with the illusion of a masterful self and would do anything to preserve that illusion.

In sum, it is the deflection of suffering that comes from confrontation with reality—the attempt to push it off on the world—which is the essence of evil. It consists in the refusal to acknowledge our own limits as finite beings, as well as the limits of others. Evil may have the character of outright sadism (taking pleasure in provoking the pain of others), or it may take the form of cultivated indifference (where others are simply not seen or heard). Of these forms, Weil notes:

> These two states of mind are closer than they appear to be. The second is only a weaker mode of the first; its deafness is complacently cultivated because it is agreeable and it offers a positive satisfaction of its own. There are no other restraints upon our will than material necessity and the existence of other human beings around us. Any imaginary extension of these limits

is seductive, so there is a seduction in whatever helps us to forget the reality of the obstacles.[34]

So while daydreaming at first glance appears benign, it fosters the construction of a character who perceives no boundaries, even when those boundaries are the edges of human lives and projects. Complete license is certainly seductive to anyone, but it necessarily "empt[ies] human lives of their reality and seem[s] to turn people into puppets."[35] Therefore, Weil, like Plato, connects injustice with falsehood and appearances. The imperative to seek truth is always an ethical one, at base.

Frequently, as we have noted, the consoling and self-expanding imagination functions in response to harm received (whether actual or perceived). But here, too, there is fictionalizing; as Weil describes it, we have only "filled an emptiness in ourselves by creating one in somebody else."[36] In order that we may not be guilty of evil, then, it is necessary that we allow ourselves to be penetrated by the reality of the world, refusing the temptations of temporary consolation that would be provided by seeking (an inherently imaginary) equilibrium. It is imperative that we not a-void. One of the cruel ironies here is that while it is deflection of suffering that defines evil, the deflector is immune to its effects. Hence, Weil writes:

> The sensitivity of the innocent victim who suffers is like felt crime. True crime cannot be felt. The innocent victim who suffers knows the truth about his executioner, the executioner does not know it. The evil which the innocent victim feels in himself is in his executioner, but he is not sensible of the fact. The innocent victim can only know the evil in the shape of suffering. That which is not felt by the criminal is his own crime. That which is not felt by the innocent victim is his own innocence. It is the innocent victim who can feel hell.[37]

Beyond this excerpt being a description of the nature of evil, we should also view it as a prescription for how to deal with suffering and even as a sense of our own degradation. She further advises, "The crime which is latent in us we must inflict on ourselves," for "a hurtful act is the transference to others of the degradation which we bear in ourselves."[38] We must never regard such a transference as a *deliverance* from evil, for "evil is not diminished but increased

in him from whom it proceeds."[39] Instead, when we refuse to trans-
fer our degradation and crime to others—and thereby "inflict" it
on ourselves—a real transformation takes place. The evil is transmuted into our own (redemptive) suffering and effectively stills the
force of violence that otherwise would be replicated as the contagion
of sin. In the same way, the tendency toward a-voidance is nourished and expanded each time we do not change the latent crime in
us to pure suffering; the imagination expands and becomes more
and more difficult to harness. What is produced from this "filling
imagination," however, is not art, novelty, beauty, or genius—evil,
it turns out, is completely mundane.[40]

Evil, contrary to public opinion and the manner in which crimes
are presented by the media, is literally *nothing new*. According to
Weil, it is simplistic and superficial. "Evil is license and that is why
it is monotonous: everything has to be drawn from ourselves," she
explains.[41] As we will describe in the next section, it is not given
to humans to create except through *decreation*, so evil is always
"a bad attempt to imitate God."[42] Any such attempt, then, reveals
the perpetrator acting in the realm of the imaginary: he acts to
obtain something that is illusory (for it can never actually deliver
him from his void, as he believes), and what he thinks himself to be
is false (for he is not creative, but *created*). So while

> imaginary evil is romantic and varied, real evil is gloomy,
> monotonous, barren, boring. Imaginary good is boring; real good
> is always new, marvelous, intoxicating . . . Evil is multifarious and
> fragmentary, good is one; evil is apparent, good is mysterious;
> evil consists in action, good in non-action, in activity which does
> not act, etc.[43]

It seems counterintuitive that goodness, deriving from "activity
which does not act," would be more "intoxicating" than assertive,
multifarious evil. But allowing the imagination to dwell on what
is evil "implies a certain cowardice," for in doing so, "we hope to
enjoy, to know, and to grow through what is unreal," Weil asserts.[44]
Additionally, to dwell on evil (by daydreaming of a limitless self) is
already to commit oneself to it; reverie, here, is considered action.
She writes, "We believe that thought does not commit us in any
way, but it alone commits us, and license of thought includes all
license."[45] From this statement, we can see the imperative of correct

orientation, for we necessarily commit ourselves to unreality (and hence evil) when we place ultimate value on mental and emotional equilibrium.

"Gravity" (*la pesanteur*)—while not equivalent with Weil's notion of evil[46]—*does* capture the nearly irresistible pull toward actions and fantasies that generate the semblance of homeostasis and themselves constitute evil. True, we sometimes submit almost unconsciously to gravity; we can "fall" into evil by negligence and inattentiveness, just as we can easily fall prey to propaganda. However, there is always the original consent to *l'imagination combleuse*. Our freedom is significant because of the choice of orientation in relation to the void: Will we impatiently deny that we are hungry for the good and resort to ersatz fillers or recognize and embrace the hunger for the good? As Weil wrote to Bousquet, the problem with daydreaming, as inoffensive as it seems, is that "it excludes love."[47] Love demands reality, which necessitates consent to void and to suffering. Clearly, then, "one does not fall into good," for true goodness and love imply attention to the abyss.[48] But what precisely is this goodness of which we are capable? And in truth, if we are defined by what God (the good) is *not*, how, in any sense, are we capable of good?

Returning the gift—Decreation

As we have argued, and as Miklos Vetö has contended, "The basic vision of Weil's metaphysics is the sinful condition of humanity."[49] This condition extends itself as an imperative for a certain manner of being oriented in the world. We have been describing this orientation in various ways thus far, including: enduring the void, transmuting latent crime into suffering, being attentive, and renouncing the filling imagination, among others. For Weil, all these particular prescriptions fall under a specific and revolutionary posture for humanity: we are to be *decreated*. "Decreated: to make something created pass into the uncreated," she tells us.[50] But what is "the uncreated"? Although Weil denies that decreation has anything to do with "destruction," and in fact, contends that the latter is only a "blameworthy substitute" for the former, the formula appears to suggest depriving (or returning?) the very *being* of something.

To become "uncreated," especially in terms of our constructions of identity, requires performing a critical genealogy of those
notions and forms of identity in a way that would denaturalize
them and render them ambiguous and relational, so that the "I"
would be decentered. But to make "something created pass into
nothingness"[51]—which is what distinguishes destruction from
decreation—requires an active self-punishing by dint of the will
and can maintain, in this way, the illusion of the autonomous agent,
and produce masochism rather than reflect true humility. This distinction is important, for the reflective undoing implied in decreation precludes the managerial activity characteristic of destruction
(and the sort of self-control that has been hailed for some time).
Genuine self-renunciation is, for example, a remembrance of our
utter dependency and vulnerability as created beings. It was for this
reason that Weil wrote, "There are but two moments of nakedness
and perfect purity in human life—birth and death."[52]
    To understand this prescription for decentering better, we must
again reflect on the void that characterizes human nature. As we
are imperfect and finite, real goodness, Weil argues, cannot origi-
nate in us and therefore cannot be willed by us. Nevertheless, paradoxically, we *can* be vehicles for the good, and this possibility
requires an extraordinary amount of effort and patience—though
Weil will characterize it as "negative" effort.[53] The only manner
in which we can "contribute" goodness to existence is by a withdrawal and renunciation of our egoistic tendencies, including, crucially, *l'imagination combleuse*. This refusal to project our selves
onto the world, signaling the decision to consent to the void, is
decreation. This is because, in Weil's metaphysics,

> We possess nothing in the world—a mere chance can strip us of
> everything—except the power to say "I." That is what we have
> to give to God, in other words, to destroy. There is absolutely
> no other free act which it is given us to accomplish, only the
> destruction of the "I."[54]

For Weil, it is the gift from the Creator to refuse the divine parent
and all that is associated with that being. We are always already
and necessarily at a distance from God, but our freedom consists
in deciding an orientation toward the supernatural (grace) or
away from it (gravity). The "power to say 'I'" is indicative of the

self-assertive orientation, the insistence on existing as if we are gods ourselves and thus lacking nothing. Ironically, this self-assertive orientation that pretends goodness derives from the "I" is only the orientation to gravity, by which our subsequent words, thoughts, and actions are predictable, unoriginal, self-serving, and cliché—all trademarks of behaviors that are *not truly free.*

It is thus that "love is a sign of our wretchedness," as Weil contends, for love is by nature an implication of our *conscious* separation from and lack of God (or the good).[55] What should be done with our existence, then, particularly if we wish to model ourselves after the origin of love and the definition of good? What it would mean to imitate God, to approximate genuine *creativity*, would be to imitate the *renunciation* of God, except that whereas God renounced being everything, "we should renounce being something. That," Weil insists, "is our only good."[56] Decreation is our only (negative) means to creating something beautiful, analogous to wiping dust off a window so light may shine through; it is when we actively impose our interests, desires, and personalities in the *intention to create* that we actually end up destroying.

Weil likens us to possessing "an imaginary divinity" that has been given to us since birth, so that we may strip ourselves of it, just "as Christ did of his real divinity."[57] When we cling to the "I" and refuse to give up this false divinity (convincing ourselves that it is real), we contaminate the scene by the distractions and the contagion of evil that attend the assertion of ego; our parochialism and narrowness blinds us to the reality of the external world and of others. Our actions should not be characterized by attempts to create, or add to the world that *is*, from our own limited designs. To do so reveals our tendency to believe that truth (goodness) can come from partial and limited beings. Such is not the case. "Creation (or manifestation)," she says, "is the act of God; preservation that of man."[58] Therefore, "we must become nothing, we must go down to the vegetative level; it is then that God becomes bread."[59]

Therefore, in relation to our existence as *created*, we should be ingrates, for we make a mistake when we accept the gift of *being* (turned away from God). This acceptance is "bad and fatal," and the gift's virtue "becomes apparent through my refusal of it," for "the self is only the shadow which sin and error cast by stopping the light of God." And Weil continues, referencing Plato's cave allegory, "I take this shadow for a being."[60] This mistake being

morally fatal, it is better to think of ourselves as vehicles, or trans-
parencies, through which pure love and goodness may pass to
others. This obligation may appear to be one of passivity, but the
renunciation of one's self is the most difficult posture to adopt and
is ironically one of the most socially subversive and threatening to
the status quo. In her *Notebooks*, Weil references an untitled story
demonstrating this effect of decreation: "Story. 'There was once a
man who became wise. He learnt how to no longer make a single
gesture or take a single step which were not *useful*. Shortly after-
wards, they shut him up.'"[61] How strange that one who acts and
speaks so economically—sparsely, that is—should be perceived as
so loud and dangerous that he would be censored. This extreme
vigilance to rein in what is superfluous and excessive in the interest
of a more productive and creative silence illuminates genuine noise
and spectacle for what it is. In our natural state, we would much
prefer the clamor.

Our religio-ethical duty by virtue of our created status, is to
be an ingrate in reference to the gift to exist outside of God—to
decreate. Decreation manifests the humility that is already in us
by nature, but that we had avoided for the sake of a false divinity. Humility consists, at least in part, in knowing the ego has no
energy of its own to create anything of real value. But character-
izing it as "the queen of virtues," Weil also states humility is "the
refusal to exist outside of God,"[62] despite the fact that God gives
us the possibility to maintain that separation and the illusions that
attend it.

Humility, like true goodness, cannot be intended or willed.
Rather, they entirely elude the will and may be considered as
effects of a previously decided orientation. Even actions and words
that may be classified as "just" are done and spoken almost in spite
of ourselves. We do not predict their manifestation, as our place
is to be the obedient intermediary between the "impossible" good
and the world, subject to necessity. For this reason, the good that
arrives via our decreation is unexpected and immensely interesting. Weil offers a metaphor:

A man coming down a ladder, who misses a step and falls, is
either a sad or an uninteresting sight, even the first time we see it.
But if a man were walking in the sky as though it were a ladder,
going up into the clouds and coming down again, he could do it

every hour of every day and we would never be tired of watching. It is the same with pure good; for a necessity as strong as gravity condemns man to evil and forbids him any good.[63]

Gravity (physical and moral) is, in other words, natural and expected. But the transcendence of this gravity is compelling. For Weil, this goodness is not merely the opposite of evil, for this would put them on the same (natural) level. Instead, she tells us, "Good is essentially *other than* evil," in the same way that supernatural justice is essentially *other than* the natural conception of justice, not a contrary.[64] Weil explains further:

> That which is the direct opposite of an evil never belongs to the order of higher good. It is often scarcely any higher than evil! Examples: theft and the bourgeois respect for property; adultery and the "respectable woman"; the savings bank and waste; lying and "sincerity."[65]

These so-called goods such as respect for property, the savings bank, and sincerity are forms of what Weil terms "degraded good." They are the relative goods—on the same level as democracy, capitalism, and religious institutions—all of which easily become idols for people who have no patience for what is not *naturally possible* and under their control. However, only such degraded good is capable of being actually violated by evil, and in this sense, degraded good *is* evil. We must renounce it as we must renounce ordinary evil, while being mindful that this inferior, relative good is much more difficult to resist than what we typically term "evil," according to Weil, perhaps because prestige and social consideration accompany the former.

Real goodness, however, is "an unfathomable marvel" that is too often desecrated at the hands of novelists and artists who render it cliché and portray evil as sensational and mysterious. We "envelop [the truth of the Good] in a fog in which, as in all fiction, values are reversed, so that evil is attractive and good is tedious,"[66] when in fact, "nothing is so beautiful and wonderful, nothing is so continually fresh and surprising, so full of sweet and perpetual ecstasy, as the good."[67] This is because the forms and manifestations of baseness are finite, for they issue from the finite (i.e., from us). We cannot, as Weil has said, pull ourselves up by our own bootstraps. So the artist, if she is to create something that can be called "beautiful" or "good," must take on "the transparency of a window pane" to allow the light of the divine to shine through.[68] This is because "matter is not beautiful when it obeys man, but only when it obeys God. If sometimes a work of art seems almost as beautiful as the sea, the mountains, or flowers, it is because the light of God has filled the artist."[69] As the divine creates, so must we decreate, according to Weil. There is harmony in this imitation, not struggle or contest, for the decreated orientation gives primacy to inspiration in human existence and, most significantly, makes love possible.

4

Love and detachment

*No man can serve two masters; for a slave will either hate
the one and love the other, or be devoted to the one and
despise the other. You cannot serve God and wealth.*

MATTHEW 6:24

*Love undefeated in the fight,
Love that makes havoc of possessions,
Love who lives at night in a young girl's soft cheeks,
Who travels over sea, or in huts in the countryside—
there is no god able to escape you
nor anyone of men, whose life is a day only,
and whom you possess is mad.*

CHORUS, *ANTIGONE*[1]

Limit of the intellect

Irving Singer once noted, "In the philosophy of love . . . I am con-
vinced that every discussion must *start* with Plato."[2] This remark
is certainly valid in the context of Simone Weil's thinking on the
subject of love and the related notion of philosophical detachment. We know that Weil read Plato as a spiritual thinker, a mystic even. She famously wrote, ". . . Then what is Plato? A *mystic*,
the inheritor of a mystical tradition which permeated the whole
of Greece."[3] These words point to the inseparability, for Weil, of

an experiential spirituality and philosophical rigor that are oftentimes assumed to be quite distinct, if not altogether contrary to
one another. It is because both are grounded in a common orientation—she names attention—that they are not at odds and, in fact,
are complementary.

But as with all of Weil's significant ideas, there is a paradox at the
base of her Platonic-Christian understanding of love. We know that
for the ancient Greeks and their Christian inheritors such as Dante,
St. Augustine, and Pascal, self-control was a central concern for living "the good life," especially when it came to matters of the heart
and flesh.[4] As we will see, in fact, self-renunciation underlies the
purest form of love in Weil's philosophy. However, the ancients also
recognized that excessive regulation of the self to the detriment of
eros precluded genuine education and therefore growth—be it moral
or spiritual. Weil, too, underscores the importance of spontaneous
desire in the formation of attention,[5] which, for her, is synonymous
with love, a desire to come into greater contact with reality.

Thus, there is a tension at the heart of Weilienne love that must
be navigated. In the erotic pulsation that stirs her to reach for
what is by definition *not present* but beyond perceptible edges—
the absent God/the absent good—she is simultaneously performing deliberate preparations for the possible arrival, reception, and
manifestation of such supernatural values. The preparatory work
is the work of the will and intelligence, necessitating philosophical
analysis and self-critique; this duty is carried out by the disciplin-
ing task-master-self who, after diligently clearing the ground of
egoistic projections and selfish desires, is one day overcome by an
experience of love that exceeds the formerly useful intellectual categories. Weil eloquently describes this possibility:

> A man whose mind feels that it is captive would prefer to blind
> himself to the fact. But if he hates falsehood, he will not do so;
> and in that case he will have to suffer a lot. He will beat his head
> against the wall until he faints. He will come to again and look
> with terror at the wall, until one day he begins afresh to beat his
> head against it; and once again he will faint. And so on endlessly
> and without hope. One day he will wake up on the other side of
> the wall.
>
> Perhaps he is still in a prison, although a larger one. No matter.
> He has found the key; he knows the secret which breaks down

every wall. He has passed beyond what men call intelligence, into the beginning of wisdom.[6]

Therefore, the love of wisdom—philosophy—is simultaneously a process of self-annihilation and liberation. Weil thought that "intelligence resides in every man,"[7] but wisdom, whose condition (according to Weil) is supernatural love, is unattainable through human effort alone. Intellectual and academic exercises ultimately reach a limit in their attempts to make contact with reality, and after this point, if we have been fully committed, supernatural love characterized by "intense, pure, disinterested, gratuitous, [and] generous attention"[8] permits the light of truth to inspire all our ideas and relations. Like Plato acknowledged, the soul bitten by such love will appear foolish, absurd, and even ignoble, but this is in part because we forget that "the best things we have come from madness [*mania*], when it is given as a gift of the god."[9]

Aside from pure love being a disciplined madness, another significant paradox will be apparent in our subsequent discussion. When Weil writes, for instance, that "it is total detachment [from the world] that is the condition for the love of God"[10] and thus the condition for the reception of (supernatural) truth and the center of Christian mysticism, we are left with the difficulty, that has long been a criticism of Plato, that such an orientation forsakes the world, its issues, and its inhabitants through an other-worldly attitude that is anything but what we would call loving. Irving Singer, for instance, remarks,

> The Platonic lover does not love *anyone*: he loves only the Good, either in abstraction or in concrete manifestations. But then . . . there is at least one kind of love that Plato's philosophy neglects. That is the love of persons, the love between human beings who bestow value upon one another, each responding to the uniqueness of the other, each taking an interest in the other as a separate individual, regardless of imperfections and apart from satisfactions that also accrue . . . If Platonism fails here, its shortcoming is very great indeed.[11]

Singer ultimately argues that Platonism *does* fail on this account, precisely because the love of ideals (which is his interpretation of Platonic love) precludes love of particular persons. Weil's own

descriptions of impersonal, detached, and universal love have
been called "evil" and "a flight from responsibility."[12] In examining the interconnected Weilienne ideas of love and detachment,
we must give serious consideration to these charges. Can love be
both impersonal/just and interpersonal/caring? Is universal love
really an avoidance of particular humans and their needs? If pure
love is ultimately a *supernatural* orientation that surpasses our will
and control, in what does our human responsibility lie? (Is ethics
grounded in religion?)

To answer these and other related concerns, this chapter proceeds
in five parts. First, we explore at greater length the Greek heritage
and ideas that have particular significance for Weil's notion of love,
especially Platonic *eros* and *mania* as read through *Symposium* and
Phaedrus. Second, we consider the implications of losing (self) control in love, and the connections between this loss and decreation,
in light of divine *mania*. Given that such decreative humility is the
basis for love, in the third section, we explicate Weilienne love in
detail, emphasizing it as a synonym for justice. One primary example of how loving attention is impossible given human nature but
paradoxically demanded as the source of justice is in the phenomenon of affliction (*malheur*). In the fourth section, then, we will
examine the implications for attentive love, given the fact of affliction, and through this analysis, explain why detachment is necessary to love. Lastly, in the fifth section, we investigate the tensions
just raised, regarding the implications of Weilienne love and the
detachment it requires for interpersonal relationships. Is Weilienne
love only frustrating to us who are selfishly inclined and prone to
the effects of moral gravity—or is it itself a kind of evil?

Platonic eros and divine mania

Arguably the two most important Platonic dialogues about
love—and which have also had the most noticeable impact on
Weil's understanding of love—are *Symposium* and *Phaedrus*.
Taken together, however, the two dialogues offer what may seem
to be conflicting accounts of the philosophic ideal of love. In
Symposium, love (which becomes synonymous with the lover of
wisdom or philosopher)[13] is cool-headed, calm, and clearly oriented toward absolute beauty and goodness. Socrates exemplifies

this love and the disposition it implies; he embodies this way of life, given Plato's descriptions, showing it as a possibility for humanity to emulate. But as Singer notes, in *Symposium,* "Though sociable and well-mannered, Socrates is emotionally cool, unimpassioned, involved in the life about him but also at a distance from it."[14] His rationality and chaste demeanor are sharply contrasted to the drunken proclamations of love, sexual overtures, and physical preoccupations of Alcibiades.

In *Phaedrus,* however, love—still understood as the philosophical spirit—is portrayed as a divine madness or *mania,* while the non-lover is castigated as boorish, uninspiring, and burdensome. Plato writes, "A non-lover's companionship . . . is diluted by human self-control; all it pays are cheap, human dividends, and though the slavish attitude it engenders in a friend's soul is widely praised as virtue, it tosses the soul around for nine thousand years on the earth and leads it, mindless, beneath it."[15] The true lover, however, "possesses the Good by enabling the Good to take possession of *him.*"[16] He has lost his own control under the influence of a radiant beauty that is reminiscent of the gods. When the lover encounters someone truly beautiful, his fearful and trembling soul, feeling itself in the presence of something divine, responds reverentially to the beloved—but in a way that looks excessive and foolish to one whose soul has not had the privilege of coming to know the divine Forms and is being rigidly monitored for the sake of self-preservation. Singer comments that we get "an inkling of possession in the religious sense"[17] in Plato's description of the lover:

> A recent initiate, however, one who has seen much in heaven—when he sees a godlike face or bodily form that has captured Beauty well, first he shudders and a fear comes over him . . . then he gazes at [the beloved] with the reverence due a god, and if he weren't afraid people would think him completely mad, he'd even sacrifice to his boy as if he were the image of a god. Once he has looked at him, his chill gives way to sweating and a high fever, because the stream of beauty that pours into him through his eyes warms him up and waters the growth of his wings.[18]

The wings—which Weil, in her Christian reading of Plato, will interpret as *grace* ("it would be impossible to state more clearly that the wing is a *supernatural organ,* that it is *grace*"[19])—enable this lover eventually to make an epistemic, ethical, and aesthetic ascent until there is (re)union with the Absolute, the source of all beauty, truth, and goodness. This growth of wings, which is both painful and joyous, is a process that happens outside of the lover's managerial will and control. The wings are divine inspiration that carry their subject to unfamiliar and unanticipated places.

Though the two descriptions of love gained from *Symposium* and *Phaedrus* appear, on the surface, to contest one another, the appropriation of these ideas into Weil's Christian mysticism reveals their possible congruence: the descriptions represent, not competing accounts of love but, arguably, two stages of the soul's ascent toward the good. In the first stage, represented by the account given in *Symposium*, we learn the importance of certain refusals, as manifested by Socrates. For instance, he refuses the lusty advances of Alcibiades for the sake of his love of excellence and wisdom. He pointedly asks his suitor: "Is this a fair exchange you propose? You seem to me to want more than your proper share: you offer me the merest appearance of beauty, and in return you want the thing itself, 'gold in exchange for bronze.'"[20] In this way, Socrates underscores what are erotic distractions: physical appearances, material concerns, preoccupations of the flesh. We then see love as beginning with renunciation of the common and earthly, and in many scenes in the *Symposium*, we find the evidence of Socrates' philosophic love: he is lost in thought, oblivious to weather, hunger, clothing, and his own health.

This first stage is one of "ground-clearing"—a forceful removal of illusion, distraction, and the falsifying imagination. Weil calls this process "training" (*dressage*) and understands that conditioning plays a role: "Training is based upon what are called today conditioned reflexes. By associating pleasure or pain with this or that object, new reflexes are formed which end by becoming automatic."[21] It is perhaps ironic that genuine love begins in the chastening of particular desires, but Weil, like Plato, understands that human nature is constituted in part by base desires that, left to their own devices, would respect no limits or reason. This is our "animal" nature. Hence, she continues with a vivid metaphor:

[Through training] we can compel the animal in us to keep quiet and not interrupt when our attention is turned towards the source of grace. Circus dogs are trained with the whip and with sugar, but much more quickly and easily with the whip, and in any case sugar is not always available. So pain is the principal method.[22]

This operation sounds violent, and, in fact, it is. The reorientation of the soul toward the good (or God, or grace, or truth) implies a simultaneous turning away from the void-fillers we have previously discussed. As we have seen, this emptying/preserving of the void is painful. It is also a voluntary process, and as Weil notes, "training is a finite operation," for "the evil within us is finite like ourselves."[23] So we are wrong if we continue to whip the animal within us when he has already become docile because then the pains are useless exercises of asceticism and even harmful to spiritual progress.

If this negative operation were the sole criterion of love, critics might be justified in calling Weil masochistic or ascetic. But if the reader will recall the previous chapter, the process of decreation was distinguished from that of "destruction," because its mode of renunciation enabled its creativity by opening to the good that is outside us. Destruction has no purpose in view other than pure annihilation or sadism-masochism, whereas decreation is the manifestation of human love, exemplified by Christ on the cross. At the second stage, therefore, after we have stilled and silenced the distractions, we become truly vulnerable to possession by the good—which Weil at times calls "grace"—provided we maintain the orientation:

> [Grace] is something that we receive without doing anything positive; except that we have to keep ourselves exposed towards [it]; that is to say, to keep our attention oriented with love towards the good. The rest, whether painful or sweet, takes place in us without our co-operation. It is the fact of this second element which proves that it is truly a mysticism.[24]

Thus, in the *Phaedrus*, the sprouting of the wings of the lover's soul and the subsequent *mania* are the events that happen *in spite of us and our self-control*. The obvious paradox is that self-disciplining is initially required for reception of the good that then subverts the whip. This is why orientation toward the good is key to this transformation; orientation toward the methods or the rituals themselves, for instance, signify an idolatry that will result in attachment to the masterful, punishing self (or masochism). As Weil puts it: "One does not play Bach without having done scales. But neither does one play a scale merely for the sake of the scale."[25]

Losing control and preparing to die

We have argued that, for Weil, love consists in two stages wherein the will disciplines the subject's base desires and falsifying imagination to bring about an orientation toward the good, which it is incapable of creating. Eventually, the will that has brought about this direction is overcome and rendered powerless by that good that is outside of its control and prediction. An important transformation occurs in this moment: the sovereign subject, who even in her self-disciplining practices had a *hold* on her world and herself, is deposed by the mysterious and rupturing movement of grace. (The phenomenon of grace is described in greater detail in Chapter 6.) That is, the once possessive subject *is possessed*, but the effect of this transformation is the emergence of a radical (non)-subject whose protective boundaries and static identity have been troubled. It is to this issue that we now turn, for the obvious question is: How could love continue, if there is eventually no subject remaining who consents to love? Must we not *hold on to ourselves*? And, in terms of our physical bodies, aren't we obliged to actively master their impulses and affects to be responsible and truly loving partners?

To explore the tensions underlying these questions, we now turn to an unexpected area of scholarship—at least, unexpected in the context of Weil's religious philosophy. Recognizing that much has been written in contemporary Continental feminist philosophy about experience of controlled and disciplined embodiment, it is helpful to assess some of these insights in light of the aspect of religious love that is grounded on *losing* control and consenting to a *porous* experience of embodiment. We know that for feminists, especially, a fundamental issue of ethical and political concern is not only the cultural context that mass-produces homogenizing and digitally altered images of female beauty but also the ways in which women's bodies are subsequently inscribed upon, monitored, and then read. In particular, feminists such as Sandra Lee Bartky and Susan Bordo, drawing on Michel Foucault's *Discipline and Punish*, argue that the female body epitomizes the "disciplined" and "docile" body in its mundane daily rituals, preoccupations, and postures. Moreover, moral evaluations have been applied to the degrees of somatic control, discipline, or continence that people (women especially) demonstrate. There is also a recognition from these philosophers that "self-control" cannot be divorced from the broader political institutions and the pervasive and anonymous systems of power that are unconsciously internalized so that people happily police themselves. As Foucault remarks, "The body is also directly involved in a political field; power relations have an immediate hold upon it; they invest it, mark it, train it, torture it, force it to carry out tasks, to perform ceremonies, to emit signs."[26] Under this recognition, self-control is not so benign since it colludes with a wider system of domination, and a lack of self-control—or what Aristotle calls *akrasia*—begins to appear ironically as a more conscious and liberated way of being.

Akrasia turns out to be surprisingly relevant to our understanding of Weilienne love, but it is negatively characterized by Aristotle as a sort of "weakness of the will," an "effeminacy," or in some cases, "impetuosity."[27] Often widely translated as "incontinence," it is generally understood to indicate a lack of self-mastery or self-control. To be afflicted with *akrasia* is not, for Aristotle, as shameful as being wholly vicious, for even though one committed vicious acts, they were preceded by an internal struggle to act virtuously; *akrasia* is a result of poorly formed habits but with intellectual understanding of what is morally correct. (It is no surprise that Aristotle associates *akrasia*/incontinence with effeminacy given the values of ancient Greek culture, but subsequently, the association of *akrasia* with feminine qualities has remained largely unchanged.)

But even today, beyond our philosophical heritage in which earlier figures such as Plato, Aristotle, St. Augustine, and Descartes identified the feminine with nature and nature with irrationality, unpredictability, and uncontrollability, we judge the *health* and *continence* of a physical body to be directly related to one another, and furthermore, assume a person's moral and spiritual character on the basis of this notion of "health." There is an unspoken imperative to always *be in control*, especially of one's body. In recent

studies on female urinary incontinence, for example, researchers
noted the paradox of embodiment:

> While Christian tradition conceives of the body as weak flesh,
> the location of sin, it is also an instructive site of moral purpose
> and intentions, with health the sign of moral well-being. In this
> context, women move from innocent transgression to intentional
> adult immorality and accede to the legitimacy of loss of social
> membership as a consequence. "If they knew you had a problem
> with your bladder, I think they would judge you differently;
> they would think you had some fault. If you can't control your
> bladder, how much control do you have over the rest of your
> life?" (Dawn, [the interviewee])[28]

Ironically, the researchers concluded that "women associate incontinence not only with lack of physical and social control, but also
with *willfulness*," just as children who are "naughty" intentionally
breach and reject "appropriate social behavior."[29] In a different
context, Susan Bordo describes the way in which thin bodies (signifying control over fat) are read in our culture: "Thinness represents
a triumph of the will over the body, and the thin body . . . is associated with 'absolute purity, hyperintellectuality and transcendence
of the flesh.'"[30] Conversely, "fat . . . is associated with the taint of
matter and flesh, 'wantonness,' mental stupor . . . mental decay,"
and a weak will.[31] Whether the incontinent body is read as actually being *willful*, or as in most cases fickle and loose, it is always
associated with some sort of moral degradation or deviancy.

The seemingly unfortunate association of women's corporeality
to the uncontrollable and the subsequent lived feminine experience
of body as "porous" and "seepage," serves as a constant reminder
of the impossibility of the discrete and self-sufficient agent and may
help reveal the illusion of static self-identity that serves the ego and
prevents love. Though coming from a different line of thinking than
Weil's, Elizabeth Grosz reminds us that the experience "force[s]
megalomaniacal aspirations to earth," and "demonstrate[s] the
limits of subjectivity in the body."[32] What Grosz reveals, then,
is the possibility for a radical revaluation of *akrasia*: rather than
being a sign of moral degradation, it is a condition of humility,
of (literal/physiological) openness to the world, that is, for Weil
an ethical receptivity. It does not permit the false and problematic

idea of sovereignty that we too often assume in relation to others or to our selves, or the corresponding colonizing demeanor that seeks conversion of the other to the same. In this way, experienced bodily incontinence could be read as a gift that can translate to the analogous release of the tyrannical self and therefore a negation of the tendency to dominate the world we encounter. Of course, because of the dominant paradigm, which reads incontinence in a negative light, virtues such as humility will be obscured and mis-read until, perhaps, in an unavoidable vulnerability due to neces-sity, one experiences a communion with the world or with another person that was formerly impossible.

In light of these considerations, we propose that Weil's idea of training (*dressage*), which is the first stage of love, paradoxically leads to consent to and acceptance of (bodily) incontinence—not only for women—that reveals the illusion of the bounded self or ego. Therefore, although training makes use of the will, when ori-ented correctly, the discipline does not produce an amplification of the will, but it is already preparation for its release. Training, that is, reflects the Platonic characterization of philosophy as a preparation for and learning how to die, and it engenders humil-ity rather than self-assuredness. Although Weil did not address or describe the particular lived experiences of the male or the female body in any significant way, mainly because of her commitment to impersonality and the universal human condition that transcends sexual distinctions and concerns, she did articulate general themes of human experience that reveal her perspective on the self as a controlling agent and the obstacles to a genuinely moral orienta-tion that such a self generates. For her, the practice of training undermines the sovereignty of the self, without thereby suggesting that one be subject to natural powers or collude with a system of oppression and force. And it is precisely the deposing of the self that enables and is the sign of love. Anne Carson describes the deposition of self in love in a similar way:

All at once a self never known before, which now strikes you as the true one, is coming into focus. A gust of godlikeness may pass through you and for an instant a great many things look knowable, possible, and present. Then the edge asserts itself. You are not god. You are not that enlarged self. Indeed, you are not even a whole self, as you now see. Your new knowledge of possibilities is also a knowledge of what is lacking in the actual.[33]

What Carson means by "the edge" is the alterity of the other person or the recognition of genuine externality and the "not-me." In Weilienne terms, this edge may be another person, or it may be the reality or necessity of the world that triggers recognition of the void—in short, the distance between creation and Creator.

That is, Weil acknowledges an essential feature of human existence that sets up imaginary boundaries between ourselves and the world: "We are born in order to 'identify' ourselves . . . [but] one is never oneself. One is always something else," she writes in her *Notebooks*.[34] Elsewhere, we have noted that she describes this condition as carrying around "an imaginary divinity"[35] that must be shed. We gravitate toward such identities because they lend a sense of certainty and stability, a presumption of the centrality of our projects, a "security" to our existence, and a preservation and even extension of our natural human limits. In short, the "imaginary divinity" is equivalent to the feeling of autonomy, self-sufficiency, and independence in identity that lends itself to the construction of incontinence (and thereby supernatural love) as a morally degraded state.

As formerly noted, Weil recommends renunciation of this illusion in a process she calls decreation, and which is clearly a central part of training:

> It is as a limited being that one must renounce the self, and for this purpose all that is necessary is to recognize all limited things as being limited. If I were to think of everything which is limited as limited, there would no longer be anything in my thoughts which emanated from the "I."[36]

As we have shown, for Weil, decreation is the process of making the created *uncreated*, unraveling our constructed and reified identities to which we have become attached. This process is more often than not inspired by undergoing experiences of marginalization or encountering, in a significant way, one who is "marginal." As bell hooks describes it, "For me this space of radical openness is a margin—a profound edge. Locating oneself there is difficult but necessary. It is not a 'safe' place."[37]

But significantly for Weil, this risky displacement through decreation requires a corresponding participation of the body in that change.[38] She thinks it is not by accident that Plato describes genuine education, in the *Republic*, as a reorientation of the whole soul, necessitating a revolution of the body: "But whereas we can turn our eyes in a new direction without or almost without using the body, it is not so as regards the soul. The soul cannot turn its eyes in a new direction without turning entirely in that direction."[39] While intelligence, in its limited way, can sharpen its focus on any given natural phenomenon, *wisdom is not attained until the ideas penetrate the body*, in a process not unlike the one Rilke called "blood-remembering."[40] This is what training accomplishes, according to her.

Since we have a tendency to set up barricades around an illusory ego, our natural attempt to overcome this temptation is to amplify the will and *resolve* to be more humble or to intellectualize humility. Weil recognizes the contradictions in these decisions. Instead, she offers *dressage* or "training" as the practice of "transforming the sense of effort into a passive sense of suffering."[41] To employ the will and intellect and assert control against the self for its own sake is paradoxically to preserve that very self and illusion one is trying to combat; the mechanism to evade this trap must be wholly other. Recall her admonition: "Whoever takes up the sword shall perish by the sword. And whoever does not take up the sword (or lets it go) shall perish on the cross."[42] In this light, the training that is required to avoid the ego's insistent presence is a gradual release of oneself, or in other words, the *losing* of control and, thus, a preparation for death. For the loss of control is really a death for us. Again, it is impermissible that one "choose the cross," for this does not carry us "beyond the will."[43] However, when we renounce the controlling self in a *negative way*—by *not* resisting the reality of suffering or by *not* turning away from the socially marginalized, for example—we begin the process of "uncreation" that leads beyond ourselves via an ethical orientation characterized by loving attentiveness.

Weil tells us, "Note that although this training is a voluntary process, and therefore a natural one, it is only performed because the soul has been touched by the memory of the things above and its wings are beginning to sprout. *And it is a negative operation*."[44] Elsewhere, she describes this training as having to "accomplish the possible in order to touch the impossible."[45] That is, love as the training of our desires where we are somatically affected ushers in a higher form of love wherein the subject, through his attentiveness, serves as the vehicle for the transmission of the good, beauty, and truth that are external to him and require his eclipse. He appears to lose his wits, sense of balance, and what has been deemed "sane" about him. In actuality, he is finally making contact with reality and thereby regaining his sanity in the midst of an insanely deluded and desensitized world.

Before we delve into the issue of this higher form of love as attentiveness to the reality of the world, we should further consider the value of bodily suffering and vulnerability in training, as Weil understands it. As we have noted, her view is that "the body plays a part in all apprenticeships."[46] We have something to learn from pain. "On the plane of physical sensibility, suffering alone gives us contact with that necessity which constitutes the order of the world," she writes, clearly referencing Christ's mediation on the cross as a model for us.[47] That contact with necessity permits us to be "wholly sensitive" to the universe, in a way that pleasure does not. That contact is also requisite for philosophy as a preparation for dying: "There is no philosophical reflection without an essential transformation in sensitivity and in the practice of living, a transformation that has an equal importance for the most ordinary and the most tragic circumstances of life."[48] It is not that we seek for suffering (or "choose the cross,") but when it comes to us, as Weil writes, "we have to open the very center of our soul to it, just as a woman opens her door to messengers from her loved one. What does it matter to a lover if the messenger be polite or rough, so long as he delivers the message?"[49] We must not make the mistake of concluding that Weil advocates submission to human abusers or tyrants; in fact, openness to reality and the subsequent sensitivity will prompt resistance to and rigorous critique of human violence and force, while the escapist imagination may in fact diminish the level of cruelty in the oppressor out of fear or convenience.

The broken or incontinent body (whose margins have been blurred) appears to be a qualified messenger of necessity, and an acknowledged helpmate of philosophy, reminding us, as it does, of our limits, finitude, dependency, and vulnerability in a way that circumvents and precludes a prideful self-centeredness. In this way,

Weil affirms, "So it becomes quite evident that philosophy does not consist in the acquisition of knowledge, as is the case with science, but in a change of the soul entirely."[50] Training, then, is not successful if it only results in different behavior through conditioning and habituation; it must really effect a change in desires and therefore a reorientation of the soul toward the good. But this good is not experienced as a tangible *something*, but as a void, or an absence. This is why the process of reorientation and the subsequent new outlook will be felt as emptiness that many will perceive as suffering.

We spoke earlier of a revaluation of *akrasia* and meant by that its potential for ethical conditioning. It may be, too, that *akrasia*, given this revaluation, is not necessarily experienced as strictly *painful* but as the opening of new possibilities. Weil describes this phenomenon: "Pain is the color of certain events. When a man who can and a man who cannot read look at a sentence written in red ink, they both see the same red color, but this color is not so important for the one as for the other."[51] How literate we are in terms of making connections between events, noting necessary relationships, and recognizing the limits of our own intelligence will determine to what extent we are *pained* by the development of love and its mastery of us. Thus, the question will be for us: How will we read the incontinent—or crucified—body, once we have contemplated its value in the philosophical orientation that is synonymous with love?

What is important in the experience of incontinence is not any particular sensation of pain, but the process and effect of *undergoing*, of *pathos*. To be sensitive to the universe, we need only recognize our innate marginality and void; to be just, however, we must go farther. Recall Weil's definition of moral innocence, personified by Christ: "To be innocent is to bear the weight of the entire universe. It is to throw away the counterweight. In emptying ourselves we expose ourselves to all the pressure of the surrounding universe."[52] Without a doubt, pain often accompanies this disposal of the counterweight and consent to bear the weight of the world; laying down the sword exposes us to persecution, as it did Christ to crucifixion. But the effect of the orientation is of secondary importance to the orientation itself and the potential for the expansion of love through the attentiveness it awakens.

Just attention

With the reorientation of the soul toward the good, self-control is finally displaced. It is not needed, however, because a new power has been submitted to, and the managerial self would only get in the way. This fact is what Socrates, as the true lover, recognizes in *Phaedrus*. Carson explains:

> Socrates' central argument, as he goes on to reevaluate madness, is that you keep your mind to yourself at the cost of closing out the gods. Truly good and indeed divine things are alive and active outside you and should be let in to work their changes. Such incursions formally instruct and enrich our lives in society; no prophet or healer or poet could practice his art if he did not lose his mind, Socrates says (244a–45). Madness is the instrument of such intelligence. More to the point, erotic *mania* is a valuable thing in private life. It puts wings on your soul.[53]

This argument, especially in Socrates' context, is quite radical and subversive. Whereas those who advocate self-control stockpile reinforcements against any erotic takeover and thus protect the status quo, Socrates casts love as a risk and adventure; "he unfolds himself for flight."[54] The loss of self for the sake of inspiration and recollection of what is divine is not an evil, as the traditional Greek attitude would have it,[55] but is central to the philosophic spirit and anything that would be called "education." But it also offers no predictable results or natural safety: "If we want to have a love which will protect the soul from wounds, we must love something other than God."[56] For Weil, this radical and impossible love of God/the good implies a detachment via the renunciation of all possible ends—"a renunciation that replaces the future with a void, as the imminent approach of death would do."[57] The impossible love that is oriented toward a void is nothing other than what Weil calls "attention." Let us examine this posture in more detail and see how it is synonymous with justice.

For Weil, attention is the *decreative* release of self to receive the world in all its reality. Paradoxically, this (passive) letting go of self and accompanying control is simultaneously a "creative" *action*: attention sees what is invisible (as the Good Samaritan saw the bleeding, anonymous, dirty man in the ditch) and hears what has been deprived of a voice because the din and smog generated from our maintenance of control has finally cleared. "Those are the sounds and images," bell hooks tell us, "that mainstream consumers find difficult to understand. Sounds and scenes which cannot be appropriated are often that sign everyone questions, wants to erase, to 'wipe out.'"[58] And we who have been so "centered" seek to eradicate these encounters, these voices, because we are destabilized by them—our solidity and our protective borders are troubled. However, Weil warns that before reaching the stage of attentiveness, "we must have worn down our own will against the observance of rules" in that practice she called training.[59] This is why Weil argues that if attention can be called an effort, "it is a negative effort," one that consists of suspending thought, agency, and will, and leaving us "empty, waiting, not seeking anything, but ready to receive in its naked truth the object that is to penetrate [us]."[60] The most precious gifts are obtained, she suggests, by waiting for them, and they come to us as a surprise.

She offers an example that is familiar to many of us of the mysterious effects of waiting attention:

> Suppose I have had a thought and have forgotten it two hours later. . . . I direct my attention for a few minutes towards an empty space; empty but real. Then suddenly the thought is there, beyond all possible doubt. I did not know what it was, and yet now I recognize it as being what I was waiting for. An everyday experience, and an unfathomable mystery.[61]

This strange yet recognizable experience demonstrates the paradoxical efficaciousness of quieting the frantic and frenzied mind. Attention, for Weil, looks nothing like what we call attention today, when we urge schoolchildren, for instance, to *pay attention*. That command is meant to get students to go on an active search for answers, to focus—that is, to "zoom in" narrowly on a particular topic to the exclusion of others. It is an understandable prescription in a cultural landscape filled with distractions. Yet Weil's idea of attention recommends a relaxing of the mind, not for lack of seriousness, but for the sake of openness to relations and ideas the subject's own efforts would have excluded, whether consciously or unconsciously.

The posture of attentiveness, then, may be compared to hungering—a refusal to fill the void. It is through this enriching emptiness that one may be penetrated by reality because the usual defenses, projections, and deflections have been surrendered. Rather than eating, then, attention is *looking*: "Method for understanding images, symbols, etc. Not to try to interpret them, but to look at them till the light suddenly dawns."[62] This method has important implications for the ways in which mysteries and experiential ambiguities have been interpreted by humans in our active quests for certainty. Theology, in fact, is arguably one such attempt to construct meaning and impose order by interpreting events that transcend natural understanding through narrative projections and system-building. As Huston Smith contends:

> It was not the disciples' minds that were first drawn to Jesus. Rather . . . it was their experience—the experience of living in the presence of someone whose selfless love, crystalline joy, and preternatural power came together in a way his disciples found divinely mysterious. It was only a matter of time, however, before Christians felt the need to understand this mystery in order to explain it to themselves and to others. Christian theology was born, and from then on the Church was head as well as heart.[63]

As Smith goes on to describe, it is natural that our experience of invisible or inexplicable events should give rise to symbols and then conceptualizations of those symbols, as the mind actively seeks comprehension through what is familiar to it already. Theology *is* this systematization of our interpretations, which may explain why Weil reads the Gospels as a conception of human life rather than as a theology. The former mode of reading preserves mystery. A theology, by contrast, given Smith's account, is necessarily a product of inattention but has the unfortunate effect of granting a *pretense* of knowledge; theologies offer consummation and illusions of being "full" for the spiritually hungry.

Unfortunately, in the same way that religious sacraments are confused with social ceremonies, love is often confused with consumption, attachment, and even active conquest. This is not to say that we are to refrain from human interactions or searches for meaning, but we should make every effort to refrain from consumptive attitudes and actions so that love may be possible. Weil writes, "A gambler is capable of watching and fasting almost like a saint," but "there is a great danger in loving God as the gambler loves his game," which is to say, with attachment and a consumptive demeanor.[64] To love something or someone is simply to desire their existence independent of ourselves, our intrusions, and our interferences. And Weil eloquently describes this state:

> The beautiful is a carnal attraction which keeps us at a distance and implies a renunciation. This includes the renunciation of that which is most deep-seated, the imagination. We want to eat all the other objects of desire. The beautiful is that which we desire without wishing to eat it. We desire that it should be.[65]

Hence a soul loves in emptiness, in hunger. Contrary to our modern self-help mantras that insist on one's own fulfillment/satisfaction/health in order to love another, Weil declares that the prerequisite to real love is void, sensitivity to suffering, renunciation of greedy attachments, and even renunciation of the desire for consummation—whether physical or intellectual.

Moreover, the filling imagination must be countered by attention because the former leads us away from the present toward future "rewards." This is why attention involves a detachment from all goals and projects—that is, a replacing of the future with a void, so that we do not escape into our projective imaginations to a-void what stands before us. In the same way that we do violence to others by demanding that they be the creatures of our imaginations, we also do violence to the present by making it subservient to a future where we believe these rewards await us. As we have described in Chapter 2 in the case of eschatological thinking, we seek an eventual equilibrium, some sort of compensation, and thus shun the recognition of our inherent vulnerability. In seeking refuge in the future, we become unable to love, as love requires reality and is a receptivity to that reality, which is to say *attention* to reality's absolute presence that has no guaranteed happy endings.

It is for these reasons that, as previously noted, Weil counters: "We must prefer real [present] hell to an imaginary [future] paradise."[66] Such a preference, so against our nature, and demanding a kind of detachment that comes only from a long period of training, is the orientation of attention. It is accompanied by an attitude of waiting and patience, a sort of perseverance at the void. While it does indicate a detachment of sorts in the attentive person, loving attention does *not* excuse one from the world; in fact, it involves her all the more. As Weil explains:

> But the detachment in question here is not without its object; detached thought has as its object the establishment of a hierarchy among values, all values. Thus it has as its object a way of life, a better life, not somewhere else, but in this world and right now, for the values placed in order are the values of this world. In this sense philosophy is oriented toward life; it aims at life through death.[67]

But this explanation of philosophical detachment only begs several questions: What values are illuminated by attention? What is the "better" way of life that is the object of detachment? If the attentive person epitomizes openness and vulnerability to reality, is she equipped with the energy to respond to the needs she perceives—or has the eclipse of herself disabled any response-ability? Simply put, how does the attentive person weigh the demands of justice and care? (Or is it possible that these traditionally juxtaposed ethical concepts are reconciled in Weilienne attention?)

Indeed, in many contemporary philosophical discussions of justice and care, these two concepts are described in ways that emphasize their distinctness from one another; care and justice are seen as two separate moral orientations, involving different emphases, expectations of situations, virtues, vices, and often entailing different actions. Even their contraries—injustice and uncaring neglect—are also understood as being separate, even if related, issues. For example, Sara Ruddick in her essay, "Injustice in Families: Assault and Domination," argues that under the care perspective, "exemplary wrongs involve indifference, neglect," or inattentiveness, whereas from the justice perspective, wrongness is defined by a lack of the "virtues of restraint and detachment," which signal the presence of domination and assault.[68] What this means for her is that there may be "little correlation" between the tendencies to be inattentive/neglectful and assaultive. She describes this distinction in the context of motherhood: "Some mothers, for example, are indifferent, inattentive, even frankly neglectful, but do not assault their children. Other mothers are protective and attentive, yet engage in assault."[69]

Weil would argue that this divorcing of domination (as injustice) and inattention (as uncaring) is imagined, and that to be inattentive *is* to be unjust and violently so, given her understanding of attention. Although Ruddick makes reference to Weil as support for her argument, she unfortunately misappropriates Weil's ethical philosophy. There are two major questions, then, that require investigation: How is it that inattentiveness is *not distinct* from domination/violent injustice in any morally significant way? And, how is one able to cultivate this attentiveness that entails both care and justice? The responses to these questions will reveal a revision of the traditional notion of inattentiveness such that our sense of responsibility will be heightened in times that would otherwise be assumed banal. Because of the stricter demands of attentiveness seen in this light, explaining its means of cultivation becomes a moral imperative, as well, and our analysis will reveal that the development of attention is simultaneously an ethical and an aesthetic process,[70] mirroring the fact that Platonic love (which is its inspiration) is love of the good and the beautiful.

One of the reasons that Ruddick and others institute a division between neglect (uncaring) and domination (injustice) is because the former is assumed to be passive—a *lack* of doing—whereas the latter is seen as active harm. This passive-active distinction abounds in philosophical debates on different ethical dilemmas (for instance, passive versus active euthanasia), but the divide is often shown to be superfluous, arbitrary, and a cause of harm more than clarity. Take for instance Peggy McIntosh's discussion of "privilege" as "unearned advantage and conferred dominance" that is accorded to whites, males, and heterosexuals, among other categories—we might add "Christians" to the list—in the United States.[71] Privilege, she says, is like an "invisible knapsack" that such groups carry around and are oblivious to. But the word "privilege" carries the connotation of being something everyone should want and strive toward, and it gives its possessors seeming permission to dominate and control (i.e., to be *unjust*) simply by virtue of belonging to that group. In our mundane way of seeing things, one who is simply privileged is not guilty of *doing anything* and is therefore not "unjust." It may be that they are oblivious to the plight of those suffering from oppression, but this is assumed to be an unfortunate effect of a desirable status rather than injustice defined as aggression toward or intrusion upon the other.

However, even McIntosh's description makes clear the active aspect of privilege: with privilege, one is permitted dominance and power to control. Moreover, in this station, one is more liable to see only "active" and explicit forms of oppression as problematic, and to be blind to their own oppressive stances and "embedded" forms of oppression (no less active). As a white woman, McIntosh writes,

> In my class and place, I did not see myself as racist because I was taught to recognize racism only in individual acts of meanness by members of my group, never in invisible systems conferring unsought racial dominance on my group from birth. Likewise, we are taught to think that sexism or heterosexism is carried on only through individual acts of discrimination, meanness, or cruelty toward women, gays, and lesbians. . . .[72]

Still, the question remains as to whether "permission to dominate" can be identified with *being domineering* or *being unjust*. At first glance, it would appear to be an unwarranted equivocation. Nevertheless, the inattentiveness that accompanies such privilege makes certain (unjust) actions inevitable, and other (loving) actions impossible.

It is Weil's understanding of the nature of attention, on the one hand, and the power to dominate, on the other, that leads us to be suspicious of divorcing privileged obliviousness from outright acts of domination. Attention, for her, is a radical renunciation of our own projects, desires, biases, and ambitions in order to be truly receptive to the reality of others and the external world. Attention "lets otherness be."[73] Because it involves a bracketing of self-centered aims and images, the attentive person is able to see what is (because of our self-preoccupations) usually invisible and hear what is usually silent or muffled sound. For Weil, attention characterizes artistic geniuses, then, as much as it does saints; it is creative and inspired by virtue of our decreation. It rids us of the clichés and obscurities caused by our persistent egos, and it reveals to us the "knapsacks of privilege" we carry unconsciously. As we have described in Chapter 3, we are naturally constituted by void, but everything in our being revolts against recognizing this. We

described how the "filling imagination" functions to disguise this
nature, but there is a more passive aspect to our natural state, too,
that makes attention nearly impossible. As Weil contends: "We
are born and live in *unconsciousness*. We are unconscious of our
misery. . . . The degradation of affliction always has this effect:
the soul clings to it until it is no longer capable of detaching itself
(*ersatz* of resignation)."[74] We are attached, that is, to our captivity
in ignorance and feel hatred for sources of illumination that bring
things into proper perspective. We become actively aggressive
toward anything (real) that challenges our imagined centrality.

Thus, fantasy—or daydreaming or *l'imagination combleuse*—
is the enemy of attention, for Weil, and our usual mode of consciousness is a fantastic one because of the ego's natural tendency
to protect itself through imagined narratives and deflections of all
sorts. This is also what injustice is. However, when we renounce
the falsifying and fantastic imagination, a "transformation then
takes place at the very roots of our sensibility," says Weil.[75] She
describes the transformation via analogy:

> It is a transformation analogous to that which takes place in
> the dusk of evening on a road, where we suddenly discern as a
> tree what we had at first seen as a stooping man; or where we
> suddenly recognize as a rustling of leaves what we thought at
> first was whispering voices. We see the same colors; we hear the
> same sounds, but not in the same way.[76]

To give another example, many of us could relate to the kind of
change of perspective effected after traveling abroad for this first
time. We see our native country, our habits, our religion, and our
attitudes about other nations differently; we smell and taste our own
cuisine differently; we begin to experience time differently, and we
hear our music differently. These transformations occur because of
a rupture and subsequent detachment from what was familiar and
taken for granted as being *the definition of what is most real*. Our
neat categories become absurd in the face of unexpected encounters, and we realize the extent to which we had been at the center
of our supposedly sacred narratives. In this way, attention grants
the reality of what has been deprived of being, such as the Good
Samaritan did before the naked, bleeding, and anonymous fellow
lying in the ditch on the side of the road in the famous Gospel

story. Clearly for Weil, attention brings an epiphany; but does the imagination entail the sort of violent objectification that Ruddick characterized as injustice? Is inattention synonymous with (active) domination? The answer to these questions lies in Weil's depiction of evil, as described in Chapter 3. Recall the way in which she characterizes the root of both sadistic assault and the convenient neglect of one who suffers: "There are no other restraints upon our will than material necessity and the existence of other human beings around us. *Any imaginary extension of these limits is seductive, so there is a seduction in whatever helps us to forget the reality of the obstacles.*"[77] In other words, when we are inattentive, human lives are emptied of their reality and people are turned into puppets. Inattention is active in the sense that it consists in (imaginarily) extending our limits, through and over the existence of others, who should serve as our limits. This happens not only in cases of war and slavery (or assault and domination) but also in the more common cases of our egotistical projections of our desires that result in our *not seeing or hearing* the affliction and needs of others.

Therefore, it is characteristic of inattention to wield power actively over others. Weil often compares our self-satisfying delusions (or, the obliviousness of privilege) to wielding a sword, in the complete license it appears to permit: "The sword affords deliverance . . . from the intolerable weight of our obligation."[78] In light of this metaphor, ego-defensiveness is a *violent* posture and cannot be resistant to the temptation of force. She cites Thucydides, who described the necessity by which humans command wherever they are able and have power:

> Possibility and necessity are terms opposed to justice . . . Possible means all that the strong can impose upon the weak. It is reasonable to examine how far this possibility goes. Supposing it to be known, it is *certain* that the strong will accomplish his purpose to the extreme limit of possibility. It is a mechanical necessity.[79]

To refuse to see the limitation manifested by others and to contemplate only what is possible for us to accomplish within a particular context is the meaning of inattention. Without doubt, this singular and exclusionary focus is the initiation of the automatic and mechanical expansion of our projects, and it implies the absence of respect for the being of others as ends-in-themselves. In Ruddick's own words,

> From the perspective of justice, relationships require *restraint* of one's own aggression, intrusion, and appropriation, and *respect* for the autonomy and bodily integrity of others. . . . A primary temptation . . . is to flout the rules of fair play, taking whatever you can get, what you are strong or lucky enough to be able to exact.[80]

Clearly, inattentiveness (understood here as disregarding the reality of other persons in favor of self-aggrandizement) is then synonymous with injustice, and the corollary, that attentiveness (or in Ruddick's terms, "care") is justice, is also true. As Weil puts it, "We have invented the distinction between justice and charity [*caritas*]"[81] because our more convenient notion of justice dispenses us from the constant vigilance demanded by attention.

Have we, in our industrialized late-capitalistic societies, made ourselves more immune to the void and to the hunger that signals it? Certainly, now we have more and easier access to false foods, as it were, (via the instant gratification of digital technology and of mass-produced material surplus) than ever before. Have we not descended into a vortex of sensing entitlement not-to-suffer, of not-to-feel-hunger? Instead of looking or attending, arguably we have taken up the consumptive posture of voyeuristic watching (of spectacles).[82] Even Weil, writing in the early 1940s, recognized: "The talking cinema is very much like [Plato's] cave. Which shows how much we love our degradation."[83] This latter activity is not one of openness, for we go into watching with expectations, usually expectations of entertainment.[84] Watching is also an activity that protects power, privilege, and obliviousness on one side while on the other side, certain groups of people are subjected to illusory fabrications (i.e., violence) at the hands of those who fashion these distractions. In the urgency of subsequent a-voiding, in our lust for control and power and the suppression of love, we have become the personification of one side only of the cold steel of the metaphorical sword; we *are* the side of brute violence and aggression:

Contact with the sword causes the same defilement, whether it be through the handle or the point. For him who loves, its metallic coldness will not destroy love, but will give the impression of being abandoned by God. Supernatural love has no contact with force, but at the same time it does not protect the soul against the coldness of force, the coldness of steel . . . If we want to have a love which will protect the soul from wounds, we must love something other than God.[85]

We need to release the handle of the sword if we wish to be attentive, though of course, the release itself would imply attention. This release is none other than the divine *mania* (what Weil calls "supernatural love") elucidated in *Phaedrus*. Clearly, this reorienting is risk-filled: releasing the handle of the sword may mean that we find ourselves quickly at the point, and as we have demonstrated, for Weil this release is exemplified by the Crucifixion. Again, modern psychology calls this move "masochistic."[86] But Weil tells us, "This is not any kind of masochism. What excites masochists is only the *semblance* of cruelty, because they don't know what cruelty is."[87] Conversely, the one who attends to reality *knows* affliction and suffering and the absence of God, this other side of cruelty. It is in this tangible absence of the good that we must wait and be irresistibly *impelled* to action. Haste and distractions are, in this state, perpetual temptations. But as Weil warned, "Alas for her if she gets tired and goes away. For the two places where God and humanity are waiting are at the same point in the fourth dimension . . ."[88] This point is the mid-point between life and death, the good and the necessary, the possible and impossible, the human and divine. This is a no-man's land, an intolerable ambiguity. This is the place of Antigone, of Socrates, of Jesus, of all such mediators. It is the place and experience of the cross—that is to say, being "nailed down" to the present, in exile—where there is a peculiar but unrecognizable advantage in the nourishment of our attention.

Affliction and the impersonal

To complete our analysis of loving attention as justice, we ought to consider the fact of what Weil called *malheur* (roughly translated as "affliction" and embodied, par excellence, by the crucified

Christ)[89] as a large part of what constitutes human reality and is perhaps the strongest challenge to attention—both for the victim and the attendant. First, in a surprising statement, Weil tells us that the love of one who is afflicted is comparable to the love of beauty, as both have a tendency to inspire renunciation and thus are great occasions for the cultivation of attention. She writes, for instance, "Beauty is a fruit which we look at without trying to seize it. The same with an affliction which we contemplate without drawing back."[90] Of course, while the phenomenon of affliction may be spiritually useful in this way, this does not mean that it is something to be desired or sought, as is the case with beauty. Moreover, Weil tells us: "I should not love my suffering because it is useful. I should love it because it *is*."[91] But there is something else that links real beauty and affliction and is essential to their very being: both beauty and affliction carry an element of *impersonality* in themselves, such that eventually the impersonal also becomes the character of one who attends to these phenomena. What does Weil mean by "impersonality," however? And how could impersonality constitute attention—that is, love—to *this person*? Beyond these questions, we must also consider the other tendency of affliction— its supreme ability to produce flight from the void.

Weil knew, and we are aware, that in this world, some people will attract our notice ("either through the hazard of circumstances or some chance affinity") and others will remain anonymous to us, escaping our gaze, or at most, we will see them "as items of a collectivity."[92] When Christ said that we have to love our neighbor, the example he gave as an illustration of that commandment was that being who was anonymous and forgotten, lying naked and bleeding on the roadside. Thus the love directed toward him would be, according to Weil, "completely anonymous, and for that reason, completely universal love."[93] Because humans are unequal in terms of their relations to the things of the world, it is imperative to give respect to that which *is* equal and identical in all humans, namely their "unquenchable desire for good."[94] In this way, we remember that what is to be attended to (and thus loved) in another is her *hunger*, or void; this is, after all, the reality of the human creature, and "love needs reality."[95] To do this, however, is paradoxically to direct one's attention *beyond* this world, because the universal human reality is linked to the supernatural reality, its origin. The human void, that is, implies "a reality outside the world . . . outside space and time, outside man's mental universe, outside any sphere whatsoever that is accessible to human faculties."[96] The void is only the universal absence of God—the inverse reflection of the supernatural. According to Weil, by virtue of directing our minds with attention toward that supernatural, we are able to make real contact with the universal center and essence of the human being who is afflicted, thereby enabling good to work through us. Those who love in this way are the sole intermediaries for true goodness to manifest in our earthly existence.

So for Weil, this universal aspect of humans that is the link to the other reality is "sacred," and it is what goes by the name of the "impersonal."[97] It is given an elevated status in part because all errors that we commit (including what are called "sins") are tied to the human personality, whereas "perfection is impersonal" and on the level of anonymity.[98] Thus, when we turn with loving attention to another human, it is because we have first detached from the temporal things of the world to turn entirely toward God, an altogether impersonal and self-renouncing experience in itself. Moreover, since "affliction is anonymous before all things" and "deprives its victims of their personality and makes them into things,"[99] if we can turn attentively toward one who is afflicted (which is to say, toward her impersonality, or her yearning for the good), we are prevented from consuming or assimilating her into ourselves or our own limited experiences. Why? Emptiness, by definition, cannot be eaten, but must be regarded. It is then that we are forced to remember our own hunger and, therefore, what absolutely unites us with the rest of humanity. For Weil, this should also be the effect of our contemplation of Christ's suffering on the cross—not satisfaction (by viewing it as a means to the resurrection), but a consent to suffer with others in the face of necessity (compassion).

Recognition of this commonality in humans by attending to the supernatural is "the only possible motive for universal respect," according to Weil.[100] This is because if we keep our attention tied to the horizontal plane of existence and the world of facts (rather than to verticality, or the good), we become unconsciously susceptible to prejudice, self-interest, proximity, convenience, pleasure, and all sorts of factors that preclude a nonpartisan (real) perspective and response. What is required by this supernatural attention demands *everything* of us:

The entire soul—including therefore its sentient and carnal part which is rooted in the things of sense and draws life from them. It must be uprooted. And this is death. . . . The loss of anything or anyone we are attached to is directly experienced as a sense of dejection which corresponds to a loss of energy. And what we have to do is to lose *all the vital energy which is supplied to us by all the things and all the people we are attached to.* . . . Thus it is total detachment that is the condition for the love of God, and when once the soul has performed the motion of totally detaching itself from the world so as to turn entirely towards God, it is illumined by the truth which comes down to it from God.[101]

But the obvious question here is, what does it mean to turn the attention toward God (or the supernatural), especially if this is something we cannot, by definition, and by our limitations, know?

In some sense, God cannot be an "object" of attention, for conceptions of God and theologies are necessarily artifices, as we have argued at length. Our attention, or love, cannot have God for its *direct object*, since "God is not present to the soul and has never yet been so."[102] What *is* possible is indirect or implicit love of God, which is ultimately "destined to become the love of God."[103] Such implicit love of God, as for example, the creative attention to the afflicted, is the fulfilling of the commandment "Thou shalt love the Lord thy God," and is the only sensible meaning of it, according to Weil.

We appear to have run into a contradiction: On the one hand, we must love God directly and detach ourselves from earthly, sensible things; on the other, God *cannot* be a direct object of our love, so we must turn to the world to love God implicitly—the only way we can. But there is no contradiction. What we attend to, for instance, in another person, is of a supernatural/universal order: the impersonal longing for the good. This sort of attention *is* a detachment from the temporal and perishable, for the yearning is an eternal one. In the same way, when we attend to the impersonal necessity of the natural world, we share in a universal perspective that is a reflection of the supernatural: "Christ tells us to contemplate and imitate the lilies of the field and the birds of the air, in their indifference as to the future and their docile acceptance of destiny; and another time he invites us to contemplate and imitate

the indiscriminate distribution of rain and sunlight."[104] The effect
of such attention to what is impersonal in the world is similar in
both cases: we are displaced from our imaginary center of the universe, and with us, our false ideas of time, our parochial hierarchy
of values, our sense of what is real and what is not—all the convenient projections of our ego are put in their proper place, which is to
say, as merely one among others.

However, there is a special problem when it comes to attending
to the afflicted. As Weil rightly notes, oftentimes, when we encounter someone who is afflicted, we are practically *unable* via our own
natural efforts to give this person any moment of attention. We can
scarcely look in their direction. Weil writes:

> Thought revolts from contemplating affliction, to the same degree
> that living flesh recoils from death. A stag advancing voluntarily
> step by step to offer itself to the teeth of a pack of hounds is
> about as probable as an act of attention directed towards a real
> affliction, which is close at hand, on the part of a mind which is
> free to avoid it. But that which is indispensable to the good and
> is impossible naturally is always possible supernaturally.[105]

It is true that an encounter with affliction, whether experienced
directly or indirectly through empathy, can, by virtue of its horror,
induce a flight into unending distractions and deflections of reality.
Weil acknowledges: "Whoever endures a moment of the void either
receives the supernatural bread or falls. It is a terrible risk but one
that must be run, even during the instant when hope fails. But,"
she adds, "we must not throw ourselves into it."[106] The last clause
is crucial, for the seeking out of affliction implies the retention
of control, power, and will in manipulating force; by definition,
then, one is unable to bring affliction upon oneself. We may be
able to bring *suffering* upon ourselves, but not affliction, because
part of what distinguishes affliction is the component of real social
exile—it is something externally imposed and therefore truly bitter. As Weil says, "[Affliction] is quite a different thing from simple suffering. It takes possession of the soul and marks it through
and through with its own particular mark, the mark of slavery."[107]
More precisely, she states:

> There is not real affliction unless the event that has seized and
> uprooted a life attacks it, directly or indirectly, in all its parts,

social, psychological, and physical. The social factor is essential. There is not really affliction unless there is social degradation or the fear of it in some form or another.[108]

Ironically, then, the afflicted one who is the literal embodiment of the living dead—a monster[109]—makes it nearly impossible for one who looks at her for only a second to engage the imagination, to make "a suitable adjustment of the mind."[110] The veil has been ripped away. The only option left is complete a-voidance—looking away. How, then, is it possible to turn with love toward the one who is afflicted?

On one level, this action *is* impossible. As we have seen, our thought naturally revolts from contemplating affliction, and our tendencies of self-preservation keep it at bay. Also, Weil notes that affliction cannot be communicated to those who have not experienced it, and "as for those who have themselves been mutilated by affliction, they are in no state to help anyone at all."[111] "Thus," she concludes, "compassion for the afflicted is an impossibility."[112] But of course, Weil does not mean that such compassion is a literal impossibility and that we are excused from it; it is only an impossibility on the *natural level* of human effort. Here we must recall an important lesson in the cultivation of attention (manifested in this context as "compassion"): if one has desired to be attentive in such situations already, as evidenced by the training undertaken to clear away distractions, then supernatural energy will make the impossible possible. In this context, her words regarding training—"we have to accomplish the possible in order to touch the impossible"[113]—take on new meaning. And this applies to the afflicted one as well:

> The soul has to go on loving in the emptiness, or at least to go on wanting to love, though it may only be with an infinitesimal part of itself. Then, one day, God will come to show himself to this soul and to reveal the beauty of the world to it, as in the case of Job. But if a soul stops loving it falls, even in this life, into something almost equivalent to hell.[114]

The phenomenon of affliction as a test of attention is an extremely precarious one. But if an original consent to the void has been made, the development of love and attention grows exponentially in confronting atrocity and degradation, for "affliction compels us to recognize as real what we do not think possible."[115] Again, the description of this phenomenon's potential for the growth of attention can be prescriptive in *no way*. We raise the issue only to suggest, as Weil does, that it reveals our a-voidance and (dis)orientation to ourselves, in a most concrete way. "One can only accept the existence of affliction by considering it at a distance," she tells us.[116] (This claim appears verified by the well-known contemporary phenomenon in which masses of people flood internet sites promising to show gory videos of human cruelty and torture, as an apparent source of amusement.)[117]

However, the distance itself is not the problem, as long as there is attention; the problem is the looking away, which may take the form of a consumptive imagination: "Sin is not a distance, it is a turning of our gaze in the wrong direction,"[118] which is to say, away from reality and its inherent connections, and toward personal aims that have become inflated, including the transformation of everything into a spectacle for our entertainment. And this turning away from reality, though itself constituting a choice, means that a person gives himself over to the laws of moral and spiritual gravity, where "he thinks that he can decide and choose, but he is only a thing, a stone that falls."[119] In turning away from the "supernatural light" that illuminates the real irreducibility of affliction and the impersonal order, the mere spectator becomes obedient to those blind and mechanical laws of gravity, where his subsequent choices are only semblances of choice. It is important to note this irony: a man flees the scene of affliction through his imagination, presumably because the objectness and abjectness of the afflicted fill him with the horror of losing his own *person* (i.e., his freedom), but this is precisely what he loses in turning away.

On the level of attention that can really "look" at affliction (having been prepared by training in solitude and exercises of self-effacement), freeing love is truly made possible. Here is where decreation happens, and where false gods flee the scene, for affliction is felt as the irreducible and unavoidable absence of God. Consider Weil's example of attending to an afflicted other, which is also a perfect example of the refusal to consume him as a spectacle:

> One of two [humans] is only a little piece of flesh, naked, inert, and bleeding beside a ditch; he is nameless; no one knows anything about him. Those who pass by this thing scarcely notice it, and a

few minutes afterward do not even know that they saw it. Only one stops and turns his attention toward it. The actions that follow are just the automatic effect of this moment of attention. The attention is creative. But at the moment when it is engaged it is a renunciation . . . The man accepts to be diminished by concentrating on an expenditure of energy, which will not extend his own power but will only give existence to a being other than himself, who will exist independently of him. Still more, to desire the existence of the other is to transport himself into him by sympathy, and as a result, to have a share in the state of inert matter which is his.[120]

We see here that creative *attention,* which is really a decreation, causes us to be transported *into* the afflicted Other, rather than the reverse, which is caused by the imagination: transporting the unconsenting Other into *us* and our fantasies. Thus, loving and attending to the Other means that we accept diminishment of our egos, for it is a necessary consequence any time we are truly open to the reality of other persons. In this loving, we also detach ourselves from any possible return from the beings we love. According to Weil, loving our neighbor means being able to ask him, "What are you going through?" "It is a recognition the sufferer exists," she contends, "as a man, exactly like us, who was one day stamped with a special mark by affliction."[121] In other words, to love is to embrace the void of another without trying to fill it with our own finite and limited human (pseudo-)solutions and easy consolations; after all, even these well-intentioned tactics too often are meant to help us forget our own hunger.

Hunger (or the void) *is* our universal reality, as we have seen:

The danger is not lest the soul should doubt whether there is any bread, but lest, by a lie, it should persuade itself that it is not hungry. It can only persuade itself of this by lying, for the reality of its hunger is not a belief, it is a certainty.[122]

Though we may not think we wish to possess the being we approach, the distance effected by self-renunciation is necessary to maintain our humility before, and hence our love for her. Again, we must love in the other what is real. Weil reminds us, "To be able to love in our neighbor the hunger that consumes him and not the food he offers for the appeasement of our own hunger—this implies a total detachment. It implies that one renounces feeding on man and wants in the future to feed only on God."[123]

Still, there remain questions about the lived experience of this detached and impersonal love—for both the lover and the recipient. Is this supernatural love ultimately satisfying to humans' needs? Can universal love account for the real complexities of interpersonal relationships with *particular* others? In recent decades, there has been much criticism of theories of love such as the one just presented. As we will demonstrate, critics argue that this impersonal love amounts to an abdication of responsibility and avoidance of genuine commitment to the complexities of human relations. How might Weil respond to these serious charges?

Facing the other?

If love is conceptually a paradox for Simone Weil, in her personal life it was arguably "an ordeal."[124] While many, such as Father Joseph-Marie Perrin, marveled at "her love for the disinherited of this world" in all the forms it took, the same has also noted an "interior problem": "Kind and merciful as she was," Perrin wrote, "she would sometimes tend to make the exacting demands of a merciless logician."[125] Gustave Thibon remarked that "she was inwardly founded on love like those volcanoes of the arctic regions of which the lava is hidden under a covering of ice."[126] Weil herself, in writing to one of her pupils in the spring of 1935, during the time of her employment at the Renault factories, confesses,

> I can tell you that when, at your age, and later on too, I was tempted to try to get to know love, I decided not to—telling myself that it was better not to commit my life in a direction impossible to foresee until I was sufficiently mature to know what, in a general way, I wish from life and what I expect from it.[127]

It is entirely apropos that this "problem" was evidenced in both Weil's writings and in the records we have of her short life, for there was rarely, if ever, a bifurcation between these two aspects in her.

Describing the rarity of the authentic unity that typified her life and thought, E. W. F. Tomlin tells us, "The false mystic is concerned with elaborating what he has seen, or with trying to define and convey the emotions which accompanied his vision. Simone Weil is solely engaged in the seeing."[128] Thus, what she *sees*, that is, what she *attends* to, will by necessity and definition come to inhabit her being and hence will resist objectification. For instance, Weil readily admitted that there were ideas that would not let her rest, words that had the innate virtue of illumination and edification, but not consolation—"vertical" words such as *God*, *truth*, *justice*, and, significantly for our purposes here, *love*.[129] Such words imply a risk and a danger, because there is the constant temptation to elaborate and posit conceptualizations through associating them with the horizontal and familiar. But because these words refer to absolute perfection, for Weil, and "are the image in our world of [the] impersonal and divine order of the universe," we should not try to make them conform to our limited paradigms, since their realities are beyond conceptualization.[130] Rather, we must accept them as "uncomfortable companions," and in finding associated ideas and actions in the light they shed, come to abolish "everything in contemporary life which buries the soul under injustice, lies, and ugliness."[131]

Love, then, being one such "uncomfortable companion" for Weil and being described as *light* and not consolation,[132] will naturally be found mystifying not only to the intellect but also to the lived experience. Rush Rhees is one scholar who openly struggled with Weil's notion of purity, especially in its implications for love. In letters to his friend, M. O'C. Drury, and in notes never intended to be published,[133] Rhees confronted the difficulties—both theoretical and practical—that he imagined would ensue from a total acceptance of Weil's love philosophy. In fact, as we noted earlier, Rhees goes so far as to write that this pure love "in her hands . . . goes to ways which are . . . in a deep sense evil."[134] There are four major points of his critique we have identified that lead him to the conclusion that Weilienne love is quite possibly evil, and which need to be addressed. Although D. Z. Phillips makes an important point in saying, "Rhees's concentration on difficulties counters the easy tendency for religious admiration of Simone Weil to lead to an uncritical acceptance of everything she says," her insights regarding the nature of supernatural love are more nuanced than they

tend to be presented by critics such as Rhees.[135] While we do not pretend that there are any final resolutions to the challenges, it seems
clear that Rhees neglected to consider important factors, not only
chez Simone Weil but also in broader philosophical and historical
frameworks. For instance, as we will describe, the social activism of
another early twentieth-century female philosopher, Jane Addams,
provides some pertinent parallels to Weil's thinking about universal
love. Nevertheless, there are others like Rhees who would provide
strong challenges to Weil's perspective on love—including those
who emphasize "interpersonal" religious ethics, like Emmanuel
Levinas, and those who emphasize care ethics, like Nel Noddings.
We will examine possible critiques from these figures, in addition
to Rhees's, and proffer Weilienne responses.

    To begin, Rhees stated or implied the following four challenges,
which we will subsequently examine closely because they represent
the most common objections raised to Weil's idea of impersonal
and supernatural love. First, Weil's notion of pure love involves
an indifference to the temporal life of others and self, whereas
many think that in loving a particular person, one "ought to hope
that things will go one way" and not another for them.[136] Second,
charity and compassion necessarily require some form of attachment.[137] Third, wanting to be physically near the beloved does not
necessarily mean wanting to possess (or consume) them, but rather
this may really indicate a love *for* them and not a love *of the possession* of them.[138] Finally, cutting attachment to the world is a
"flight from responsibility"; it "disregards the dependence of others on you," and it is "evil."[139] Furthermore, Rhees claims that Weil
ignores the suffering inherent in intimate relations (e.g., marriage
or parent-child relationships), instead focusing her discussions on
love of strangers and love of God, throwing into question whether
she could love humans as humans.[140]

    In general, Rhees' problems with Weil's notions of purity and
love are arguably more (self-)disclosive of the human attachment to
attachment itself, rather than suggestive of something "evil" inherent in Weil's thought. By carefully and philosophically revisiting
themes central to Weil's ethical-religious account of love, such as
the void, detachment, "gift,"[141] charity, and distance, we do not
attempt to *solve* the perplexities of pure love in Weil's writings and
life but to *dissolve* some of the problems that are unnecessarily
projected onto the issue.

The first problem Rhees identifies concerns the practical consequences of Weil's contention that pure love must be a detached love. For example, she writes,

> Every desire for enjoyment belongs to the future and the world of illusion, whereas if we desire only that a being should exist, he exists: what more is there to desire? . . . In this sense, and on condition that [love] is not turned toward a pseudo-immortality conceived on the model of the future, the love we devote to the dead is perfectly pure.[142]

Indeed, as we have seen, for Weil, love is simply the desire for the *existence* of a being, without the escape into the (imaginary) future. But Rhees ponders, "It would seem to follow [from this] that if you love someone, you ought not to be concerned about what may happen to him while he is alive. You ought not even to care whether in his life he is going to come nearer to God or to be degraded."[143] For him, love entails that we *ought* to hope that things will go one way, and not another.

One might simply respond that Rhees confuses an "is" for an "ought." That is to say, just because we often *do* hope for particular things for those we love does not imply that we *should*. But why shouldn't one do so? Weil makes it clear that "the future is a filler of void places."[144] Hoping, as a futurally oriented phenomenon,[145] would be tied up, according to Weil, with the workings of the imagination, in its projections for certain ends, either for oneself or for another. Therefore, in hoping, one would not be fully attentive to the present existent, and while we may *believe* ourselves to be participating in the good, we have in fact allowed ourselves to be distracted from reality, where we could have become intermediaries for the good. Perhaps this only demonstrates Vance Morgan's point about Rhees: "Rhees' problem with Weil," he writes, "is on a *metaphysical* level and is an example of an interpreter attempting to understand a text from within the confines of a particular metaphysical framework, when the author of the text is writing from within the confines of an entirely different framework."[146]

Indeed, rather than *hoping* for good, it is for humans to turn their attention and love toward "the reality that exists outside the reach of all human faculties," and in so doing, to become mediators through which good can descend from there and come among one's fellows.[147] As we have shown, to love is to be just. Hence it is not merely a metaphysical difference for Weil and Rhees, but it follows from Weil's understanding of this love of reality that all persons would be established as equals in their capacity to attend to what transcends contingency and particular contexts. Hoping for a particular end for another, then, is not only escapist but also short-sighted, presumptuous, and self-satisfying; for in hoping, I hope *that*, and am thereby transferred to another reality—that is to say, unreality. It is no surprise that "hope" is one of those words that is (and has been) easily appropriated by political campaigns, for the politician seeking election desires nothing so much as to have his constituents forget about the present. Instead of hoping, waiting (without knowing for what) or "listening ceaselessly" is the mode by which one becomes a vessel for true goodness. Only by renouncing every form of the imagination—hoping included—do we preserve the interior void, a condition for love. As Weil asks, "If we accept no matter what void, what stroke of fate can prevent us from loving the universe?"[148]

Regarding his second critique, in questioning the theoretical soundness of Weil's notion of loving in the void, Rhees insinuates that charity and compassion necessitate *some* form of attachment, thus throwing doubt on whether love is really always "detached." He writes, "Sometimes Simone Weil speaks as though *all* attachment were something like the attachment of a miser for his treasure. But of course she cannot hold to this line, since it makes nonsense of charity, of compassion, and so on."[149] In order to assess whether Rhees is correct in his insinuation, we must first give an account of authentic charity, or benefaction, and then proceed to its implications for pure love.

When one is charitable, one gives a *gift*. Jean-Luc Marion, in his "phenomenology of givenness," has had this to say about what constitutes a gift:

> The gift, to be given, must be lost and remain lost without return. In this way alone does it break with exchange, where one gives only to have it repaid (with a marginal profit) . . . [I]t is a question of the pure and simple loss involved in giving with abandon. . . . Hence the paradox: the gift must be lost for me, but not for everybody. It's necessary that an Other receive it and definitely deprive me of it.[150]

From Marion's compelling description of a gift, we see that detachment is a necessary ingredient of charity; otherwise, when one is
attached, (even to the intended beneficiary!) what one engages in
is not properly *giving*, or benefaction, or charity, but some sort of
controlled economic exchange. If one is attached to the Other who
receives, there is necessarily a return to self in the so-called giving;
"investment" would be a more appropriate label. Pure love, on the
other hand, would *compel* the giving, such that it would not even
be recognized as such. Weil cites the disciples: "Lord, when was it
that we saw you hungry and gave you food, or thirsty and gave you
something to drink?"[151]

Giving, for Weil, would involve the Hindu mandate to be
detached "from the fruits of action . . . to act not *for* an object but
from necessity."[152] She tells us, "Every act should be considered
from the point of view not of its object but of its impulsion. The
question is not 'What is the aim?' It is 'What is the origin?'"[153] And
clearly, for her, the origin should be God. Hence, "[w]e should not
go to our neighbor for the sake of God, but we should be impelled
toward our neighbor by God, as the arrow is driven toward its
target by the archer."[154] Nowhere in this depiction of charitable
action would attachment be a possibility. Again, this is not simply
a metaphysical matter, but an ethical one as well. What would it
mean for there to be an attachment, even to the Other, in the act
of giving? Would the recipient not feel the constraint of the attachment, and if so, are we not *buying him*? Weil tells us, for instance,
"Almsgiving when it is not supernatural is like a sort of purchase.
It buys the sufferer."[155] Thus, it becomes clear that real loss, which
cuts the cords of attachment, is necessary for the gift to be pure.
Weil writes, "Benefaction is permissible precisely because it constitutes a humiliation still greater than pain, a still more intimate
and undeniable proof of dependence."[156] This mention of dependence would seem to contradict what we have established concerning the absence of attachment in giving. But she continues, "The
dependence, however, must be on fate and not on any particular
human being. That is why the benefactor is under an obligation to
keep himself entirely out of the benefaction."[157] Real charity, then,
issues from a detached and pure love, which is to say, from a desire
to do what justice demands and thus not only does not necessitate
attachment but also absolutely precludes it.

For Weil, consenting to distance from the beloved is key to a pure or "supernatural" love, one not tarnished by attachment, modification, domination, submission, or the desire for possession. So it is in this context that Rhees makes his third objection, "If I do not want to be separated from the person I love, this need not mean that I want to possess him (or her)."[158] He goes on to protest Weil's analogy of this desire for proximity with the miser's love of a treasure, arguing that although the miser may make sacrifices to keep the money, "he does not make sacrifices for *it*; he does not have a love for *it* in the way in which you love the woman who is yours, and for whom you make every sacrifice."[159] In other words, he questions why the desire for proximity would imply a desire for consumption.

As we have noted, Weil does often compare love with hunger; of course, for her, pure love would be evidenced by *looking* antithetical to *eating*. Can one, in fact, have a pure love for something that one dares to approach? Weil thinks that by "remain[ing] quite still" we actually unite ourselves with that which we desire.[160] It is this way with God, for instance: we do not dare approach Him, but paradoxically, by our self-renunciation it is possible to be closest. The approach itself is an assertion of self and suffices to bring one the sort of satiation and consolation that arises from a consumptive posture. Anytime distance is reduced, love (i.e., hunger) is conquered. But this is precisely the danger, for it is the hunger that is real: "We imagine kinds of food, but the hunger itself is real; we have to fasten onto the hunger."[161] What this means is that as finite, fallible creatures, our remembrance that *this is our constitution* is of utmost importance. In constantly seeking proximity to the beloved, we ironically forget our essential hunger, for this is the paradoxical nature of desire that Emily Dickinson expresses in the last stanza of her poem, "I Had Been Hungry": ". . . so I found / that hunger was a way / of persons outside windows, / the entering takes away."[162] Though we may not think we wish to possess the beloved we approach, the distance is necessary to maintain our humility before, and hence our love for her.

Simone Weil is not the only woman to have been criticized for finding her vocation in serving the world beyond and even to the exclusion of, intimate and familial relations. In his fourth critique, Rhees saw in Weil a "tendency to ignore the relations between two persons . . . which are the relations of just *these* individuals" and thereby to ignore the suffering that would be inherent therein.[163]

Care ethicists, such as Nel Noddings, are also highly suspicious of notions like "universal love" because of the propensity toward abstraction and abstention from the practical world. Noddings worries about the caring that retreats from the tending to particular persons by going

> . . . toward other objects of caring—ideas, animals, humanity-at-large, God—[such that] her ethical ideal is virtually shattered. . . . Our ethic of caring—which has been called a "feminine ethic"— begins to look a bit mean in contrast to the masculine ethics of universal love or universal justice. But universal love is illusion. Under the illusion, some young people retreat to the church to worship that which they cannot actualize; some write lovely poetry extolling universal love; and some, in terrible disillusion, kill to establish the very principles which should have entreated them not to kill. Thus are lost both principles and persons.[164]

If this neglect of persons is true, can it be justified? Jane Addams, another social activist of the early twentieth century who felt called to "higher claims" argues, by contrast, "The stern [ethical] questions are not in regard to personal and family relations, but *did ye visit the poor, the criminal, the sick, and did ye feed the hungry?*"[165] Addams believed that the two interests, personal and social, did each have a real moral basis and a right to its own place in life; however, these interests are bound to collide tragically, unless family and close friends are educated to recognize the broader social claim as legitimate. Hence, for Addams, the responsibility lies with the family and the spouse to adjust to the more expansive and inclusive ethic.

While Addams argued on the basis of a democratic humanism that "to attain individual morality in an age demanding social morality . . . is utterly to fail to apprehend the situation,"[166] as we have seen, Weil explains impersonal attention on a *religious* basis: in order to truly love those here below, our love must "detach itself completely from creatures to ascend to God," pass "through God as through fire," to then come down again "associated with the creative love of God."[167] As we have pointed out, however, since God cannot be a direct object for our love, Weil actually means that we attend to the universal human void which is sacred. She explains:

We have a heavenly country, but in a sense it is too difficult to love, because we do not know it; above all, in a sense, it is too easy to love, because we can imagine it as we please. We run the risk of loving a fiction under this name. . . . Let us love the country of here below. It is real; it offers resistance to love. It is this country that God has given us to love. He has willed that it should be difficult yet possible to love it.[168]

Her maddening paradox of the imperative to love what is here below while detaching from its particulars to ascend to a supernatural commonality points to the extraordinary difficulty of resisting idolatry—which we commit either by imagining the supernatural or absolutizing the natural. The orientation of love is, for Weil, as challenging as the proverbial camel who passes through the eye of the needle, or more to the point, "the rich man [who enters] . . . into the kingdom of God." When the disciples expressed their dismay at this illustration, wondering how they could then be saved, Jesus responded: "For mortals it is impossible, but for God all things are possible."[169] Weil does not deny the importance of interpersonal relations, for they are essential in avoiding pure abstractions and fictions: "In all departments of life, love is not real unless it is directed toward a particular object; it becomes universal without ceasing to be real only as a result of analogy and transference."[170] The point is, we ought not to privilege certain relations and persons above others by making exceptions, special excuses, et cetera, because the ego is always involved in such rankings. In addition, such privileging shows that we have fallen under a conceit that select people, concerns, and relations are *more real* than others. By contrast, our love of a particular person must leave impartiality intact and preserve the autonomy in ourselves and others; these qualities are of an impersonal order. Weil provides a helpful example to illustrate this transference: "As a geometrician looks at a particular figure in order to deduce the universal properties of the triangle, so he who knows how to love directs upon a particular human being a universal love."[171] This detached love does not diminish the beloved but in fact is like a vision that refuses to be distracted by what is inessential and accidental about a person—the very same qualities that the ego exaggerates and uses as the basis of discrimination.

If this detachment brings about resentment and abandonment on the part of our comrades in our personal lives, we can be certain that they "are no true friends of God," Weil remarks.[172] "Our neighbor, [and] our friends . . . do not fall to the level of unrealities after the soul has had direct contact with God," she continues, distinguishing herself from Plato. "On the contrary, it is only then that these things become real. Previously they were half dreams. Previously they had no reality."[173] So despite Rhees' claim that cutting attachment to the world constitutes a flight from responsibility and is evil in its apparent disregard of "the dependence of other people on you,"[174] it seems that real justice is possible only through this impersonal attention. The temptation to give preferential treatment to one's closest friends, and to leave the ego intact in doing so, is too great otherwise. It *would* be uncomfortable for the average human to accept that "love is not consolation," but "light"[175] and that loving truth (which is a mandate) entails enduring the void. What may be perceived as fleeing responsibility, as disregarding the dependence of others, may in fact be the result of the sort of attachment that should itself become enlightened. We are tempted to label the discomfort and personal neglect we feel from the saint's detachment as evil, but is the evil not in us? Weil reminds us, "The sin in me says 'I'. . . . Evil makes distinctions, prevents God from being equivalent to all."[176]

Still, are there not other philosophies on love that extol the singular uniqueness of particular persons in relationships as central to the ethicality of the engagement? Emmanuel Levinas is clearly one such philosopher who, by taking a phenomenological approach to the encounter with the Other, reveals the "height" and "infinity" (or vertical dimension) that manifests in the experience of that irreducible alterity. We generalize here some key points from his work, *Totality and Infinity*, for the purposes of this contrast to Weilienne love. For Levinas, broadly speaking, it is the encounter with *difference* or alterity of the Other—the fact that he is irreducible to the Same (the subject, me)—that founds the religio-ethical dimension and thus my responsibility for the Other. In fact, "preexisting the plane of ontology is the ethical plane,"[177] for Levinas, insofar as relation and encounter are primary, whereas abstraction, systematizing, and totalizing are secondary.

In the encounter, the Other comes to me as "absolutely foreign," and this strangeness is the property of his freedom, his distance from me. As Levinas notes, "The absolutely foreign alone can instruct us. And it is only man who could be absolutely foreign to

me—refractory to every typology, to every genus, to every charac-
terology, to every classification. . . ."[178] While Weil also emphasizes
the importance of distance between two persons to preserve autonomy and the capacity for free consent, goodness is only possible
in a relation when there is a recognition of what is *common* in all
people—the impersonal hungering. Levinas does say that "to recognize the Other is to recognize a hunger," but he goes on to say,
"To recognize the Other is to give. But it is to give to the master,
to the lord, to him whom one approaches as 'You' in a dimension
of height."[179] Levinas thus describes the experience of the Other as
one of divinity (or, in his term, "infinity"). Weil, on the other hand,
reserves that level of alterity/mystery for the supernatural—which
we only know by its absence. Other persons *are* limits to us and
our projects, but only on the basis of the common *link* to the good,
by virtue of their desire for the good. That is, there is mediation
(exemplified by the Christ figure) between the immanent and transcendent in Weil's philosophy, whereas, for Levinas, "[t]he dimension of the divine opens forth from the [particular] human face"[180]
in an unmediated way.

Beyond this difference, we also know that for Levinas, there is a
distinction between the ethical dimension and that of the uniquely
loving or erotic relationship. In the latter, Levinas describes an
ambiguity wherein desire (a tending toward the absolutely other,
characteristic of the ethical relation) and need (a tending toward
satisfaction and consummation for the self) are joined. In the loving
relationship, that is, Levinas emphasizes the additional element of
enjoyment of the Other and, therefore, a return to self in consum-
matory experiences. He writes of the ambiguity: "Love remains
a relation with the Other that turns into need, and this need still
presupposes the total, transcendent exteriority of the other, of the
beloved."[181] Weil, however, is unequivocal in her denigration of
carnal love, but more to the point, she warns of the destructive
influence of the element of "need" admitted into any friendship or
relationship. "To soil is to modify, it is to touch," she says, describing the disfiguring effects of power exerted in any relationship,
including the erotic caress.[182] And, "In all human things, necessity
is the principle of impurity."[183] The problem is precisely that lovers
want to possess, to enjoy the Other, to reaffirm the self through the
Other. In this light, Levinas' description of the (feminine) beloved
is telling:

The beloved is opposed to me not as a will struggling with my own or subject to my own, but on the contrary as an irresponsible animality which does not speak true words. The beloved, returned to the stage of infancy without responsibility—this coquettish head, this youth, this pure life "a bit silly"—has quit her status as a person. . . . The relations with the Other are enacted in play; one plays with the Other as with a young animal.[184]

While philosophers like Luce Irigaray have been critical of passages in Levinas' phenomenology of eros such as this one for primarily feminist reasons, Weil would see the description as indicative of a mind that has given (in the Platonic sense) full reign to its *basest* desires and complete license to the falsifying imagination that projects animality onto the reality of a person.

Moreover, according to Levinas' description, our love is ultimately defined by its return to us. He writes, "If to love is to love the love the Beloved bears me, to love is also to love oneself in love, and thus to return to oneself. Love does not transcend unequivocably—it is complacent, it is pleasure and dual egoism."[185] In Weil's thinking on love, this is a recipe for domination and constraint within relationships—that is, injustice. The autonomy (and integrity) of the Other is compromised by the consumptive aspect of the erotic orientation, for they become a means to my self-love. Hence, for Weil, even "to desire friendship is a great fault," for it is of "the order of grace" and should be for us an unexpected and gratuitous joy. "Friendship is not," she contends, "to be sought, not to be dreamed, not to be desired; it is to be exercised (it is a virtue)."[186] This virtue requires the preservation of hunger on our part and the refusal to fill this void with another.

In the end, Simone Weil can perhaps be accused of seeking to express and live a love that is not pleasant, a love that is too great for the intellect's grasp, and too detached for the hungry ego. Despite Richard Rhees' admitted high regard for Weil and her work, when he says in various places that he *thinks* Weil is mistaken about love, one wonders whether he is not in actuality *wishing* (imagining) her to be mistaken. Such a desire would be a temptation for anyone. Weil herself recognized the tension that pure love is bound to produce. She knew, for instance, that the testing of Job was "a question of the level of love."[187] The question that must be confronted is: "Is love situated on the level of sheep, fields of corn, numerous children? Or is it situated further off, in the third dimension, *behind*?"[188] And Weil did not believe that she would pass this test, either, confessing, "I think I must love wrongly: otherwise things would not seem like this to me. My love would not be attached to a few beings. It would be extended to everything which is worthy of love."[189] This sort of love seems impossible to us, but "it is necessary to touch impossibility in order to come out of the dream world" and approach the door of the supernatural, the real.[190]

In an age where distractions are omnipresent and where self-love is touted as the foundation of all other loves, the dream world appears to be inhabited consciously and willingly. It is no surprise that we do not *see* whole races of people, whole nations, the poor, and the diseased but primarily direct our "attention" toward those who entertain us and who perpetuate our fictional worlds. It is therefore a revolutionary hypothesis that love is the selfless attending to reality. It is in this way, and no other, that love is a condition of justice, for while such love seems impossible to us, it is something we must begin to "see" in order to begin seeing those whom our preferential loves have made invisible. But it is in this way, too, that pure love (and thus, "real mysticism") is not ennobling or glorious, but crucifying. Perhaps the question Weil leaves in her wake is whether we are prepared to accept a detached, pure, and patient love as the model for our interaction with others. This "impossible" love—which for Weil is the only love—may be our greatest ethical and religious challenge, and by virtue of an inherent reference to absolute perfection, an uncomfortable companion for us as well.

5
Beauty and anonymity

*Consider the lilies of the field, how they grow; they neither
toil nor spin, yet I tell you, even Solomon in all his glory was
not clothed like one of these.*

MATTHEW 6:28–9

*Space juts out from us and translates each thing:
to succeed with a tree's essence
cast innerspace around it, out of that space
that has its life in you. Surround it with restraint.
In itself it has no bounds. Only in the field
of your renouncing does it rise as Tree.*

RAINER MARIA RILKE[1]

Decentered eye, decentered I

While much has just been said about love requiring self-renunciation
and subsequent release of control, a more thorough appreciation of
Weil's religious paradoxes can be had through examining her ideas
on the nature of the beautiful and the disposition proper to its
appreciation. As we will see, the development of a certain aesthetic
posture inclines us to be just and loving; this aesthetic posture will
be such that in beholding a work of art, for example, we will feel
displaced from our imagined centrality in the world, stopped short
in our consumptive and egocentric ways. Weil held that any love of

beauty will simultaneously be a love of and consent to our inherent limitations in the encounters with what is external to us. But as we will see, the beautiful—especially as embodied in the tragic—will also call us to *exceed* limits. Recall Weil's claim that "the beautiful is a carnal attraction which keeps us at a distance and implies a renunciation," including a renunciation of the "most deep-seated" imagination.[2] But in renouncing the imagination, we paradoxically exceed what we thought possible. In this way, we see that the beautiful object acts *on* us as it structures our mode of being in the world; at the same time, our disposition will determine what we can appreciate, to such an extent that, as we have shown in the previous chapter, attention is *creative*.

The particular comportment inherent in encountering the beautiful as depicted by Weil is shared by the philosopher Edward Bullough, and we briefly cite his view only to provide some preliminary illumination on Weil's aesthetic philosophy and its relation to the cultivation of attentiveness. According to Bullough, "the essence of the aesthetic attitude is the psychological process (or act) of *distancing*."[3] Any involvement with the aesthetic object that is purely personal or that solely fulfills our practical needs or base desires is decidedly unaesthetic. There is a famous example Bullough gives of this phenomenon, where

> the jealous husband who, at a performance of Othello, keeps thinking of his own wife's odd behavior, is attending not really to the play as such, but to its *relation to his own life*. His attitude is not duly "distanced," and is therefore not aesthetic. His involvement in the play is merely personal. . . . [Or again,] when one feels delighted by a play merely because his daughter plays a leading role therein; or by a record of *Shahnai* music just because it is being played on his stereo, the inner fabric of the play or the music is hardly given any thought, and hence the attitude is not aesthetic.[4]

What this amounts to is that the object of beauty that makes attention *possible* (for Weil tells us, "[t]he beautiful is something on which we can fix our attention,"[5]) also potentially permits a great deal of self-obsession. But the fault is not in the work of art, per se, but in our refusal to consent to the experience of hunger arising from the attraction, or void.

Any "good" that is opened to us via the aesthetic object is revealed only when we are in the posture of *looking* and not of *eating*, Weil argues. She even speculates that "vice, depravity, and crime are nearly always, in their essence, attempts to eat beauty, to eat what we should only look at."[6] Eating, of course, is analogous to giving complete license to the self-protecting imagination, that is, inattention. It wants to neutralize potential rupture in advance, to reduce all meaning in accordance with our desires. Whereas to be attentive to the thing of beauty depends upon an initial consent to preserve the void that we want desperately to fill. Crucially, there are certain experiences and manifestations of pure beauty that make the willingness to preserve the void more likely. Before giving attention to two manifestations of beauty that exemplify Weil's aesthetic-religious philosophy—anonymity and tragedy—we will now consider in further detail the aesthetic dimensions of the attentive orientation and their relation to the moral subject.

Aesthetic arrest

Interestingly, in drawing on the studies of contemporary psychologists such as Andrew McGhie and Michael and Abigail Lipson, we find that, in their view, the antithesis of attention is *self-interest* or *self-orientation*, like it is for Weil. McGhie writes, "Observations of neurotic patients suggest that their poor concentration is due, not to their being easily distracted by extraneous external stimulation . . . but rather to their preoccupation with their own inner problems."[7] And Michael and Abigail Lipson explain that "the rebound from absorbed study to self-concern . . . represents an attentional and . . . a *moral* lapse. (It is of course irrelevant whether one's attention to the task recoils to a self-orientation of positive or negative valuation: 'I have done well' and 'I have done badly' are ethically equivalent in this sense.)"[8] Weil, too, held the view that attention is an orientation directed away from oneself. "Attention alone—that attention which is so full that the 'I' disappears—is required of me. I have to deprive all that I call 'I' of the light of my attention and turn it on to that which cannot be conceived."[9] "That which cannot be conceived" here stands for any of the Platonic absolutes, as we have seen—the good, beauty itself, truth, and of course, for Weil, the supernatural/God. The mistake, then, is to treat as absolute temporal phenomena in our hunger for the tangible and immediate, for such gratification conduces to self-obsession.

The moment, that is, *I* begin to neglect the *relativity* of such objects for the sake of my self and my desire for comfort, *I* cease to be attentive, and *I* turn away from the object in its reality and turn toward illusion (and an illusory self.) It is not difficult to see that the orientation toward illusion and the orientation toward reality are mutually exclusive and that the lacking of one suggests the presence of the other: so it is with attentiveness and distractedness. These orientations are not entirely determined by their objects, although some objects (such as expensive and luxurious products) tend to stimulate the deceitful imagination more easily and conjure illusions about the self more quickly.

However, we had also formerly said, in relating Pascal's views on diversion and the influence thereof on Weil's concept of *l'imagination combleuse*, that it is *distraction* that consists in avoiding oneself and escaping into external stimuli. Recall his statement: "A king is surrounded by people whose only thought is to divert him and stop him thinking about himself, because, king though he is, he becomes unhappy as soon as he thinks about himself."[10] Though seemingly contradictory, these two theories (the psychologists' and Pascal's) on attention are actually complementary. When the inattentive person is absorbed with him/herself, it is the *imaginary or false idea of a reified self that is the object of fixation*. The *true* self (mediocre, limited, porous, incontinent, mortal—in short, the void) inspires fear and disgust, such that even the king seeks to be disturbed, as Pascal says. And Weil points out that one *cannot* be truly self-centered, given the nature of the self: "If we could be egoistical it would be very pleasant. It would be a rest. But literally we cannot."[11] We cannot truly love ourselves, according to Weil, because of our finitude, experienced as wretchedness. However, this inability to be an egoist, while exposing this humiliated nature, is also the source of our "greatness," in that this should compel us to attention, to look beyond ourselves. Furthermore, attention, while being decidedly *not* self-concerned, *is* reflective of the attending subject in a way that avoids dishonesty, illusions, and imaginings of royalty. Consider Weil's metaphor of the painter:

> A painter doesn't draw the place where he himself is. But looking at his painting, I know his position in relation to the things he has

drawn. On the contrary, if he represents himself in his painting, I know with certainty that the place he shows himself to be isn't the one where he is.[12]

In other words, if we make ourselves the object of our focus, we will of necessity represent ourselves (to us and to others) wrongly. Thus, distractedness and the workings of the imagination not only permit but also sustain illusion, reification, objectification of others, thoughtless consumption, and desecration of the beautiful.

However, the basis for the attentive orientation, as we have seen already, is rooted in a divine model, the source of transcendent inspiration. This model is unrepresentable, except by analogy. Any *good* artist, therefore, imitates divine creation via decreation: "In creating a work of art of the highest class the artist's attention is oriented towards silence and the void; from this silence and void there descends an inspiration which develops into words or forms."[13] Salomé Voegelin eloquently confirms this idea: "When there is nothing to hear, so much starts to sound. Silence is not the absence of sound but the beginning of listening."[14]

As attention and decreation are inextricably joined together, our attentiveness, being creative in its renunciation, makes it more likely that others will see reality as well. In the transparency that attention manifests, we not only become an impersonal reader of reality, without perspective, but we also cease to be the obscurity (which having a personal perspective brings) that serves as a distraction to other beings. If we carry Weil's description of attention to its fullest extent, we will see how, in being inattentive, we actively contribute to the culture of distraction: *this* is the sense in which we alter reality, but we alter it for the worse; we are not creating but destroying:

> Not to recognize and accept this impossibility of creating is the source of many an error. We are obliged to imitate the act of creation, and there are two possible imitations—the one real and the other apparent—preserving and destroying. There is no trace of "I" in the act of preserving. There is in that of destroying. The "I" leaves its mark on the world as it destroys.[15]

Thus, in giving in to distraction and noise, to the orientation of "eating" and consolation, we leave new blemishes on the world.

We also become increasingly banal and "looking" becomes more and more difficult the more we a-void. In such cases, we enter into a vicious downward spiral of objectification—of ourselves and of others—which is to say idolatry.

Distractedness is then, beyond being idolatrous, unoriginal and the antithesis of any truly aesthetic orientation. For by being an orientation that brings only idols into view, distractedness is a determinate orientation toward escape, comfort, and the familiar. Attention, however, is an orientation that reveals to us not only our own degradation but also the general complexities, subtleties, details, and nuances of life, which go unperceived in a typical self-centered state. Attention is therefore experienced as an asymmetrical and imbalanced orientation. The two ways of being obedient—to mechanical necessity (distractedness) or to God/love/ the void (attentiveness)—implicate the very constitution and moral fabric of our *beings*. We become different sorts of creatures in either becoming opaque and impermeable to the world in our distraction (like "a stone that falls"[16]) or transparent and porous in our attention. In becoming attentive, we are not only able to see what is external to us, in all its reality, but we are also able to know the reality of ourselves: our mediocrity, our finitude, our vulnerability to moral gravity, and, finally, our nothingness in the sense of the void. Here is the crucial and paradoxical point: without attention, part of the reality we cannot realize is our own distractedness, which is to say, we do not realize our own tendency to avoid the real, our moral "gravity," and, therefore, our own imprisonment to the natural attitude.

As noted earlier, Weil describes these orientations of distractedness and attentiveness as postures of "eating" and "looking," respectively. "Here below," Weil writes, "to look and to eat are two different things. We have to choose one or the other. . . . The only people who have any hope of salvation are those who occasionally stop and look for a time, instead of eating."[17] Are there conditions that assist us in this "stopping"? Plato underscored the effects of the beautiful as unique and essential to the good life: a trembling and reverential restraint of greedy impulses in remembrance of the divine. But what can rightfully be characterized as beautiful? How do we make this discernment? Does Weil give us any clues as to what could have an ennobling effect on the perceiver? What has the potential to cultivate our aesthetic-ethical-religious attention?

Weil writes that if we project our evil upon "something perfectly pure,"[18] then that object *cannot* be defiled, and will not reflect the evil back on us, but instead will effect a transubstantiation, delivering us from evil. But we rightly wonder *what* that "something" is. "That which is perfectly pure can be nothing other than God present in the world," Weil elaborates, including such things in this category as "sacred objects," "sacred texts" (such as the Lord's Prayer), "the beauty of nature when looked at for itself," and sometimes human beings and works of art.[19] Looking in particular at works of art, then, the first thing we must recognize is that *sometimes* they are perfectly pure. In what sense, then, is art an incarnation of the supernatural, for Weil?

Any work of art, or in general anything that could be called truly "beautiful," to serve as an object of attention, will necessarily remind those who contemplate it of their inherent hunger, their void. Weil clearly sees that certain objects, in their transcendent beauty, do have an ennobling effect upon the psyches of the beholders. For example, from her lectures we find: "Architecture: a child, as a matter of instinct, does not play around in a cathedral," for "what is beautiful takes hold of the body."[20] This statement suggests the seeming impossibility of distractedness—even for a child—in the presence of a work that, in its own way, is a *moral exemplar*. Like an exemplar, the cathedral has a concrete and transformative effect on those who would open themselves to it. Weil tells us that beauty "teaches us that mind can come down into nature. Morality itself tells us to act according to thoughts that are true. [But] beauty is a witness that the ideal can become a reality."[21]

Additionally, since attention can (by definition) only be directed toward what is real, there is, in Weil's philosophy as with Plato, an identification of the beautiful and the real. On this note, Miklos Vetö remarks, "Obviously this identity does not mean that the beautiful is something of the order of substance, hypostatized; the real, as we know, is only the network of necessity limiting and organizing the material world." He goes on to explain that the presence of necessity in the world is a harmony, or "order of the world." Hence, "everything that is, is beautiful, since all is in harmony with the will of God."[22] (Note: "Everything that is" refers to nature, that is, God's creation, but not necessarily to human artifice and fabrication; thus, artworks that do not reflect the order of the world will not, for Weil, be considered beautiful.) Weil does use the terms "order of the world" and "beauty of the world" inter-changeably; but what is meant by *necessity*, and how is it relevant to cultivating the attention?

There are two aspects of "necessity," according to Weil. One is that it is "exercised," and the other is that it is "endured." If "the sun shines on the just and the unjust," then the two aspects are symbolized by "the sun and the cross," she writes.[23] When one comes to realize that these two elements—as different as they may seem—are merely different sides of the same coin (of necessity), one can come to appreciate as beautiful those necessary relations that comprise the universe. The nature of necessity, then, suffices to *keep* us at a distance, for "the sun that shines on the just and the unjust" is an indifferent, impersonal one and does not foster attachments. The impersonality of the order of the world has the same effect upon humans as the many challenging disciplines in school have upon a schoolboy who prefers only one subject, and it has the same effect as the cycle of agricultural labor does on the farmer, who may often feel like a hamster inside a wheel at the end of each year.

Therefore, in contemplating the order of the world as beautiful, there is a reticence, a withholding, a noticeable absence. Beauty, as Ann Pirruccello notes, always arouses a longing for finality.[24] And Weil agrees with Kant, who said that beauty "is a finality which involves no objective . . . no good except itself, in its totality, as it appears to us."[25] We desire beauty, but when we try to possess it, we realize we still desire something, and we have no idea what that is. Thus, we are tantalized because we are given nothing that is tangible, and we do not get a sense of consummation or satisfaction from the finality of beauty. The artist, too, can have no particular intention in art, as this would be reflective of his own will. "The poet who puts in a certain particular word for a certain particular effect is a mediocre poet."[26] Art calls for our decreation, whether we are the onlooker or the artist. Weil references Eve, as a negative example, who "caused humanity to be lost by eating the fruit" and argues that the contrary posture, of looking without eating, would logically be our salvation.[27] As Pirruccello puts it:

> This kind of good that attracts us without giving us anything tangible ensures that the experience of beauty arouses our feeling of incompleteness, and while enjoying the good that beauty does

provide, we cannot help being referred to an absent goodness, an impossible goodness of which we possess no idea.[28]

This paradox of "presence and absence" in attending to the beautiful, as Pirruccello articulates it, or of revelation and reticence, is what maintains the appetite in relation to it, or the void. We will examine two types of aesthetic phenomena that stimulate, but do not fill, this void: the anonymous or "bland" art that enshrines the impersonal and the tragic.

Anonymous and bland

Weil writes that priests, if they are following their sacred duty, will emulate the saints, "principally the one veritable saint, who is Christ"[29] and thereby be inspired to convey more goodness than they themselves are capable of. She worries, however, that writers and artists—as a result of the Enlightenment mentality—champion self-reliance and personality and increasingly produce work that is excessively psychological and subjective. Perhaps for this reason, T. S. Eliot asserts that great literature (and we may extend this to art in general) must be impersonal and universal, and explains: "The author . . . is trying to affect us wholly, as human beings, whether he knows it or not; and we are affected by it, as human beings, whether we intend to be or not."[30] How are we affected by art in which the author has become nearly invisible, like an anonymous translator?

It would seem that the more "impersonal" the art is, the less likely it is to be appropriated as fuel for egoistic endeavors. For instance, it is difficult to personalize something like Gregorian music and this may explain Weil's penchant for it: "A person who is passionately fond of music may quite well be a perverted person—but I should find it hard to believe this of anyone who thirsted for Gregorian chanting."[31] In addition, in Medieval Byzantine iconography such as "Christ the Pantocrator," expressionism and indeed, *expressions* in the sacred face were discouraged due to their potential for arresting the observer at the superficial level of the representation and thus leading to idolatry. The icons themselves were to be "anonymous," and the artists were to refrain from investing their personalities in them or even signing them.[32] As Richard Kearney tells us,

[T]he beholder was not inclined to ask, "Who painted it?" or to exclaim, "What superb artistry! What beautiful facial features! What originality of expression and technique!". . . . Indeed the common practice of portraying the eyes of Christ as expressionless was an apt symbol of the icon's primary function: to invite the onlooker to travel through the vacant regard of the image towards the suprasensible transcendence of God. . . . In other words, the *theocentric* quality of the icon was evident in the fact that every effort was made to eschew worshipping the image itself so as to worship God *through* the image. The makers and beholders of icons were not to follow their own fancies but to harness their imaginations to the sacred visual types laid down by age-old tradition.[33]

In contrast to this theocentric value, the modern practice of expressionistic self-portraiture epitomized by Vincent Van Gogh naturally exemplified an anthropocentric and humanistic trend. And later, the Marilyn Monroe serigraphs created by Andy Warhol as well as Martin Sharp's "Pop Poster of Van Gogh" convey the "undecidable status" and "ambiguity" inherent in postmodern parodies. As Kearney puts it, "Our inability to definitively place Sharp's poster parody on the side of 'art' or 'pseudo-art' is itself an indication of its postmodern character. . . . [It] differs fundamentally in that it does not seek to direct the onlooker's attention toward some transcendent being but mischievously exults in its role as a playful item of popular consumption."[34]

Weil might argue that this preeminent "value" of postmodern art and the postmodern psyche amounts to a destructive nihilism. She is certainly very critical of genres that embrace a relativistic spirit and make a mockery of the notion of aesthetic standards and a hierarchy of values. She sees Dadaism and surrealism, for instance, as representing "the intoxication of total license, the intoxication in which the mind wallows when it has made a clean sweep of value and surrendered to the immediate."[35] While neglecting the power and potential for domination inherent in a definitive set of standards for aesthetic judgment, Weil perceives the greatest threat to be the "absence of value" and "non-oriented thought," such that these art movements are the equivalent, to her, of the destruction of towns and human lives.[36] Humans, she thinks, are naturally

MY LOVE of PLATO agrees OBJECTIVITY of TRANSCLS

hungry for the good, and the denial of this original orientation and desire effects a perversion of the human spirit.

Arguably, in addition to "the total absence of value as [the] supreme value,"[37] our contemporary popular aesthetic is characterized by extreme triteness and explicit "personality," which has the paradoxical effect of making it simultaneously attractive and forgettable. In fact, it has been argued that this pop art dominating our culture brings about a real decrease in the attentiveness of the beholders. For instance, Theodor Adorno in his essay, "On the Fetish Character in Music and the Regression of Listening," notes the ways in which mass music is reified through "formulas" and "standardizations" that are not based on criteria of musical proficiency, for instance, but only on what will guarantee commercial success. Ironically, however, given the commercial success, such music must be "apprehended in a distracted manner."[38] He tells us that the listeners typically show a preference for

and Adorno agrees, is. mass is t? A. NEG

> the individual instrumental colors as such. This preference is promoted by the practice of American popular music whereby each variation, or "chorus," is played with emphasis on a special instrumental color, with the clarinet, the piano, or the trumpet as quasi-soloist. This often goes so far that the listener seems to care more about treatment and "style" than about the otherwise indifferent material, but with the treatment validating itself only in *particular enticing effects*. Along with the attraction to color as such, there is of course the veneration for the tool and the drive to imitate and join in the game; possibly also something of the great delight of children in bright colors, which returns under the pressure of contemporary musical experience.[39]

Indeed, on several occasions, Adorno describes the contemporary listener who craves the so-called colorful and exciting and new (but which is actually completely familiar) as childish and undeveloped.[40] For example, he tells us, "There is actually a neurotic mechanism of stupidity in [contemporary] listening, too; the arrogantly ignorant rejection of everything unfamiliar is its sure sign. Regressive listeners behave like children. Again and again and with stubborn malice, they demand the one dish they have once been served."[41]

yes, q/as

Moreover, it is characteristic of "infantile hearing" that it demands "sensually rich and full sonority" as well as "the most comfortable and fluent resolutions."[42] In this preference, there is distaste for the unexpected and for any dissonance that causes tension. According to him, this is because such music is unable to be reified and assimilated into the listener's identity. In the context of the ubiquitous commodity, the listener feels she has no choice but to succumb to this paradigm of objectification. Adorno explains,

> The type of relationship suggested by the billboard, in which masses make a commodity recommended to them the object of their own action, is in fact found again as the pattern for the reception of light music. They need and demand what has been palmed off on them. They overcome the feeling of impotence that creeps over them in the face of monopolistic production by identifying themselves with the inescapable product.[43]

But again, there is the ironic effect of this sort of aesthetic in its requirement that we become distracted and forgetful: "Just as every advertisement is composed of the inconspicuous familiar and the unfamiliar conspicuous, so the hit song remains salutarily forgotten in the half-dusk of its familiarity."[44] Significantly, then, the preference for "style" and "color" does not awaken a taste for truly new colors or sonorities. Instead, "the atomistic listeners are the first to denounce such [truly new] sonorities as 'intellectual' or absolutely dissonant," Adorno warns us.[45] And furthermore, the "hit song" with its immediate sense of vibrancy cannot be *attended to*; it is responsible for the creation of "deconcentration" in listeners. As Adorno contends,

> If the standardized products, hopelessly like one another except for conspicuous bits such as hit lines, do not permit concentrated listening without becoming unbearable to the listeners, the latter are in any case no longer capable of concentrated listening. . . . Again and again one encounters the judgment that [such music] is fine for dancing but dreadful for listening.[46]

Because contemporary industrialized society has developed a taste (albeit self-defeating) for those "debased cultural goods," which are reified, packaged, commodified, and ultimately, *had*, we crave that which is well-defined and easily identified (but without real standard), which has a dominant taste or chorus, and which can then be violently expected, demanded, appropriated, and repeated endlessly. This amounts to a regression from listening, and thus from attention, and thus from openness to subtlety, complexity, nuance, and possibility. But there is art that precludes this fetishization and all of its consequences. Even Adorno notes, "A Beethoven symphony as a whole, spontaneously experienced, can never be appropriated."[47] But what is it about the Beethoven symphony that resists appropriation?

To avoid idolatry, degradation, and the inevitable "regression of listening" that accompanies pop art, Weil contends that a supernatural aesthetic that engenders tension, humility, and attentiveness is required. This aesthetic is primarily characterized by impersonality and will be, following Weil's terms, a sign of *genius* and genuine *novelty*. After offering a synthesis of Weil's thoughts on this supernatural aesthetic and its relation to these traits, we will show that this aesthetics has a complementary counterpart in the aesthetic of "blandness" in classical Chinese philosophies. By elaborating upon Weil's ideas through examining the insights of François Jullien with regard to blandness in classical Chinese aesthetics, we will demonstrate the broader context from which this sort of beauty can be approached and sensed, and its effects on people who partake of it. However, in attending to the complementary aesthetics of the bland, we are also drawn out of a tempting ethno- and religio-centrism in acknowledging a religious aesthetics that proceeds from "*elsewhere*," from "*beyond the European sphere*,"[48] and thereby hope to reflect Weil's own ecumenicalism, even if it is at times troubled.

"The supernatural," as we have seen in the preceding chapters, figures as a prominent part of Weil's thought. However, it is notoriously difficult to define and even her allusions to its role in human existence are unsatisfying to one who would seek to grasp it as a philosophical concept. Metaphorically speaking, it does not exhibit a "strong flavor"; if it itself is not subtle, it is at least subtly referred to. But given what we *can* say of it, "indirection" and "flavorlessness" may be the most apt descriptors. For instance, Weil frequently compares the supernatural to "light,"[49] something intangible but equally illuminating. Moreover, there is actually good reason for it being conceptually elusive: Weil writes, "The object of our search should not be the supernatural, but the world. The supernatural is light itself: If we make an object of it, we lower it."[50] Therefore, what we find in examining Weil's thoughts on the supernatural is a *sense*, an *aesthetic attitude*, conveyed through examples and metaphors of "perfect beauty" in the world. The transcendent thing of perfect beauty, which has the capacity to move the soul upward past pandemonium—and is the only thing that can do this—but which also has the capacity to lower us in humility "by a movement in which gravity plays no part,"[51] will present itself as universal and eternal, but for this reason will go unnoticed by most and be considered "unremarkable." In recalling some of her concrete examples of perfect beauty and justice (e.g., the Gregorian chants, Bach, Romanesque architecture, *Antigone*), the three values of the impersonal, the genius, and the new will be revealed as foundational to this particular aesthetic.

To understand how a beautiful thing is impersonal, we must consider Weil's identification of five sub-traits of impersonality in aesthetics. First, there is duration. "One does not grow tired of beauty," whereas "one does grow tired of what is pleasing, of what only flatters the senses," Weil claims.[52] The beautiful is something one can attend to for hours; anything that falls short of this (such as the statues in the Luxembourg, for her) is unendurable and demands either that we look away, or that we eliminate the offense.[53] Second, there is purity: beauty does give a "pure pleasure," a pleasure absolutely distinct from the one that arises from and encourages consumption. This is why real beauty "captivates the flesh" and stills the child in us "in order to obtain permission to pass right to the soul."[54] So while the beautiful is a "carnal attraction," it "keeps us at a distance" and demands that we renounce our falsifying imaginations.[55] Third, there is the element of infinity. That is, there can be no comparisons in the realm of absolute beauty; to think in terms of "better" or "worse" or any matter of degree suggests that the work is not truly beautiful, for the beautiful is the incarnation of God in matter. Fourth, there must be no element of flattery, for there can be no elevation of the ego in attending to the beautiful. Finally, as we have seen already, impersonality implies universality. Michel Sourisse notes, "Art of the first order always finds its source of inspiration and its model in the contemplation of the universe. Gregorian chant does not escape this law."[56] Indeed, for Weil, the Gregorian chant epitomizes the beautiful, perhaps surprisingly, because of its "share of monotony." This beautiful monotony, as opposed to a mechanical monotony of factory work or of the clock, finds its model in the "perfect regularity of the sky's revolutions that permits the rhythm of agricultural work, the only work that puts us directly in contact with the universe."[57]

Taken collectively, these five sub-traits constitute what we are calling the impersonal nature of Weilienne aesthetics. This quality that suffuses the Gregorian chants and the Romanesque architecture is, like the Medieval Byzantine iconography, significantly *effaced* and *anonymous* so that the object itself does not become the fixation (or idol) but instead serves as a *vehicle* for divine manifestation. The art, like the exemplar, should be empty of personality and in this sense, given the world's standards, may be quite "unremarkable" on one level. But ironically enough, impersonality allows beauty to "cry out." This crying out is a crucial function of true art, for between beauty, truth, and justice, only beauty has a voice. Weil writes, "[Beauty] cries out and points to truth and justice who are dumb, like a dog who barks to bring people to his master lying unconscious in the snow."[58] The impersonality permits this voice (and moreover, its efficacy) because it is what is sacred and perfect in a human being. Anything that issues from the impersonal is compelling and urgent because it is inherently connected to the rest of humanity; it is not a narrow interest, a personal protest. This is not a utilitarian observation; the difference in the impersonal and the personal is not one of numbers but is a metaphysical and experiential difference. It is the difference between seeing our proper place in the grand scheme of things and thinking that we are the center of the world. With the latter, our creations may be "glorious and dazzling achievements . . . which can make a man's name live for thousands of years. But above this level," Weil continues, "far above, separated by an abyss, is the level where the highest things are achieved. These things are essentially anonymous."[59]

Again, the "highest things" may in fact receive little to no attention from the public whose tastes, as Adorno notes, have been trained for the same childish dish, disguised in different dressings. But Weil is keen on this tendency and, understanding the inevitable egoism in artists that accompanies the admiration from the collective, sharply remarks that "it is precisely those artists and writers who are most inclined to think of their art as the manifestation of their personality who are in fact the most in bondage to public taste."[60] The other artists, who create from the springs of the impersonal, and who therefore practice the form of attention that is possible only in solitude, apart from the collectivity, are considered men and women of genius, for Weil. *Their* works, unlike those of their colleagues just mentioned, have real duration: "The works of authentic genius from past ages remain, and are available to us. Their contemplation is the everflowing source of an inspiration which may legitimately guide us" and "make us grow wings to overcome gravity."[61] The genius, unlike the man/woman of talent, embodies "the supernatural virtue of humility in the domain of thought."[62] This is why the inarticulate village idiot, if he loves truth, is closer to genius than the intelligent and linguistically adept person who is proud of his intelligence and talent. Weil says that this pride is analogous to the pride of a condemned man in relation to his large cell.[63]

Although the art of the genius is imbued with humility and hence an elevating power, the ascension of the soul is paradoxically due to contact with real gravity that is then transmitted by the pen, or the paintbrush, or the instrument of the artist. As Weil says, "[The geniuses] give us . . . something equivalent to the actual density of the real, that density which life offers us every day but which we are unable to grasp because we are amusing ourselves with lies."[64] The artistic genius is fully committed to revealing, and not obscuring, harsh reality. For this reason, his/her personality must be absent from the creation and the creative process. Weil gives the example, "If a child is doing a sum and does it wrong, the mistake bears the stamp of his personality. If he does the sum exactly right, his personality does not enter into it at all."[65] Our tendency, wanting to be gods ourselves, is to fictionalize, rather than to transmit a truth transparently. We embellish, we refashion, "we do not study other people; we invent what they are thinking, saying, and doing."[66] But we go even farther, as we have seen, in completely reversing values "so that evil is attractive and good is tedious."[67] And this tedium should not be understood as being synonymous with the "beautiful monotony" that characterizes the Gregorian chants. Whereas the latter has a universal and transcendent nature and is complete with finality, tedium is comparable to the "mechanical monotony" that lacks harmony and finds itself in the reign of necessity with no end. In fact, of course, it is such mechanistic evil that is old, uncreative, and repetitive, while goodness and beauty are new and resist arbitrary rules.

Art can be genuinely *new* only when it is suffused with the supernatural, which is external to us and beyond our control. One may be tempted to think that because of its impersonality (which includes universality), ideal beauty would be static and hence expected. Yet this ignores the aspect of infinity that describes transcendent art: its potential for forms of manifestation is by definition limitless. Weil writes, "Nothing is so beautiful and wonderful, nothing is so continually fresh and surprising, so full of sweet and perpetual ecstasy, as the good."[68] This is because "necessity as strong as gravity" condemns us to evil; it is all-too-natural. What is unexpected is to discover a person who is able to resist gravity. The forms and manifestations of baseness are finite, for they issue from the finite (i.e., from us). So the artist, if she is to create something that can be called "beautiful," must become transparent to allow the light of the divine to shine through. Recall that this is because "matter is not beautiful when it obeys man, but only when it obeys God. If sometimes a work of art seems almost as beautiful as the sea, the mountains, or flowers, it is because the light of God has filled the artist."[69] As we know, for Weil, the most precious and surprising gifts are obtained by waiting on them, not by effort of the will and self-assertion, though the period of training is necessary: "The weeds are pulled up by the muscular effort of the peasant, but only sun and water can make the corn grow."[70] In renouncing ourselves, we simultaneously renounce our mediocrity and are raised by attention; *we* become new. Thus it is that these three attributes of the Weilienne aesthetic—the impersonal, along with the genius and the new—describe both the artist and the art.

But we are left with the phenomenological question: *What is the sense of this impersonal aesthetic? How does it give itself to me?* Answering these questions becomes all the more problematic when one reads, "Beauty always promises, but never gives anything; it stimulates hunger but has no nourishment for the part of the soul which looks in this world for sustenance."[71] Weil has herself characterized the beautiful Gregorian chants as "monotonous," but for reasons already mentioned, this description is problematic. There is, we think, a perfect descriptor in the notion of blandness which we find quite naturally in another cultural context—that of ancient China (and in particular, the Confucian and Taoist traditions).

[cf. WHITMAN ?]

"The flavor of [the] waters is bland, but, in fact, it is not bland, it is the best flavor in the world, with which the flavor of no other food can compare. Naturally, 'those who can appreciate the flavor of food' are already quite 'rare,' but those who can appreciate the flavor of water are even more so," François Jullien writes.[72] In studying the ancient Confucian and Taoist traditions of China, Jullien has observed the underlying theme of *dan*—blandness—which significantly links various art forms (landscape paintings, music, literature, the culinary arts) to societal mores, notions of virtue, and religious values. On one level, the virtue of blandness lies in its inherent impartiality and "non-differentiation." He writes, "As long as no one flavor attracts us more than any other, and one is not favored more than another, we maintain an equal balance among all the virtual forces at work . . . Preference alone is the source of trouble."[73] In this sense, blandness reveals its Taoist roots, where singling out one "side" (or in this case, "flavor") sets up competition, strife, and enmity. But we might also consider Weil's interpretation of the "lilies of the field that neither toil nor spin" in this regard. For her, the important point is that "they have not set out to clothe themselves *in this or that color*; they have not exercised their will or made arrangements to bring about their object,"[74] and in this way, they are an image of docility and impersonality that we are to emulate. Or consider the virtue of blandness in its impartiality (characterized as "impersonality") of the Weilienne God who is the ultimate example for humans, who "maketh his sun to rise on the evil and on the good, and sendeth rain on the just and on the unjust."[75]

NB
&
NOR
&
EVIL
F

So, on one level, rather than blandness being a deficiency, it may well prove to be a positive virtue that enables detachment and reveals "the path of free, unimpeded growth, the path of what happens spontaneously."[76] Only a person's blandness would allow one to be truly open and attentive and to move in harmony with the fluctuations of the world. Interestingly, though, Jullien finds this value contrary to Christian revelation, arguing in fact that blandness places us "at the point furthest from [Christ's] Revelation." He reminds us of Christ's injunction to the disciples to be "the salt of the earth," and to always remember that if salt has lost its savor, it is "to be cast out, and to be trodden under foot of men."[77] He goes on to note that in the Christian tradition, "salt is a sacred condiment and at the same time the mark of difference—even of

categorical opposition."[78] At first glance, this analysis appears correct, especially if we consider the quality of the *new* that is supposed
to characterize Weil's Christian understanding of the beautiful and
the good. But if we understand "distinctive" and "flavorful" in this
sense of *the new*, then the problem appears to dissolve. For that
which is new in the Weilienne conception does not derive from the
individual, as Jullien insinuates, but is always already present in
the supernatural, or the Tao. When he concludes, then, that in the
Chinese aesthetic, "reality projects no meaning beyond itself" and
"blandness characterizes the real in a way that is complete, positive, and natural,"[79] we may say the same for the Weilienne God,
who is synonymous with reality and hence is also final.

On another level, blandness is analyzed as having inherent duration, both over the span of history and also within an individual's
memory. Jullien describes the phenomenon of bland music and
how it gives itself to the listener:

> The most beautiful music—the music that affects us most
> profoundly—does not, as is mentioned at the beginning, consist
> of the fullest possible exploitation of all the different tones. The
> most intensive sound is not the most intense: by overwhelming
> our senses, by manifesting itself exclusively and fully as a sensual
> phenomenon, sound delivered to its fullest extent leaves us with
> nothing to anticipate, nothing to look forward to.[80]

At this point, Jullien notes that such explicitly sensorial music fills
us "to the brim" and satisfies the metaphorical hunger for beauty.
Immediately, Weil and Adorno come to mind: Weil, who warns
against the sensation of satiety, for it is an illusion (we are empty!);
the truly beautiful will "promise" but "not give anything." And
Adorno, who in discussing music himself, acknowledges the dangers of its fetishization, which permits its gluttonous consumption
and promotes a hypocritical "deconcentration." Moreover, the
preference for "instrumental colors" is a symptom of reification,
according to him. Jullien would agree with both:

> In contrast, the least fully rendered sounds are the most promising,
> in that they have not been fully expressed, *externalized*, by the
> instrument in question . . . And it is thus that they manage to
> sustain . . . a "lingering" or a "leftover" tone. Such sounds are

all the more able to extend and deepen themselves in the minds of their hearers for having not been definitively realized; and so they retain something more for later deployment and keep something secret and virtual within. In short, they remain heavy with promise . . . Music such as this stays on in the spirit and "is not forgotten."[81]

The "lingering" or "leftover" flavor is precious precisely because it evokes "a potential, inexhaustible value, ever more desirable as it continues to avert its own consumption," Jullien continues.[82] However, "what detracts from strong flavors such as brine or vinegar is that they are fully encompassed by their identification as distinct flavors—the salty and the sour, respectively—rather than evolving into something beyond themselves."[83] Is there any better way to characterize and illustrate the brute illogic of egoism, of self-centeredness, here writ as possessing "strong flavors" and in the writings of Weil referred to as manifesting "personality"? The bland, though, as opposed to the full exploitation of sound or taste or sight, suffices to bring us, according to Jullien, "to a subtler and more fundamental grasp of reality."[84] We are recalled, that is, from our state of dispersion, distraction, and deconcentration, to a land of "shared and discreet simplicity"[85] where the artistic geniuses, rather than trying to outdo one another, work side by side in tearing the veil from the world as it is. What is revealed is unexpected and elusive, and at times, difficult to discern, and even more difficult to swallow. But it is also unforgettable for these reasons.

Tragedy and the breach

While Weil often emphasizes that beautiful art must be impersonal, "essentially anonymous," implying a renunciation of self and of the consumptive posture, she also recognizes that "greatness in our times must take a different course" than classical geniuses and artists such as Leonardo da Vinci or Bach. She hints that art in our time will only be reborn "from amidst a general anarchy," and that it will be a solitary-endeavor, with no "echo."[86] In our context, arguably, beauty might then emerge through means that are "out of order," or are even explicitly illegal. Beauty, for Weil, is the attractive, magnetic aspect of justice and truth, and as the latter are oftentimes at odds with societal norms and systems, it is easy to see why the beautiful may be quite disruptive on a social level, and traumatic on an individual level. In this sense, as Katherine Brueck puts it, "For Weil . . . the magnetic power of the beautiful bears a tragic cast."[87]

Indeed, the encounter with the tragic in art arouses our desire for seemingly impossible goodness. But it disturbs us. Tragedy reminds us of the splinter at the core of human existence that we habitually patch over and ignore, and so it does not bring consolation. Iris Murdoch tells us that "it is the height of art to be able to show what is nearest, what is deeply and obviously true but usually invisible."[88] For Weil, too, the true artist sees what is invisible and hears what is muffled to the collective and neatly managed by the bureaucracies; thus, she sees/hears the marginalized, the afflicted, the abject, and the "monsters" who exist at the limits that the rest of us refuse to acknowledge consciously. In this way, the tragic artist grasps suffering intimately (and for this reason may be considered "mad," to recall our discussion of divine *mania*). But tragedy is not the same as sorrow, and the artist does not attempt to manipulate facile emotions in her audience by conjuring up clichéd images of pain and suffering. In fact, it is notoriously difficult to capture and compose tragedy. Murdoch writes:

> The tragic art form is rare because it is difficult to keep attention focused on the truth without the author slipping into an easier sentimental, abstract, melodramatic (and so on) mode. . . . Tragedy is a paradoxical art because to succeed it must really upset us while exhibiting, but not as mere consolation, some orderly and comprehensive vista of evil and catastrophe. Death threatens the ego's dream of eternal life and happiness and power. Tragedy, like religion, must break the ego, destroying the illusory whole of the unified self.[89] (p. 121)

Weil would add on to this description that works created by tragic artists are not simply "clever" or born of "talent"; like the impersonal artists, they are genius, but the tragedians and their works are genius because of an intimacy with affliction that nevertheless is not a presentation of their *personal* experience, but a result of a self-effacing attention:

The nobleness of suffering is not to be spoken of lightly or too
often; it can too easily become mere literature in the mouth of
people who have not suffered pain that can break the very soul.
Do you realize there are millions and millions of people on earth
who suffer nearly always, from birth to death? It is a pity they
[have been deprived of] expression; they would say the truth
about suffering . . . The most beautiful poetry is the poetry which
can best express, in its truth, the life of people who can't write
poetry. Outside of that there is only clever poetry; and mankind
can do very well without clever poetry.[90]

Such truthful representations of suffering are indeed rare, but they
exist. As Weil notes, the great paradox is that the afflicted, the
victims of the greatest injustices, are often least able to communicate these truths. But they have perhaps the greatest potential to
rupture our banal experiences and force us to reflect upon the very
inattentiveness that has resulted in such injustices. However, even
here there is no guarantee of that revelation or the ensuing transformation. For example, as Cornel West has pointed out, blues
music—manifestations of the pain of oppression black people have
suffered for centuries, tinged with impossible hope—has frequently
been annexed as hip background music in upper-class white living
rooms during dinner parties, deprived of its tension, tragedy, and
real significance in this use.[91] This appropriation is certainly an
instance of inattention and is therefore unjust. Unfortunately, it
is only one of countless examples of such cultural colonization of
which the privileged and the powerful have been guilty. Following
Adorno's line of thinking, the tragic, not surprisingly, tempts those
who are "centered" to neutralize it by commercializing it and
therefore prevent against its subversive potential. Through the mill
of the culture industry, we see only simulations of human crisis.
   Sophocles' Antigone is a tragic play that greatly inspired Weil
and influenced her thinking. She thought the story sufficiently
important to retell, in a pamphlet called "Antigone,"[92] for the sake
of her factory co-workers and manual laborers in 1936. Weil's
idea was that masterpieces of Greek poetry should be available
and accessible to the masses who, she thought, would surely be
moved by the narrative and characters. In brief, the story revolves
around a young woman, Antigone, who stands in opposition to the
laws of her own country and the head of its government, Creon,
who also happens to be her uncle. Her two brothers, Eteocles and

Polyneices, following the death of their father, Oedipus, were rivals for the throne. Eteocles succeeded in becoming king, and held to the throne, causing Polyneices to be exiled. Upon his exile, he joined with foreign armies and invaded the city at stake, Thebes, whereupon the brothers came face to face and killed each other in a fight. Their uncle, Creon, then took over the throne and declared that the traitor, Polyneices, shall be left unburied, his body to be picked over by wild animals and left to rot in the weather, to reflect his dishonorable life. As Weil informs us, "Here it is important to know that for the Greeks there could never be a greater shame or dishonor than to be treated in this way after death."[93] Creon made this decision known to the citizens of Thebes and issued a warning that anyone who would disobey the decree would be put to death.

Antigone was left behind in the shadow of her brothers' deaths, along with her sister Ismene. Antigone, out of love for Polyneices and unable to endure the thought of her brother's body being treated so disrespectfully, decides she will bury him. Her sister, Ismene, ever the practical and law-abiding sibling, strongly discourages Antigone from her plan—unsuccessfully. Antigone's love for her brothers transcends human and political discriminations and reveals her orientation to something more eternal. When Creon asks her whether she dared to disobey his law and was in fact the one responsible for the illegal burial, she replies with conviction:

Yes, it was not Zeus that made the proclamation;
nor did Justice, which lives with those below, enact
such laws as that, for mankind. I did not believe
your proclamation had such power to enable
one who will someday die to override
God's ordinances, unwritten and secure.
They are not of today and yesterday;
they live forever; none knows when first they were.
These are the laws whose penalties I would not
incur from the gods, through fear of any man's temper.[94]

Subsequently, a dialogue with Creon ensues, but as Weil points out, "he judges everything from the point of view of the State," while Antigone "holds to another view which seems to her superior."[95] Ismene eventually comes to her side and wants to share in her sister's tragic fate, and Creon leads them both away.

Eventually, and despite attempts by her fiancé Haemon (who is also Creon's son) to reason with his father on behalf of Antigone and the city of Thebes, she is dragged off by the king to be sealed alive in a cave, her tomb, where she will linger, agonizingly, on the threshold between life and death. She breaks down, weeping, but receives no consolation from her fellow citizens. But the story does not end there. As Weil summarizes,

> A priest who can tell the future predicts the most terrible disasters for [Creon] if he does not deliver Antigone. After a long and violent discussion the king gives in. The cave is opened and there Antigone is found already dead, having succeeded in strangling herself. There also her fiancé is found, convulsively kissing her corpse. The young man has chosen to be entombed with her. As soon as he sees his father he gets up and in an excess of frustrated fury, kills himself before his father's eyes. The queen, as she learns of her son's suicide, kills herself also. When news of her death is announced to the king, this man who knew so well how to speak as a master breaks down, mastered by sorrow.[96]

Although one message is clear—hubris brings about devastation and destroys human lives—there is no resurrection in the end, or ʃsatisfying resolution in this story.]

Yet the protagonist, Antigone, captured Weil for many of the same reasons that Christ did. Here was a loner, absurd in her context and radical in her orientation, whose indiscriminate love leads to her exile, affliction, and eventual (unjust) demise; "it was the same love," Weil writes, "extreme and absurd, which led Christ to the Cross."[97] Antigone's virtue is precisely her immoderation, her madness. But it is a surfeit of love with an orientation to the supernatural. The tragic art of Antigone—both the character and the play itself—is the representation of the trespassing of fabricated human boundaries. Antigone embodies this border-crossing, par excellence, as William Robert eloquently describes:

> Tragedy crosses the line. It is excessive; it goes too far; that is what makes it tragic. Tragedy is not tragic simply because someone or something dies but because someone or something steps across a border and, in doing so, breaches a boundary believed to be

unbreachable. Someone or something exceeds an established limit. Therein lies the tragedy.[98]

If tragedy represents border-crossing and "puts on trial limits and limitations,"[99] we might wonder what (if anything) distinguishes it from Weil's notion of evil, understood as the imaginary extension of self over and through the (real) limits of others. But the tragic question is, as Robert goes on to ask, borrowing from Jacques Derrida, "What is it, then, to cross this ultimate border?"[100]—that is, the border demarcating life from death, between the natural and the supernatural, between human and divine law? The tragic test does not lie in, for instance, extending our own power by negating the limits of other lives, for this breach would occur on the same (horizontal, natural) plane and would not introduce any new paradigm. This was Creon's mistake. However, if we forego human comforts and even our life itself on the basis of a principle, which promises nothing in return, not even a consoling thought or word, then we have breached a limit—we have changed planes.

Antigone, again, represents this genuine breach; as her practical sister Ismene tells her, she is "in love with the impossible."[101] As Robert describes her, "Antigone is a foreigner, even at home. She is from the start . . . 'the system's vomit,' finding no place in nature or culture." Moreover, her homelessness means that "she is an aporia, a 'non-way.'"[102] She cannot be figured into a standard category or be reasoned with. Her committed orientation to the supernatural and eternal decrees, in the face of her uncle Creon, who represents human authority and brute force, is her excess and is what renders her abject. But here again, like the non-lover of *Phaedrus*, prudence and self-regulation for the sake of temporal concerns would be the refusal of the divine. Her own displacement, including her live burial, suffices to decenter us, the readers, in the same way that Weil thinks the Incarnation of Christ should. Her character, like Christ's, is a direct challenge to our complacent obedience to worldly powers and constructed boundaries. Antigone mocks our terror before that ultimate border, which we revere in our prioritizing of biological human life before all else. (In this sense, is not self-preservation the ultimate idol? How many sacrifices do we lay before this golden calf?) Were she pragmatic, "level-headed," and sensible, Antigone would not be immortal.

What we learn from Antigone is that there is an aesthetic-religious basis to her actions. She is, as she admits, in her commitment to

bury her brother Polyneices against the king's orders, "a criminal—but a religious one."[103] The orientation toward the eternal, by
definition *inspired*, manifests as a challenge to natural and human
authority and to our ordinary, manufactured ways of seeing the
world. While tragedy points to the irreducibility of affliction and
in so doing, reorients our attention to the placeless and abject, it is
also true that the beautiful can serve to *place* the excluded in a way
that is subversive to mainstream collectivities; hence Weil sought to
introduce *Antigone* to as many of the lower-class workers and societal outcasts as possible. In the end, the art of *Antigone* is a form of
pure beauty by virtue of its tragic breach; for this reason, it is experientially indigestible—we can only look, and be transformed.

"Purity," as Weil writes, in one of her many paradoxes, "is the
power to contemplate defilement," for when we are contemplating human wretchedness, we are thereby also necessarily contemplating the (absent) supernatural, which is wholly other than us.[104]
And this is precisely how "extreme purity" is defined by Weil: the
capability to "contemplate both the pure and the impure," for
"impurity can do neither: the pure frightens it, the impure absorbs
it."[105] Extreme purity in an individual, who is necessarily decreated
and has experienced exile, must be characterized by this internal
tension of holding contraries before the mind, resisting the tendency toward simplicity and ideology. She writes, for example
that "beauty is the harmony of chance and the good."[106] Beauty is,
then, the conjunction of the vulnerable, fragile, earthly, accidental, and mortal thing with an infinite love that nevertheless does
not disguise the finitude of that thing. This paradox also constitutes justice. As we have seen, the beautiful and the just can be
contemplated, but not easily consumed or fetishized. In this way,
beauty and justice are conducive to further creations and political
actions demanding that degree of attention.[107] The beautiful work
of art provides no self-confirmation but is instead a paradoxical
attraction that defers the immediacy of our egoistic projections.
Likewise, the just *polis*, inspired by beauty, is never self-satisfied
or complacent in the manner of Creon but is dialogical and would
seem to resist the static identity and tyranny that makes for an
exclusive and parochial collective.

Perversions—Fabrications of order

Despite the elements of tragedy and impersonality in the beautiful, Weil recognizes that beauty always functions first as a carnal attraction; as Plato recognized, there is an erotic pull toward physical beauty that, under the right conditions and with the proper orientation, can lead us to love of the divine. But there is always the chance that in the carnal attraction, we become fixated on the particular and foreclose any possibility of aesthetic, moral, or religious ascension. The character of Antigone, for example, is attractive to us on a certain, natural level: she is courageous and audacious. We love a good scandal and may even exhibit a morbid fascination with her punishment and death. If we take the tragedy in this dissected and distracted way, it may only reinforce our basest tendencies. For this reason, the line between the consumptive attitude and the attentive attitude may appear quite thin. Weil wonders, "If the beautiful is the real presence of God in matter, and if contact with the beautiful is a sacrament in the full sense of the word, how is it that there are so many perverted aesthetes? Nero."[108] She theorizes that what Nero (and other "perverted aesthetes") love cannot properly be called "beauty" but is a bad substitution that is more like a "demoniacal" art.[109] We suspect that tragedy and impersonality in art cannot really prevent its appropriation by a would-be tyrant; the pure can be defiled, the tragic can be sanitized, and the impersonal can be personified, for the imagination is sufficiently powerful to distort even "transcendent beauty" into a self-affirming image. A-voidance via the eating and desecration of beauty is certainly possible. While some types of art lend themselves more to consumption and perversion than others, beauty, per se, cannot promise deliverance if consent to look is refused; hence, there remains a real moral risk in the aesthetic object.

In one who consents to the tension of savoring, the beautiful begins to develop the faculty of attention; but for one who seeks immediate appeasement of this feeling of hunger, ways of establishing order among humans and things are oftentimes sought that dissipate any aporia.[110] This establishing of arbitrary order is the attempt to fabricate beauty, to construct it by dint of the will. As we know, however, beauty does not issue directly from humans any more than goodness does, according to Weil, so the assertion of creative authorship can only result in ugliness and injustice. As she rightly notes, "This desire for order is the result of a *sense* of beauty," and unfortunately, there is often a connection "between tyranny and the love of beauty" even though the latter becomes perverse.[111] She continues: "Apart from war, the instrument for increasing his power, Louis XIV was only interested in festivals and architecture. Moreover war itself . . . stirs man's sense of beauty in a way that is vital and poignant."[112] For instance, journalist Chris Hedges describes in his book *War is a Force that Gives Us Meaning* the almost incredible disillusionment that faces *victims* of war in times of *peace*, when the ordered and meaningful world that characterized their comradeship in struggle disappears due to irrelevance. In his introduction, he gives an account of an encounter he had with a woman and her friends in Bosnia, in the fall of 1995, a few weeks after the war had ended:

> . . . All she and her friends did that afternoon was lament the days when they lived in fear and hunger, emaciated, targeted by Serbian gunners on the heights above. They did not wish back the suffering, and yet, they admitted, those days may have been the fullest of their lives. . . . [What they expressed was] the disillusionment with a sterile, futile, empty present. Peace had again exposed the void that the rush of war, of battle, had filled. Once again they were, as perhaps we all are, alone, no longer bound by that common sense of struggle, no longer given the opportunity to be noble, heroic, no longer sure what life was about or what it meant.[113]

In a similar vein, Weil writes, "Revolutionaries . . . if they didn't lie to themselves, would know that the achievement of the revolution would make them unhappy, because they would lose their reason for living. And it is the same with all desires."[114]

As another recent example, one may recall Radovan Karadzic, the former leader of the Bosnian Serbs who was indicted for war crimes in 1995 and is "held responsible for the three-year siege of Sarajevo, leading to the deaths of as many as 10,000 civilians." Karadzic has famously been interested in poetry, even attempting to become a renowned poet himself. But unsurprisingly, "A critic in the mid-1980s gently noted that Karadzic was 'not very successful' with his poetry, because of his tendency to engage in 'verbal narcissism.' Karadzic himself regarded his poetry as brilliant, however, and told the chief psychiatrist at the mental health clinic where he worked that he was destined to become 'one of the three most important poets writing in the Serbian language.'"[115]

If the attraction to beauty is so closely tied to the desire for order and therefore sometimes, perversely, tyranny and a lust for war, what can be looked upon as a safeguard to prevent the dangerous distortion? Sadly, there is nothing that can keep one from attempting to fabricate or consume the beautiful. But it is imperative to understand that the attempt to impose self-generated order, especially when manifested as war, exclusion of human beings from a city, abuse of a family, marginalization of a minority, et cetera, results in

> [the severing of] every bond of poetry and love between human beings and the universe. It is to plunge them forcibly into the horror of ugliness. There can scarcely be a greater crime. We all have a share by our complicity in an almost innumerable quantity of such crimes. If only we could understand, it should wring tears of blood from us.[116]

That is, there is a contagion to ugliness, as there is to beauty. This understanding depends greatly upon our cultivation of this aesthetic-ethical-religious posture of attention we have been describing. Our complicity in subjecting others to ugliness and despair is precisely our inattention that reinforces and enlarges our own appetite for power and our corresponding hatred of others' limits, as well as our attempts to create beauty by "seeing" connections that do not exist, or by projecting ourselves into the poem, play, or painting, or by forging meaning based on egoistic illusion. "Bad artists," as Iris Murdoch argues, "are useful to tyrants, whose policies they can simplify and romanticize, as in Stalinist-style art."[117] We might add that bad artists are *themselves* tyrants, in the sense that their creations have a disfiguring effect on the psyches of their fellows, by adding to the pull of gravity in the world. Nevertheless, even the most beautiful and accurate representations of tragedy cannot inspire justice if we refuse to look. But when we *do* look, and as the training of attention begins through our contemplation of divine paradox, we become capable of not only encountering beauty on deeper levels but also of being a vehicle for it, too, through maintaining contact with what is impossibly real. Such inspiration, Weil concludes, "if we know how to receive it, tends—as Plato said—to make us grow wings to overcome gravity."[118]

6

Possibility and impossibility

Should we continue in sin in order that grace may abound? By no means! How can we who died to sin go on living in it? Do you not know that all of us who have been baptized into Christ Jesus were baptized into his death? Therefore we have been buried with him by baptism into death, so that, just as Christ was raised from the dead by the glory of the Father, so we too might walk in newness of life.

ROMANS 6:1–4

They tell you we are dreamers. The true dreamers are those who think things can go on indefinitely the way they are.

SLAVOJ ŽIŽEK, speaking at Occupy Wall Street protests, Zuccotti Park, October 10, 2011

Violent interruption

What counts as interruption in a cacophonous and amplified milieu? What arrests the gaze in a landscape of billboards and brightly flashing advertisements? What, moreover, can still our self-defensive imaginations, depose our stubborn senses of false sovereignty, and resist our greedy assimilations of phenomena into a self-preserving symbolic order and nexus of meanings? Is there anything that refuses being flattened onto the screen of competitive commensurability—becoming another commodity—where value is ascribed on the basis of popular consensus or else the power of capital? What can awaken us from our anesthetizing political dreams?

These questions, admittedly, arise from a suspicion that, after all, the paradoxical ideals described in the previous chapters are simply *not possible* in our complex and disoriented world, even if they are desirable. Simon Critchley characterizes modern post-Kantian philosophy as beginning, "not in an experience of wonder at what is, but from an experience of failure and lack."[1] Philosophy, that is, begins in disappointment with the world, as we sense that things are not simply wonder-full. This experience is not reducible to an awareness of the multitude of crises plaguing the world—wars, violent suppressions, environmental catastrophes, and so on—but is also constituted by the sense that the solutions being proposed are disguised derivatives of the problems themselves. Our paradigms are not subjected to rigorous critique, but are often only reaffirmed: in response to problems created by various technologies, we offer technological fixes; threats of nuclear armament from countries whose interests do not align with ours reveal our own blood-thirst and eagerness for war; in response to our distracted students we serve up "innovative educational models" and "multimodal tools" claiming that many learn best by video gaming, texting, and Facebook postings.[2]

For Simone Weil, these predictable responses to perpetual problems are only the signs of the force of gravity; it *is*, in fact, impossible for us to emerge from these destructive cycles—except through grace. However, Weil's idea of grace is not a simple one; like the other significant aspects of experience already discussed in previous chapters, grace is paradoxically encountered. More than representing a mere promise of deliverance from the laws of moral gravity and necessity that permeate the natural world, grace also is the violent and unexpected rupture that opens the space for what, in worldly terms, is "impossible." Weil writes of two movements of grace—"the ascending movement" and "the descending movement of the second degree of grace."[3] This chapter will offer an elaborated phenomenological description of these two movements of grace and, in so doing, will reveal significant ethical characteristics of the subject created by grace. We will describe the two movements of grace as two stages that, taken together, comprise a paradox: (1) Death, or the decreative event, followed by, (2) Recreation, or subjectivating inspiration.[4]

After detailing grace as a process of decreation-recreation, we will propose three descriptions of the subject formed by the workings of grace. First, the decreative event of grace serves as a challenge to current structures of identity, meaning, and law, and to any objectification of the experience that would provide any claims to knowledge. The subject of grace is therefore de-posed from secure and privileged identity and scenes of power. Second, this rupture of grace ensures that certain options or "possibilities" are no longer counted as such. Instead, the subject is left with a radical choice between incommensurate orientations, and this choice constitutes the subject's only freedom. Finally, the recreating aspect of grace inspires in the subject an orientation toward the impossible, that which is inconceivable within current paradigms and systems, and this new subject becomes the vehicle for genuine creativity. The subject who has been de-posed by grace and subsequently flooded by new illumination does not therefore settle for what is conveniently pragmatic, nor does she fall to the temptations of fatalism or nihilism. Only grace can generate works that reveal and present the formerly invisible, give voice to the previously inaudible, and offer beautiful and truthful answers to the once-insoluble.

The first movement of grace—Death, or the decreative event

It is curious that even though Weil writes of two distinct movements of grace, one "ascending" and the other "descending," she offers the general declaration that "grace is the law of the descending movement."[5] It is, in other words, a sort of energy that, like gravity, comes down, but, unlike gravity, can have this effect without natural force or weight. In what sense, then, can the first ascending movement be consistent with a general law of descent?

The ascension Weil refers to is in the context of an allegorical description of creation. That is, the first (ascending) movement of grace points to God's withdrawal or renunciation from being *all* so that something else (creation) might exist. The supernatural, as we have seen, is a transcendent reality paradoxically constituted by self-limitation for the sake of the existence and freedom of others. Being left to ourselves in the absence of the supernatural, we humans can perform a similar self-renunciation and forgoing of power to bring about greater alignment with this reality, but we cannot do this with our own finite efforts. "Not to exercise all the power at one's disposal is to endure the void. This is contrary to all the laws of nature. Grace alone can do it."[6] In more general terms, ascension here implies the vacuum or void left because of the withdrawal of pure goodness from creation for the sake of our existence and freedom; our human experience is that of an elemental absence, sometimes acutely perceived in a particular event or situation that destabilizes our constructed securities and habituated mental defenses. Otherwise, we forget our finitude and limitations, and in this way, we deny the independent reality of everything else. The first movement of grace is only that which reminds us of our *created status*.

A common interpretation of Weilienne grace, however, is that it is the other "side" of waiting for and desiring pure goodness, or the *reward* of humbled patience. She has contended, for instance, that if we "leave a vacuum . . . a supernatural reward results."[7] Does this not mean that if we, too, renounce ourselves, our prejudicial desires, our sense of unlimited power, and our projects, we can rightfully expect to be satisfied by grace? The supernatural reward *seemingly* refers to the second movement of grace that descends to fill the void and will be further addressed in the next section. But here it is important to recognize that for Weil, grace first stimulates the original void, and in this sense, the first movement of grace is experientially distinct from the second. She writes, "Grace fills empty spaces, but it can only enter where there is a void to receive it, and it is grace itself which makes this void."[8] She goes on to describe, "First there must be a tearing out, something desperate has to take place, the void must be created." And then, referencing St. John of the Cross, she hints: "Void: the dark night."[9] But a qualification is needed here, for we have previously said that void is inherent in and constitutive of our very being. What then, would it mean to say that the first movement of grace *creates* the void?

One must understand that Weil recognizes the ease and frequency with which the void is forgotten and filled by humans bent on manufacturing illusions of self-sufficiency and even royalty for themselves. Thus, whenever she speaks of a void being "created" or "made," she is referring to an *event* that shatters our illusions and complacencies and has the potential to call us to a universal but unspeakable truth about our situation. To borrow from Alain Badiou, we might understand the event as a *supplemental* happening that we, with our usual ways of understanding the world, cannot account for. The event is unpredictable and uncontrollable, and it "compels us to decide a *new* way of being."[10] The event is a singular encounter, and it exceeds the margins with which we have circumscribed politics, sex, culture, religion, and even our understanding of ourselves. The event itself is sensed as something precarious and tenuous because it cannot be subjected to our previous frameworks of knowledge; in fact, it is what makes a *hole* in our knowledge. That is, it resists objectification, and because we cannot assimilate and compartmentalize it into our assumed nexus of meanings, our sense of psychical, emotional, and social stability and certainty is shaken. We experience a death to self. In short, a void is (re)created—or, more properly, the void is stimulated so that we become aware of it. This awareness of the void is the initiation of our decreation by the event, the first movement of grace.

We must remember that Weil's depiction of decreation entails a willing renunciation on the part of the person; it is not simply destruction suffered passively. While it is true that grace initiates the recalling and thus opening of the void, it is *possible* to have built up such a system of deflections and rationalizations, or to have embraced such a deterministic theology, that no matter what interruptions of grace arrive on the scene, every rupture initiated will be so quickly filled by the workings of the imagination that "events" are scarcely noticed and the narcissistic ego remains intact. Miklos Vetö characterizes the self-protective ego in the following way:

> The whole sphere of the self is maintained by a centripetal force greedily sucking in reality, and the more one nears the center, the more powerful is the force. . . . The self is a violent contraction paralyzing and crushing the beings and things it encounters. Such an attitude serves the purpose of destroying the world, leaving there a trace of the self; it never helps us to understand the world.[11]

This destructive attitude is only aided by the faculty of imagination. Weil writes that "the imagination is continually at work filling up all the fissures through which grace might pass."[12] As we have seen, this imagination is the producer of fictions, generally by flattening and simplifying phenomena, that is, depriving them of their reality. This procedure always has the effect of (falsely) confirming our own sense of centrality and our own blind desires. However, genuine decreation is "imitation of God's renunciation in creation," a willingness to strip ourselves of our "imaginary divinity."[13] In such cases, we really suffer the loss of the false sense we carried around that we were the center of the universe; we feel the loss of control, we see the idiocy and narrowness of our desires, we perceive our mediocrity, and we feel our own finitude and mortality. The event humbles us in an unexpected and excruciating way, and we feel as if we were dying.

Those who are visited by events and who are open to suffer the grace of decreation are often falsely charged with being masochistic. The label is reflective of our contemporary tendency to medicalize and psychologize every aspect of humanity, but it also serves as a convenient buffer to and defense of an imperative to be attentive to the world. But such an imperative should not be confused with an active "seeking out" of pain and suffering, as we have seen. It is ultimately only through decreation that one can make contact with pure good, and "the cross" certainly *seems* to fall under the category of decreation. But what does Weil mean when she says that we "should not be able to choose to imitate [Christ]"?[14] Here, despite all appearances, she is not denying our ability and responsibility of *orienting* ourselves such that we are open to whatever befalls us, but the authenticity and mystery of the Crucifixion (and of a decreative event in general) is located, for Weil, in its pure bitterness, absent of any notions of romantic martyrdom. The event is never self-imposed but always arrives in spite of ourselves, and we are undone by it.

The second movement of grace— Recreation, or subjectivating inspiration

We are decreated by the first movement of grace, but we are also recreated by a second movement of grace that visits an attentive orientation. The eventual interruption is only the beginning of the story, for something—consent to the void and to being a vehicle for the good—is required of us. As Badiou tells us and Weil would no doubt agree, "There is no instantaneous salvation . . . The subject has to be given in his labor, and not only in his sudden emergence. 'Love' is the name of that labor."[15] Weil frames this imperative to love in the work of arresting the imagination that was described in Chapter 4 as *training*: "We must continually suspend the work of the imagination filling the void within ourselves. If we accept no matter what void, what stroke of fate can prevent us from loving the universe?"[16] Insofar as we are faithful to and persevere in the space created by the rupture, rejecting easy consolations and clearing away void-fillers, we become increasingly able to respond to the genuine needs of the world—response-able, or a *responsible subject* who no longer engages in fabricating her own self-affirming reality, but instead lovingly attends to the impersonal Real.

Earlier, we alluded to the notion that the second (descending) movement of grace might indicate a supernatural reward that comes down to one who has suffered the initial rupture of grace. But the descent here actually refers to the consented and committed attention and its necessary effects that feel like the impossible, impractical, excessive, or absurd answers to our most pressing crises. Badiou's words in describing what he calls "the ethic of a truth" may be helpful in understanding Weil's second movement of grace. He writes, "Do all that you can to persevere in that which exceeds your perseverance. Persevere in the interruption. Seize in your being that which has seized and broken you."[17] The requirement here is to "not give up" by deflecting the unfamiliar and unassimilable revelations and returning to the ordinary ways of approaching the world. But for Weil, this perseverance in the void that goes by the name attention is unnatural for us and, again, is experienced as *impossible*, for we want very much to grasp onto something tangible, known, or stabilizing when we have been riven by an event. It is for this reason that she writes, "Any attempt to gain this deliverance by means of my own energy would be like the efforts of a cow which pulls at its hobble and so falls onto its knees."[18] Nevertheless, we are responsible for annihilating that sense of need for homeostasis, including the times that we feel we are owed something when we have been harmed or else when we have done good for others.

There is good reason, therefore, to question whether this "supernatural reward" should be regarded as any kind of guarantee of relief and whether it could, properly, be *expected*. As

Weil herself writes, "Every kind of reward constitutes a degradation of energy,"[19] and in saying this, she is giving voice to the fact
that an anticipated return on a good deed deprives that deed or
that patience of its energy of grace. Badiou articulates a similar
point when he writes that grace "is what comes *without being
due.*"[20] Unlike Weil's idea of gravity, which pulls us quite naturally
toward a filling of the void or establishing of equivalence, the second movement of grace requires an unnatural (or "supernatural")
desire, and *it is a desire liberated from objects* (including objects of
knowledge), such that "there is an unspeakable wrench in the soul
at the separation of a desire from its object."[21] This excruciating
desire-without-an-object *is* synonymous with consent to the void,
consent to the loss of experienced equilibrium, the forgoing and
forgetting of reward or desert.

　　Grace is present and enables further attentiveness where one has
left that vacuum and where "other wages" have been refused. As
we will later describe in detail, it is only through such active renunciation and attentiveness that we become certain kinds of responsible subjects; the mode of self-preservation, however, is antithetical
to our ethical subjectivation. Our inclinations to self-preservation
and self-enhancement signify our relapse to the un-*event*-full
world, the mode of being prior to subjectivation. Badiou describes
this irony well:

> The ordinary behavior of the human animal is a matter of what
> Spinoza calls "perseverance in being," which is nothing other
> than the pursuit of interest, or the conservation of self . . . To
> belong to the situation is everyone's natural destiny, but to belong
> to the composition of a subject of truth concerns a particular
> route, a sustained break, and it is very difficult to know how this
> composition is to be superimposed upon or combined with the
> simple perseverance-of-self.[22]

The route of the "sustained break" is simultaneously what grace
permits and requires for its constitution of the attending subject.
But when we become impatient for a return on our investment
(when we begin, even, to *think* in those terms!), and when we turn
in desperation to earthly energies and void-fillers in general, Weil
tells us that we become "incapable of thinking and doing anything
but evil."[23] Counterweights, such as self-congratulation, revenge,

rationalization, and self-pity, must all be cast aside. The importance of the receptivity and continued consent to grace alone cannot be overstated.

We should note here that there is a danger that lurks in involving grace in a formulaic ethical prescription, however. Precisely because grace exceeds our power, control, and effort, we should refrain from thinking that we can order or dictate its arrival in any way. Weil explains the proper orientation: "We must give up everything which is not grace and *not even desire grace*."[24] In desiring grace as an end, there is a strong temptation to objectify it, to have some-*thing* in mind, and to carry the conceit of being able to control its presence. In such cases, we foreclose the possibility of real openness and vulnerability to the advent of events. We think of our own spiritual station, instead of doing the work of love, which necessitates an orientation toward what is exterior to us. Paradoxically, receptivity to grace will entail detachment from the idea of grace. This is perhaps one of Weil's most profound spiritual insights, as when she warns: "The presence of God in us has as its condition a secret so deep that it is even a secret from us. There are times when thinking of God separates us from him. Modesty is the condition of nuptial union."[25]

The question now becomes: What is it to think and act in accordance with the event of grace, if we are not to think *about* grace, or even desire it? What is it to seize the seizure? In our perseverance and endurance of the void created by the event, a resurrection of sorts takes place; a new order is established that breaks radically with old ways of behaving, speaking, seeing, thinking, and believing. A process of subjectivation is initiated insofar as we are faithful to the rupture of the event. What is this new being? What constitutes the new world order?

The deposed

In Weil's writings, as we have noted, grace can appear as a sort of nourishment or "supernatural bread" that enables loving attentiveness. What is remarkable about this conception is that this energy must paradoxically function as an anti-food, or an emptiness, that maintains the void. Weil states, for instance, that "we should not

ask for earthly bread," where earthly bread represents all manner of void-fillers, alternative sources of energy and incentives
for action, such as "money, ambition, consideration, decorations,
celebrity, power, [and even] our loved ones."[26] In addition, we may
consider dogmas, fixed identities, religious communities, trite art,
and ideologies as examples of earthly "fillers," whose function is to
generate complacent self-satisfaction. One reason these sources of
energy, or "other wages," should be regarded with caution is that
we ourselves are able to find and often secure them, and this gives
us the illusion that our being "carries the principle of its preservation within itself."[27] Weil describes the danger inherent in filling
the void:

> The soul knows for certain only that it is hungry. The important
> thing is that it announces its hunger by crying. A child does not
> stop crying if we suggest to it that perhaps there is no bread.
> It goes on crying just the same. *The danger is not lest the soul
> should doubt whether there is any bread, but lest, by a lie, it
> should persuade itself that it is not hungry.* It can only persuade
> itself of this by lying, for the reality of its hunger is not a belief,
> it is a certainty.[28]

Thus the crying, which is to say the supplication, is *morally* important, for it represents an attitude that recognizes the reality of our
finitude and our inability to be self-sufficient; it counteracts every
tendency toward egoism. That "lie" that says we are not "hungry"
is for Weil the beginning of selfishness and evil.

Similarly, Weil observes that, in a general sense, she is devoid of
"the principle of rising" within herself.[29] That is, she says that only
by directing her attention toward something real and something
better than herself can she be "really raised up."[30] She writes, "No
imaginary perfection can draw me upward even by the fraction of
an inch."[31] She makes clear that this attention or "thought direction" is not to be confused with the "suggestions" that are only
imaginative projections:

> If I say to myself every morning, "I am courageous, I am not
> afraid," I may become courageous, but with a courage which
> conforms to what, in my present imperfection, I imagine under
> that name, and accordingly *my courage will not go beyond this*

imperfection. It can only be a modification on the same plane, not a change of plane.[32]

The change of plane—epitomized, as we have just seen, by Antigone's "breach"—arrives only through the advent of grace, or "the supernatural," for by definition, grace exceeds the limits of our conceptions. Additionally, grace illuminates what, on a natural level, is considered impossible and extreme. In fact, for Weil, contradiction is the criterion of the real in the context of this higher plane, for

> ... we cannot by suggestion obtain things which are incompatible. Only grace can do that. A sensitive person who by suggestion becomes courageous hardens himself; often he may even, by a sort of savage pleasure, amputate his own sensitivity. Grace alone can give courage while leaving the sensitivity intact, or sensitivity while leaving the courage intact.[33]

The method of "suggestion" alluded to here is tantamount to an effort of the will, for Weil. It is ineffective when it comes to the acquisition of virtues, which would appear to cancel one another out, for *we do not know how to strike the balance,* except by compromising to some extent one or the other. This is why Weil says that saintliness is characterized by the "simultaneous existence of incompatible things in the soul's bearing," or a "balance which leans both ways at once."[34] For this to be possible, the person has to have been "wrenched apart,"[35] or *deposed by grace.*

While for Weil, "we can only advance horizontally"[36] when we set out with our own intentions, we must also realize that forgoing active attempts at melioration does not mean that we are purely passive in the face of injustices—a common misunderstanding, to be sure. The obvious question, then, is: Following our deposition, what is our proper disposition if we are not to make an active search and not to orient ourselves in a particular direction? Her response to her own question affirms the importance of the emptiness of attention, even to the point of agnosticism. Weil utilizes another analogy of a child to explain our proper posture, though here, the natural tendencies of the child may prove a handicap. She says that a child, who has lost his mother in the street, will run about in all directions, crying, and looking for her, but this is the wrong approach. If he had the sense and courage to stand still, wait on her, and call out for her, she would find him sooner, Weil tells us. But the analogy is not quite sufficient, for Weil says that in our case, we must "not [even] call upon someone," for "we still do not know if there *is* anyone; but cry out that we are hungry and want bread."[37]

Again, what is essential for us to know is only that we are hungry; it is not necessary or useful to believe that there is a Provider, or even that there is bread. It is the hunger that we can be certain is real, that characterizes our deposed disposition and that opens the door to grace that makes our attention creative and responsible. But Weil writes, "All those who believe that food exists, or will one day be produced, in this world, are lying."[38] Being attentive, then, precludes thinking in terms of a particular object and certainly forecloses any thoughts or bets on salvation. As we saw in Chapter 1, if we take on a search for God, and it appears our search has succeeded, the result, Weil writes, can only be illusory, and what we have found will be a false God. The proper comportment for attention transcends the horizontal effort and the intentional framework. Such consent to the void does involve an ethos of quietude and stillness that goes against our nature, but this religious orientation is not one of *quietism*, inaction, and complete passivity, for consent simultaneously necessitates active engagement, or what Weil called *action non agissante*.

One comparison she uses is of solar energy (representing grace), which works against physical gravity, permitting animals and vegetation to grow and rise vertically. It is the only power that can overcome gravity. Even other sources of mechanical energy, like coal and petroleum, ultimately derive from this primary resource. A good farmer will arrange everything "in such a way that the plants capable of using [solar energy] and transmitting it to us will receive it in the best possible conditions."[39] In like manner, our active efforts should only be geared toward clearing away the pervasive void-filling distractions, in order that we might receive the original source of energy that may one day yield fruit. In other words, we are "to dispose our soul so that it can receive grace," but even this effort is made possible by the initial movement of grace.[40] Attention, therefore, is the opening to vertical—that is to say, genuine—progress. What is produced by way of this progress is without precedent and beyond prediction.

Attention consists, as we know, in a *looking*, without discrimination and without perspective, at everything, pleasant or unpleasant, and a noting of the connections and relationships between disparate phenomena. To do this, however, is very difficult, because our perceptual faculties tend toward resolving ambiguities, imposing discrete distinctions, establishing hierarchies, and emphasizing those phenomena that reinforce what the ego has already assumed about itself and the external world. Because the "I" does not want to suffer or be compromised in its projects, it rebels against this perceptual generosity, and this rebellion consists in evasion and the strengthening of the imagination that aids it. This is where, again, the muscular, active effort called "training" actually has a role. Like the good farmer who consistently pulls up the weeds that block solar energy,

[t]he only effective and legitimate use of our muscular efforts is to keep at bay and suppress whatever may prevent us from looking up; they are negatively useful. The part of the soul which is capable of looking at God is surrounded by barking, biting, destructive dogs. They must be controlled by the whip.[41]

Weil goes on to say that this training is a condition for spiritual ascension, but of itself, it does not enable one to rise. Again, it is only grace that is the elevating power, and "God comes when we look towards him," and "to look towards him," she explains, "means to love him."[42] As we have seen, to love God also means to endure the void and to appreciate the distance between ourselves and the Good: to consent to a deposition of self. This, then, is what it really means to keep one's eyes turned toward God.

While there is a proper employment of the subject's agency in clearing distractions away, we cannot forget that Weil thinks that by "remain[ing] quite still" we actually unite ourselves with that which we desire.[43] It is this way with grace, for instance: we do not dare make the approach, but a patient and unobstructed hunger for the impossible is the only avenue for realizing the Good. Recall Weil's simile:

God and humanity are like two lovers who have missed their rendezvous. Each is there before the time, but each at a different place, and they wait and wait and wait. He stands motionless,

nailed to the spot for the whole of time. She is distraught and
impatient. But alas for her if she gets tired and goes away. For
the two places where they are waiting are at the same point in
the fourth dimension . . .[44]

What this means is that as finite, fallible creatures, our hunger
for the Good is of utmost importance, for the creative attention
made possible by grace follows desire. This is a desire deprived of a
proper *object*, for objects turn the hunger into a *means*. When the
desire becomes a mere means to an end, the intentional structure
dictates base motives and energies, and even the most seemingly
charitable gestures become tainted by our greed. For instance, she
warns us about self-conscious charity: "God is not present, even
if we invoke him, where the afflicted are merely regarded as an
occasion for doing good."[45] Weil offers us, therefore, a challenge to
"love on empty," writing,

> A man has all he can do, even if he concentrates all the attention
> of which he is capable, to look at this small inert thing of flesh,
> lying stripped of clothing by the roadside. It is not the time to
> turn his thoughts toward God. Just as there are times when we
> must think of God and forget all creatures without exception,
> there are times when, as we look at creatures, we do not have
> to think explicitly of God. . . . There are times when thinking of
> God separates us from him.[46]

Here we are brought back full circle to the importance, in Weil's
philosophy, of grasping that grace requires an abstinence from any
opiate or energy that can be named or conceived as "God." But
we also "must not seek the void, for it would be tempting God
if we counted on supernatural bread to fill it."[47] The point is that
in our lives, we encounter, on a regular basis, realities that leave
us feeling cold, frustrated, and empty. We must not run from the
void that we come to recognize (in these situations) as constitutive
of our individual selves and of human existence in general. When
we do cry out for the supernatural bread, or "grace," or "light,"
we must understand that what we petition for is not a compensation in the usual way. There will be no quick consolation, and
no self-affirmation, that anesthetizes us from the trauma. When
there has been a compensation provided by the imagination (like

saying to oneself, "God has a reason for this evil; it is part of a master plan," or "By my suffering, I advance spiritually,") then grace is refused. Weil explains this character of grace and its prevention by making reference to the Gospel of Matthew: "That is why we read in the Gospel, 'I say to you that these have received their reward.' There must be no compensation. It is the void in our sensibility which carries us beyond sensibility."[48] What is being requested, then, is the ability to *endure* the emptiness; that is, the petition for supernatural bread, or grace, is actually the petition for an *increased capacity for attentiveness*.

This supernatural bread is, then, nothing tangible. In fact, it may very well be silence: "It is when from the innermost depths of our being we need a sound which does mean something, when we cry out for an answer and it is not given us, it is then that we touch the silence of God."[49] Often, however, we attempt to convert this form of the supernatural bread into something tangible, something we can consume; the temptation to create an idol is nearly irresistible. "As a rule our imagination puts words into the sounds in the same way we idly play at making out shapes in wreaths of smoke."[50] Naturally, we fool ourselves in attempting to make grace something we can consume and attach ourselves to. But in fact, for Weil, we can only desire the impossible.

The clear perception of our real situation and the problems that exist therein provides no consolation for us. Instead, by virtue of the view we have accessed, we find ourselves (de)positioned at a crossroads: we can resign ourselves to hopelessness with the growing sense of our own impotence, or we can maintain attention to the difficult and perplexing realities, without succumbing to temptingly facile answers.

The radical choice

"We see the same colors; we hear the same sounds, but not in the same way," Weil wrote, describing the transformative effects of renouncing our imaginary centeredness in favor of sustained attention.[51] By the grace of an event that initially ruptures our imagination, we begin to perceive situations in an altogether new light perceiving, that is, the real problems that face us. In emerging from the world of dreams, the subject is not self-preoccupied but realizes that problems issue from her very self-centeredness and her refusal to accept and respect the being of others and the world around her. According to Weil, this epiphany leaves us with one essential choice, though it may be manifested in an infinite number of ways: "to desire obedience [to God] or not to desire it."[52] What does this option mean for us?

As we have noted, grace is what shatters our normal ways of functioning and thinking. These "normal" ways, however, are constricted by forces of what Weil calls gravity, the pull toward moral baseness comprised by self-centeredness and the failure to recognize one's own limits, or the overt denial of the reality of others. This gravitational force is so powerful that our ways of being outside of the event (and hence, outside of grace) are nevertheless constituted by a kind of obedience—but it is obedience to nature, or "mechanical necessity." Hence, Weil writes, "If a man does not desire [obedience to God], he obeys nevertheless, perpetually, inasmuch as he is a thing subject to mechanical necessity."[53] But the event reveals a "new necessity . . . constituted by laws belonging to supernatural things," and in this new situation, "certain actions become impossible for [the subject, while] others are done by his agency, sometimes almost in spite of himself."[54]

In other words, the attentiveness made possible by the rupture highlights the distance and incommensurability between former and present ways of being; they are no longer seen as being constituted by differences of "degrees" but are radically opposed. As part of this transformation, many old problems are seen as superfluous and dissolved, while new (real) problems are illuminated. In recent years, philosophers such as Simon Critchley, Alain Badiou, and Slavoj Žižek have described the task of philosophy as "the invention of new problems," the deciding, that is, of what the important problems are.[55] The "TV philosopher" who talks about the problems as they are presented by network news, who engages in the debates in the prescribed terms, has done a great disservice to the task, for, as Badiou writes, "the sole task of philosophy is to show that *we must choose*."[56] He means that we must choose between two incommensurate types of thought, two terms devoid of any relation, illustrated by Socrates on the one hand and the sophist Callicles on the other, who argues that "might makes right" and that the happy man is a tyrant.[57] Thus, the problems as presented by Callicles (or the world) are not the real problems, and the solutions to these will naturally be beside the point. The real philosopher, then, will always appear as "a stranger, clothed in his new thoughts," and the philosophical commitment will always have a foreignness about it because it is unfamiliar to the banal categories.[58]

Before we turn our attention back to Weil, a further clarification is warranted about what makes the philosophical commitment a "strange" one. Badiou offers a helpful example from the end of Book IX of Plato's *Republic*. As Badiou describes it:

> At the end of Book IX, Socrates is discoursing with some youths, as always, and some among them say to him: 'This whole story's very nice, but it will never be realized anywhere.' The critique of utopia was already in place. So they say to him: 'Your Republic will never exist anywhere.' And Socrates replies: 'In any case, perhaps it will exist somewhere else than in our country.' In other words, he says that it will take place abroad, that there will be something foreign and strange about it . . . Genuine philosophical commitment, in situations, creates a foreignness . . . And when it is simply commonplace, when it does not possess this foreignness, when it is not immersed in this paradox, then it is a political commitment, an ideological commitment, the commitment of a citizen, but it is not necessarily a philosophical commitment.[59]

What Badiou identifies by the exemplar of Socrates is the apparent impossibility of this new vision. The new paradigm does not square with what we already know and experience. Indeed, the philosopher frustrates us by offering paradoxical situations and impossible worlds; our totalizing knowledge, which is a form of power, is interrupted by something we cannot anticipate or lay claim to.

For Weil, the "philosophical commitment" is, paradoxically, both a precursor (insofar as it is "training") *and* a consequence (insofar as it is the deciding of the rupture) of grace. In this new committed way of being, even contemplation of former ways of acting and speaking does not make them inevitable and, in fact, makes them impossible if it is true attention that is given. Conversely, the decreative deposition of the subject that accompanies attention to just actions not only makes such actions possible, but it also makes them necessary; in other words, the actions that ensue from a void not filled (made initially possible by grace) will give themselves as unavoidable and cause us to be "strange." Although attention itself implies a self-renouncing consent, the actions that follow from attentiveness to the Good are not exactly *willed* on our parts. Weil describes this sort of action:

> There are cases where a thing is necessary from the mere fact that it is possible. Thus to eat when we are hungry, to give a wounded man, dying of thirst, something to drink when there is water quite near. Neither a ruffian nor a saint would refrain from doing so. By analogy, we have to discern the cases in which, although it does not appear so clearly at first sight, the possibility implies a necessity . . . We should do only those righteous actions which we cannot stop ourselves from doing, which we are unable not to do, but, through well-directed attention, we should always keep on increasing the number of those which we are unable not to do.[60]

So in Weil's paradigm, one's activity is only efficacious and righteous when compelled by what one *receives*, namely by the inspiration of grace; for her, it is erroneous to insist that a genuinely good deed originates in the self. There is clearly a paradox in the mandate to *do* that which we are *unable not to do*, but the important point is the choice of consent to the attentive/philosophical orientation whereby grace makes real moral progress possible:

> God has provided that when his grace penetrates to the very center of a man and from there illuminates all his being, he is able to walk on the water without violating any of the laws of nature. When, however, a man turns away from God, he simply gives himself up to the law of gravity. Then he thinks that he can decide and choose, but he is only a thing, a stone that falls.[61]

The initial choice of orientation determines everything. There is, in Weil's account, freedom to reject grace, but there is no freedom in what follows from that consent to gravity: one's tendencies and base habits only become calcified and a necrotic rigidity takes over. One may argue that the orientation and consent to grace permits

no more freedom, since it has been described as a different kind of
"obedience" (to God). However, because this disposition is characterized by openness and lack of *object* that fixates it, the scope of
what is possible through the attentive being is virtually limitless.
She can even, as we detailed in the previous chapter, be counted
a genius in her creativity and insight, being a conduit for works
that are genuinely beautiful and new, because of her consent to the
supernatural orientation.

This consent to grace is extraordinarily difficult. Weil compares
the process following our consent to the implantation of a seed
within us. To nurture the growth of the seedling, "we cannot avoid
destroying whatever gets in its way, pulling up the weeds, cutting
the good grass, and unfortunately the good grass is part of our
very flesh, so that this gardening amounts to a violent operation."[62]
Our consent to grace, that is, entails that our will and intelligence
be employed *only* for the sake of checking our selves, uprooting the
conditions and comforts that aid our forgetfulness and our negligence of the reality the event revealed. The consent itself, whose
essence involves the renunciation of all manner of distractions, is
experienced as unnatural, since the ego naturally tends to rein-
state its mastery and control of situations. Even the most pious
and well-intentioned persons are subject to the mechanical laws
of gravity and may ironically "compensate" themselves for their
"spiritual poverty."

The essential choice with which we are presented in no matter
what situation can be put in the following way: Will we be faithful
to the revelation of the phenomenon as it stands with our interests
and desires put into abeyance, or will we cloud our own perception and pervert our response by projecting ourselves onto what is
revealed? To achieve the disinterestedness of the former orientation
means, again, that we must not *will* actions in the usual, intentional
way, for the sake of a desired end. If grace has had anything to
teach us so far, it is that good arrives beyond the scope and power
of our selves. In every case of a truly good deed, the origin of the
action will be something exterior to us, something that eludes our
will, something that seemed impossible. But this fact should not
deter us, for "impossibility is [only] the door of the supernatural.
We can but knock at it. It is someone else who opens."[63]

The impossible

We have been speaking of the event of grace that convokes us to a decreated orientation characterized by attentiveness or persever-ance in the void. It is important to recognize that for Weil, the arrival of grace may become manifest in an unlimited number of ways but always in forms that destabilize our norms, expectations, and even our very agency and will. It is because of this last quality that we can speak of the subject of grace becoming recreated as the vehicle for truly insightful, new, and revelatory works. This is a paradoxical subject, then, whose active intentionality is challenged and replaced by an impersonal anonymity. But until and unless this transformation happens, the individual's actions are subject to the effects of moral and spiritual gravity and will therefore preclude any good, beautiful, or truthful results.

As the second movement of grace descends to be revealed to the attentive being who has consented to the first movement, norms and expectations are not reestablished but continue to be exceeded and upset. The fruits of grace, in the process of blossoming from a deposed and attentive subject, are surprising even to that subject:

> With all things, it is always what comes to us from outside freely and by surprise, as a gift from heaven, without our having sought it, that brings us pure joy. In the same way, real good can only come from outside ourselves, never from our own effort. . . Thus effort truly stretched toward goodness cannot reach its goal; it is after long, fruitless effort which ends in despair, when we no longer expect anything, that, from outside ourselves, the gift comes as a marvelous surprise.

Paradoxically, this (passive-active) receipt of grace simultaneously enables genuine "creativity": grace allows the attentive subject to see the things deserving of the names "good," "beautiful," and "true," and their facilitators are rightly called geniuses by virtue of that attentiveness to the world. Therefore, subjects of grace demand the impossible, for as Weil writes, *"the good is impossible."*[64]

The subject whose formation is initiated by the event of grace will, without the ordinary protective consolations in place, become highly dissatisfied by the forces at work in the social realm, including what is offered by politicians' rhetoric, or committees, or news analysts, or popular self-help prescriptions. The slogans and lies fail to ring true anymore, and they fail to amuse. She can no longer humor small talk, whose intention is to keep everyone comfortable. Nor is she content with condescending handouts or even pay raises when they are meant to supplant real justice. She can see behind empty promises made to the afflicted, and see the ways in which they are being used as pawns by the powerful. Yet as stated previously, she is also prevented from desiring or seeking grace itself: "The object of our search should not be the supernatural," Weil writes, "but the world. The supernatural is light itself: if we make an object of it we lower it."[65] Thus, this subject *does* seek real and meaningful contact with the world, but the problem is that what is discovered as needed when she makes this contact departs so radically from what exists, or from what options are popularly prescribed, that her desires are labeled "impossible," or else, she lacks the language to articulate them. She becomes, she feels, like the idiot vagrant stammering before the magistrate who knows she will never be listened to.[66] In any case, idols—ersatz divinities, final solutions, reductive answers, static categories, and self-affirming religions—are laid aside when she is awakened by the event of grace. All such sacred cows and the borders that protect them are troubled by the interruption of the event.

The "Occupy" protests that began in mid-2011 on Wall Street have been famously characterized by their lack of definite character or reducible creed and by their seemingly absurd demands. This lack of ideology or representative has proved frustrating for politicians and pundits alike who have tried to get a "handle" on the movements. But two philosophers in particular, who have supported and spoken at sites of protest, have articulated in different terms what we are calling the rupture of idols and have the potential—despite their own philosophic distance from her—to shed light on Weil's conception of grace as it relates to the hunt for the impossible. Slavoj Žižek, for instance, gave the following illustration:

So what are we doing here? Let me tell you a wonderful, old joke from Communist times. A guy was sent from East Germany to work in Siberia. He knew his mail would be read by censors, so he told his friends: "Let's establish a code. If a letter you get from me is written in blue ink, it is true what I say. If it is written in red ink, it is false." After a month, his friends get the first letter. Everything is in blue. It says, this letter: "Everything is wonderful here. Stores are full of good food. Movie theatres show good films from the west. Apartments are large and luxurious. The only thing you cannot buy is red ink." This is how we live. We have all the freedoms we want. But what we are missing is red ink: the language to articulate our non-freedom. The way we are taught to speak about freedom—war on terror and so on—falsifies freedom. And this is what you are doing here. You are giving all of us red ink.[67]

In other words, we have been living in a dream world. And the words that will capture the truth of the situation will be foreign to the dreamers. Weil puts it: "It is necessary to touch impossibility in order to come out of the dream world. There is no impossibility in dreams—only impotence."[68] And along the same lines, Judith Butler had this to say at the protests:

People have asked, so what are the demands? What are the demands all of these people are making? Either they say there are no demands and that leaves your critics confused, or they say that the demands for social equality and economic justice are impossible demands. And the impossible demands, they say, are just not practical. If hope is an impossible demand, then we demand the impossible—that the right to shelter, food and employment are impossible demands, then we demand the impossible. If it is impossible to demand that those who profit from the recession redistribute their wealth and cease their greed, then yes, we demand the impossible.[69]

In Weil's terms, the event of grace falsifies the ordinary language of demands that we are accustomed to speaking and upon which we have depended for a long time. Grace illuminates a situation in such a way that we acutely understand the necessity for the "red ink," new frameworks that gesture to the impossible. Weil writes,

In order to provide an armor for the afflicted, one must put into their mouths only those words whose rightful abode is in heaven, beyond heaven, in the other world. There is no fear of its being impossible. Affliction disposes the soul to welcome and avidly drink in everything which comes from there. For these products it is not consumers but producers who are in short supply.[70]

These other-worldly words welcomed by the afflicted are not necessarily signifiers of *the answer* that will resolve current crises; instead, the event of grace may produce a discourse that captures for us in a novel and illuminating way the problem itself, purified of distracting rhetoric and influence. Understanding the problem precisely, even without knowing the answer, will enable us to recognize charlatans, sophists, and partial solutions for what they are. As Weil explains analogically, "We see that which is opaque through the transparent—the opaque which was hidden when the transparent was not transparent. We see either the dust on the window or the view beyond the window, but never the window itself . . . The reason should be employed only to bring us to the true mysteries, the true undemonstrables, which are reality."[71] The reason that casts aside illusory and simplistic identities, definitions, and ideologies is a product of the subjectivation triggered by the event. In this subjectivation, we do not *see* the event of grace in the sense that we grasp an object; what *can* be perceived are real problems that convoke us to response and depend upon our committed attention.

Conclusion:
Educating paradox

*You desire truth in the inward being; therefore teach me
wisdom in my secret heart.*

PSALM 51:6

*. . . Consumerist reading isn't the only kind there is. It's also
possible to read religiously, as a lover reads, with a tensile
attentiveness that wishes to linger, to prolong, to savor, and
has no interest at all in the quick orgasm of consumption.*

PAUL J. GRIFFITHS[1]

In this book, we have attempted to bring some of Simone Weil's
most profound religious insights into the foreground without,
thereby, diminishing the fruitful tensions in her thought. There is
always a challenge in faithfully presenting the ideas of another,
which is nothing more nor less than the challenge of attention
itself with its hermeneutic difficulties: How does one facilitate but
not get in the way of the object's presentation to others? In other
words, how can we illuminate an idea, a thinker, or a phenomenon
without also casting ourselves (or at least our own symbolic frameworks) in the spotlight? We understand the need for creating a real
opening to and *desire for* the reception of new ideas, especially
those that rupture preexisting categories. However, as Don Ihde
explains the conundrum,

> The paradox consists in the fact that without some—at least
> general—idea of what and how one is to look at a thing, how
> can anything be seen? Yet, if what is to be seen is to be seen
> without prejudice or preconception, how can it be circumscribed
> by definition?[2]

Though Ihde is referring specifically to the "hermeneutic circle" that is an ever-present concern in phenomenology, at base, this paradox is a question about education, about how to be the Socratic midwife in the delivery of philosophic wonder.

Remembering that for Plato education is a complete reorientation of the soul toward the good, implying a transformation of our desires, Weil underscores the importance of joy in learning as an indispensable precursor to spiritual purity and hunger that "draws God down."[3] The educator, then, seems to be tasked not only with presenting real problems and tensions to her students in such a way that they are stimulated to pursue the love of wisdom themselves, but she must also prevent herself from becoming an obfuscation and distraction for her students, in the process of teaching. Weil expresses this latter concern:

> May I disappear in order that those things that I see may become perfect in their beauty from the very fact that they are no longer things that *I* see.
>
> I do not in the least wish that this created world should fade from my view, but that it should no longer be to me personally that it shows itself. To me it cannot tell its secret which is too high. If I go, then the creator and the creature will exchange their secrets.[4]

It is, undoubtedly, a strange image of teaching wherein the teacher departs in order that the author/creator and the student may "exchange their secrets." It is also, perhaps, too simple. The educator *does* have a role to play in being a "midwife" or a "mediator," but this role implies its own paradox, as we will see.

For Weil, the sole purpose of education is the growth and cultivation of attention that may one day contemplate (the absent) God. In light of this, it is worth noting that nearly any subject can be conducive to this development—physics, Latin, philosophy, ballet, et cetera—so long as the student undertakes the challenges presented in a patient and vigilant way. In fact, Weil informs us that subjects for which we lack natural aptitude may be an especial benefit to this cultivation of attention, provided we do not get frustrated and give up. Wrestling with problems or translations, for example, trains the will for its eventual quieting by external inspiration. The student learns not only the particular content—physics equations and applications, for example—but more importantly, she learns humility in the focusing upon present problems:

> If we concentrate our attention on trying to solve a problem of geometry, and if at the end of an hour we are no nearer to doing so than at the beginning, we have nevertheless been making progress each minute of that hour in another more mysterious dimension. Without our knowing or feeling it, this apparently barren effort has brought more light into the soul.[5]

However, for this process to take place, the material must be given to the student *as a problem, or a paradox*. Of itself, this presentation should not involve any fabrication, for Weil contends that "all truth contains a contradiction."[6] In saying this, she does not mean something nonsensical, like *truth is illogical*, in this narrow philosophic sense. In fact, she tells us, "It is not the role of philosophy to suppress [contradictions]," for "far from being an imperfection of philosophical thought, [contradiction] is an essential characteristic without which there is no more than a false appearance of philosophy."[7] Instead, contradiction is to be experienced as obstacle to habituated thought and preconception, so that it functions as a "loosening" agent with respect to our attachments. Or, to put the experience of paradox in religious terms: "Contradiction experienced to the very depths of the being tears us heart and soul: it is the cross," or the preparation for the death of the "I," which is the heart of philosophy and study in general.[8]

Just as work capable of cultivating attention requires, according to Weil, an infusion of poetry, and poetry, to be authentic, must reveal contact with fatigue, hunger, and thirst,[9] so education must preserve at its center paradox and aporetic tension. We betray our disciplines *as disciplines*, that is, when we pretend that answers are simple, straightforward, and easy. When we ask rhetorical questions of our students rather than genuine questions—that is, questions that are genuinely questions *for us*—we mislead them and are misled ourselves. Again, this is not a prescription for the kind of relativism that treats all speculations and interpretations as valid, sound, and relevant. Too often, we make the mistake of thinking that truth that is difficult (or impossible) to grasp is the same as the nonexistence of said truth. This mistake is most likely the result of our impatience. Undeniably, Weil thinks that there *is* truth, and that we must strive toward it: "When we set out to do a piece of work, it is necessary to wish to do it correctly," and when we have failed, we must examine our mistakes squarely and attentively, "without seeking any excuse or overlooking any mistake or any of our tutor's corrections, trying to get down to the origin of each fault."[10] As educators, then, we must be willing to grapple with the real obscurities in a text, with our own intellectual shortcomings (even in front of a classroom), and with the silences following our questions that signal contemplation and growing attention.

In short, real teaching, we argue, is not a *skill or set of skills*, as it is so often characterized in the specialized "education" departments and offices of institutions of higher learning today. Rather, to be an educator is to be *oriented* attentively, in the various contexts this book has explored. The teacher is, then, an exemplar of attention; in addition to the problematic material she introduces to her students, she shows her own love of wisdom—not as a performance, but as an actual engagement with necessity and the good that constitutes decreation. As Plato understood through the figure of Socrates, education is an erotic enterprise in which the desires of students are transformed by the beauty evident through the mediator—their teacher. But beauty makes its appearance only via the *eclipse of the person* who teaches; her loving orientation must have the character of impersonality, by the mere definition of attention. In this light, Weil offers a further analogy for her teaching, one that, in this instance, does not involve her wholesale disappearance:

> To be what the pencil is for me when, blindfolded, I feel the table by means of its point—to be that for Christ. It is possible for us to be mediators between God and the part of creation which is confided to us. Our consent is necessary in order that he may perceive his own creation through us.[11]

It is not necessary to conclude from this that good teachers only teach explicitly religious matters, such as "Christ" or "God." As we have seen, instruction of such religious concepts *qua* conceptualizations would of necessity be illusory, as they do not give themselves to us in that way. Weil's point is that, as mere vehicles for the unfolding of reality, we must be wary of being taken as more than mediators.

We are all familiar with the sort of teaching that centers on a "cult of personality." Many talented and charismatic educators who take real interest in their students' lives and projects become, often despite their contrary intentions, the focus and motive for these students' academic energies. In many cases, apparent philosophical interest is sparked and maintained when the *personality* of the teacher captures the curiosities and imaginations of students whose interest in the subject, subsequently, becomes tied up with the teacher's interest *because* it is the teacher's. In Chapter 5, we described the primary way in which the love of beauty can become perverted—namely, by "getting stuck" at the level of the physical, personal, and particular, rather than understanding that it is the gateway to divine beauty, beyond our imagination. The problem, then, with the cult of personality in teaching, is that students get "stuck" at this entry level of the personal, and their efforts become entirely wrapped up in accompanying superfluities, such as whether or not they are "liked" by their teacher, or how "interesting" or "entertaining" the teacher is, apart from any serious consideration of the problems presented. We do not intend to suggest that such distractions are always caused by the educator; as with beautiful artworks, there is always sufficient capability in people for imaginative disfiguring and fictionalizing that even purity is no guarantee of an attentive observer.

The educator finds herself in a paradoxical and precarious position. She realizes that she exemplifies a particular orientation that is at odds with much of the rest of the world, and that the purpose of education (if we follow Plato and Weil) is to inspire this (re)orientation in others. But can there be an *impersonal exemplar*? Is not the exemplar, by definition, a particular *person* who has arrested the imaginations of others? According to Anthony Steinbock, "Exemplars are not norms, but 'personal models' on the basis of the value seen in the content of the exemplar."[12] But an educator who embodies the supernatural orientation of attention will not handle the material in her lectures as *material*, strictly speaking, but as the living, changing, and life-impacting contradictions that call for continual struggle and even suffering. Education, despite what many students would like to believe and what many universities advertise, necessitates suffering: "Suffering, teaching and transformation. What is necessary is not that the initiated should learn some*thing*, but that a transformation should come about in them which makes them capable of *receiving* the teaching."[13] As we have seen, becoming attentive from a state of dispersion and distraction is crucifying, in that it demands self-renunciation. Becoming a genuine student, just like becoming a genuine educator, is a process of decreation.

Thus if we approach our lectures with a certain lack of self-consciousness—not stupidity, and not false innocence, but a complete investment in the themes being discussed, and moreover, with a hunger for truth—students will most likely imitate this direction as well and become equally and impersonally invested in the problems; the light that emanates through the void cannot be consumed. In such cases, our exemplar has become, paradoxically, an "impersonal model" of attentiveness, effaced and anonymous in the sense that her personal characteristics or quirks are no longer "given," but instead, her methods and meditations are seen—which are not, properly speaking, *hers*. In this way, the orientation is "supernatural" while also thereby representing "true philosophy" because it "doesn't construct anything; its object is already provided,"[14] though not given to us immediately. There is "a special way of waiting upon truth,"[15] therefore, that counters our tendency—whether as students or teachers—to be too hasty and active in seizing upon ideas, or in thinking that we can generate the final answers. (At best, these will be temporary; at worst, they will lull us into complacency.) It is not that we stop searching or hungering when we wait, but we cease grasping impatiently for whatever "byte" of information comes our way and can fill in a false blank. Indeed, education was never, until just recently, about *information* at all.

Students, in their turn, as they learn this practice of waiting, cease to think of their seemingly fruitless struggles in terms of "dead time" or "wasted time." That is, they become attentive in their orientation and no longer fixate on the metaphorical finger pointing to the moon. Certain incentives also disappear from their energies: grades, accolades, career trajectories, potential earning power—in short, the very "rewards" that our university administrators promise to potential students, in selling education (as a product, of course). Given these incentives that are so aggressively pawned onto students, it is nothing short of a miracle if they are eventually able to forget the soulless economy of corporatized education and come to recognize the "need that their life should be a poem."[16] By addressing this need, which, in any case, will never do away with the tensions or the voids, we educators also enable students to be able to ask important questions. These questions are always genuine questions, never cynical or rhetorical. These questions, by the emptiness that gives rise to them, can give life and, by the decreative disposition that founds them, can be creative. Perhaps the most important question they are enabled to ask, according to Weil, is: "What are you going through?"[17]

If such a scenario sounds hopelessly idealistic, then we should also heed Weil's words: "An educational method which is not inspired by the conception of a *certain form of human perfection* is not worth very much."[18] This form of "human perfection" strongly resembles, we would argue, the impersonal exemplar who attends to the paradoxes of this world. In such a person, there would exist "a focal point of greatness where the genius creating beauty, the genius revealing truth, heroism and holiness are indistinguishable."[19] It is important to remember that in contradistinction to the *leader* or *authority* of secular hierarchy, the *exemplar* has no followers but only "'emulators' in a relationship of emulation" who come to love, esteem, hate, and scorn what the exemplar loves, esteems, et cetera.[20] In light of this, it is easy to see why the exemplar is "not a goal after which one strives" but is rather the goal-determiner for the emulator.[21] Weil underscores the importance of this particular role when she says, "All men are ready to die for what they love. They differ only through the level of the thing loved and the concentration or diffusion of their love."[22]

On this basis, a true pedagogy of paradox is possible. T. S. Eliot, who considered Weil to be a saint if not a genius, recognized that many will not agree with her views; some, in fact, will violently disagree with them. "But," he wrote, "agreement and rejection are secondary: what matters is to make contact with a great soul."[23] In the case of Simone Weil, we, her readers, may expect a soul that eludes, frustrates, and even withdraws to the point of unrecognizability, but in this way, she carries us to impossible heights.

NOTES

Introduction

1 FLN 147.
2 Alain Badiou, "Language, Thought, Poetry," in *Theoretical Writings*, ed. and trans. Ray Brassier and Alberto Toscano (London and New York: Continuum, 2006), 239.
3 Ibid. 239–40.
4 NB 37.
5 NB 29 and WG 63.
6 Rainer Maria Rilke, *The Notebooks of Malte Laurids Brigge*, trans. Stephen Mitchell (New York: Vintage International, 1990).
7 We borrow the metaphor of "ripe fruit" to describe the product of Rilke's "blood-remembering" from John J. L. Mood. See: Rainer Maria Rilke, *Rilke on Love and Other Difficulties*, trans. with commentary John J. L. Mood (New York: W.W. Norton & Company, 2004), 111–13.
8 Ibid. 112–13. Emphasis added.
9 Ibid. 112.
10 Badiou, "Language, Thought, Poetry," 241.
11 Ibid.
12 Ibid.
13 Ibid. 242.
14 Maurice Blanchot, *The Infinite Conversation*, trans. Susan Hanson (Minneapolis and London: University of Minnesota Press, 1993), 106.
15 GG 98.
16 Blanchot, *The Infinite Conversation*, 107.
17 Ibid. 108.
18 FLN 147.
19 WG 130.
20 Leslie Fiedler, "Introduction," in WG xxvii.

Chapter 1

1 Sappho, *The Poems*, trans. Sasha Newborn (Santa Barbara, CA: Bandana Books, 2000), 27.

2 Gershom Scholem, *On the Kabbalah and Its Symbolism*, trans. Ralph Manheim (New York: Schocken Books, 1996), 32.

3 Ibid. 32–3.

4 Ibid. 5–6.

5 WG 47. There exists a cottage industry of biographers and commentators who obsess over Weil's Jewishness, or more generally attempt to psychologize her as a means of "understanding" her thought. With respect to the former obsession, many go so far as to insist that Weil's relationship with her Jewish identity is *the* central question in coming to know her thought. See, for examples: Palle Yourgrau, *Simone Weil* (London: Reaktion Books, 2011), esp. Chapter 8 "On the Jewish Question"; Thomas R. Nevin: *Simone Weil: Portrait of a Self-exiled Jew* (Chapel Hill, NC: University of North Carolina Press, 1991); and Robert Coles, *Simone Weil: A Modern Pilgrimage* (Woodstock, VT: Skylight Paths Publishing, 2001), esp. Chapter 3 "Her Jewishness." For an insightful discussion of the question of whether Weil could be "released" from her Jewish ethnicity by argument or otherwise, see Richard Bell, "Simone Weil, Post-Holocaust Judaism, and the Way of Compassion," in Richard H. Bell, *Simone Weil: The Way of Justice as Compassion* (New York: Rowan & Littlefield, 1998), Chapter 9.

6 WG xv. We will take up Weil's thinking about Judaism in the next chapter.

7 Whereas Weil learned to read ancient Greek at an early age, she never really learned Hebrew—although she did go on to learn other languages in her study of religion, such as Sanskrit.

8 WG 22.

9 Ibid. Emphasis added.

10 Ibid. 24. Emphasis added.

11 See: Simone Pétrement, *Simone Weil: A Life*, trans. Raymond Rosenthal (New York: Pantheon Books, 1976) and Gabriella Fiori, *Simone Weil: An Intellectual Biography*, trans. Joseph R. Berrigan (Athens, GA: University of Georgia Press, 1989).

12 T. S. Eliot wrote, "We must simply expose ourselves to the personality of a woman of genius, of a kind of genius akin to that of the saints" ("Preface," in NR viii). Or, for instance, even her critic Emmanuel Levinas said of Weil, "She lived like a saint and bore the suffering of the world" (Emmanuel Levinas, "Simone Weil against the Bible," in *Difficult Freedom: Essays on Judaism*, trans. Seán Hand [Baltimore,

MD: The Johns Hopkins University Press, 1990], 133). Her niece,
Sylvie Weil, has recently published an autobiographical account of her
experiences growing up in the shadows of such a "saint"; see: Sylvie
Weil, *At Home with André and Simone Weil*, trans. Benjamin Ivry
(Evanston, IL: Northwestern University Press, 2010).

13 Leslie Fiedler, "Introduction," in WG xv. Accounts of Weil's childhood
are especially prone to such flourish, reminiscent of stories of saints'
divinely inspired speech and miracles. For example, Weil was a sickly
child and in October 1913 she came down with influenza. She was
ordered to lie still on her back for long periods of time. As Gabriella
Fiori writes it, "She does so 'without any complaint whatsoever,'
as her *dumbfounded* mother observes" (Fiori, *Simone Weil*, 15;
emphasis added). Or, in November 1914, her mother Selma is again
left speechless when her daughter—then aged five-and-a-half—was
shivering cold while being bathed, calmed herself and asked, "Why
are you trembling you carcass?" (Ibid.).

14 WG 24. Emphasis added. Elsewhere she writes, "I have never once had,
even for a moment, the feeling that God wants me to be in the Church.
I have never even once had a feeling of uncertainty" (Ibid. 31).

15 See: E. Jane Doering, *Simone Weil and the Specter of Self-Perpetuating
Force* (Notre Dame, IN: University of Notre Dame Press, 2010) and
Sylvie Courtine-Denamy, *Three Women in Dark Times: Edith Stein,
Hannah Arendt, and Simone Weil*, trans. G. M. Goshgarian (Ithaca,
NY: Cornell University Press, 2000).

16 WG 142.

17 Well after her death, stories started to circulate that Weil had in fact
been baptized by her close friend, Simone Deitz, *in extremis* on her
deathbed. For a full account and analysis of the plausibility of this
story, see: Eric O. Springsted, "The Baptism of Simone Weil," in *Spirit,
Nature, and Community: Issues in the Thought of Simone Weil*,
Diogenes Allen and Eric. O. Springsted (Albany, NY: State University
of New York Press, 1994), 3–18.

18 WG 4–5. Later in the same letter she writes, "I love the six or seven
Catholics of genuine spirituality whom chance has led me to meet in
the course of my life. I love the Catholic liturgy, hymns, architecture,
rites, and ceremonies. But I have not the slightest love for the Church
in the strict sense of the word, apart from its relation to all these
things that I do love" (Ibid. 8).

19 "I think that only those who are above a certain level of spirituality
can participate in the sacraments as such . . . I think I am below this
level . . . I consider myself to be unworthy of the sacraments" (Ibid. 5).

20 Ibid.

21 See: E. Jane Doering and Eric O. Springsted, eds, *The Christian*

Platonism of Simone Weil (Notre Dame, IN: University of Notre Dame Press, 2004).

22 Plato, *Republic*, BK VII in *The Complete Works of Plato*, ed. John M. Cooper (Indianapolis, IN: Hackett, 1997).

23 GG 53.

24 Ibid. 55.

25 Ibid. 56. Emphasis added.

26 Ibid. 61.

27 Ibid. 115. See also: Bartomeu Estelrich, "Simone Weil on Modern Disequilibrium," in *The Relevance of the Radical: Simone Weil 100 Years Later*, ed. A. Rebecca Rozelle-Stone and Lucian Stone (New York: Continuum, 2010), 3–17.

28 LP 45.

29 It is useful to compare this point to what Freud wrote in his essay "The Future of an Illusion" namely: "Where questions of religion are concerned, people are guilty of every possible sort of dishonesty and intellectual misdemeanor. Philosophers stretch the meanings of words until they retain scarcely anything of their original sense. They give the name of 'God' to some vague abstraction which they have created for themselves." Sigmund Freud, *The Freud Reader*, ed. Peter Gay (New York: W.W. Norton & Company, 1989), 705.

30 GG 60.

31 "The Great Beast is the only object of idolatry, the only *ersatz* of God, the only imitation of something which is infinitely far from me and which is I myself" (Ibid. 164).

32 Ibid. 57.

33 Plato, *Phaedo*, 64a in *Complete Works*.

34 LP 44.

35 Ibid. 38–9.

36 GG 165.

37 Cf. n. 28.

38 Plato, *Republic*, BK VI, esp. 493a–4a.

39 Plato, *Republic*, BK VI, 494a in *Complete Works*, 1116.

40 Plato, *Republic*, BK VI, 493b–c, 1115. Emphasis added.

41 It is worth noting Neil Postman's interpretation contrasting George Orwell's and Aldous Huxley's dystopian novels, *1984* and *Brave New World* respectively. He feared that Huxley was more correct than Orwell in that the latter envisioned an external force would be required to suppress free thinking and activity, whereas the former, Huxley, thought that it would be those very things that humans enjoy—are amused by—that will lead to their own undermining. See: Neil Postman, *Amusing Ourselves to Death: Public Discourse in the Age of Show Business* (New York, Penguin, 1985), vii–viii.

42 GG 166.

43 "A crowd—not this crowd or that, the crowd now living or the crowd
   long deceased, a crowd of humble people or of superior people, of
   rich or of poor, &c.—a crowd in its very concept is the untruth, by
   reason of the fact that it renders the individual completely impenitent
   and irresponsible, or at least weakens his sense of responsibility by
   reducing it to a fraction." Søren Kierkegaard, *The Point of View for
   my Work as an Author: A Report to History and Related Writings*,
   trans. Walter Lowrie (New York: Harper & Brothers, 1962), 112.
44 GG 165.
45 WG 11.
46 Ibid. 5.
47 GG 166.
48 SWA 235.
49 Matthew 4:8–11.
50 WG 12.
51 For an incisive philosophical discussion of the self-help movement, see
   Charles Guignon, *On Being Authentic* (New York: Routledge, 2004).
52 GG 167.
53 As Alain Badiou writes, "The very idea of a consensual 'ethics'. . . is a
   powerful contributor to subjective resignation and acceptance of the
   status quo." Alain Badiou, *Ethics*, trans. Peter Hallward (New York:
   Verso, 2001), 32.
54 See Chapter 2 for an extensive treatment of Weil's ideas concerning
   other religious traditions.
55 WG 32.
56 Ibid. 12.
57 For a detailed account of the historical tracings of Weil's thought as
   a direct response to the rise of Hitlerism, see Doering, *Simone Weil*,
   Chapter 3.
58 WG 37. See also her remarks: "I should like to draw your attention to
   one point. It is here that there is an absolutely insurmountable obstacle
   to the Incarnation of Christianity. It is the use of the two little words
   anathema sit. It is not their existence, but the way they have been
   employed up till now. It is that also which prevents me from crossing
   the threshold of the Church" (WG 33) and "The Thomist conception
   of faith implies a 'totalitarianism' as stifling as that of Hitler, if not
   more so. For the mind gives its complete adherence, not only to what
   the Church has recognized as being strictly necessary to faith, but
   furthermore to whatever it shall at any time recognize as being such,
   the intelligence has perforce to be gagged and reduced to carrying out
   servile tasks" (LP 38–9).
59 Doering, *Simone Weil*, 78.
60 "[A] nation as such cannot be the object of supernatural love. It has
   no soul. It is a Great Beast" (GG 169).

61 Elsewhere Weil emphasizes the point that behind identitarian
    abstractions "there is an actual human group"; that is, there are real
    human beings who breathe, suffer, and die (SWA 235).
62 A fruitful comparison can be made between Weil's thinking on this
    issue and Albert Camus'. In his "Letters to a German," Camus argues
    that one can love one's country, but, for him, true patriotism requires
    that citizens "conquer themselves first." As he writes, "I cannot believe
    that everything must be subordinated to a single end. There are
    means that cannot be excused. And I should like to be able to love my
    country and still love justice." Albert Camus, "Letters to a German,"
    in *Resistance, Rebellion, and Death*, trans. Justin O'Brien (New York:
    Vintage, 1974), 5–6.
63 GG 169.
64 WG 11. Again, this is reminiscent of Camus who wrote, "We had
    much to overcome—and, first of all, the constant temptation to
    emulate you [Nazis]. For there is always something in us that yields
    to instinct, to contempt for intelligence, to the cult of efficiency. Our
    great virtues eventually become tiresome to us. We become ashamed
    of our intelligence, and sometimes we imagine some barbarous state
    where truth would be effortless" (Camus, "Letters to a German," 7).
65 SWA 221.
66 Ibid.
67 Ibid. 222. Emphasis added. See also: A. Rebecca Rozelle-Stone and
    Lucian Stone, "The 'War' on Error? Violent Metaphor and Words
    with Capital Letters," in *The Relevance of the Radical: Simone Weil
    100 Years Later*, ed. A. Rebecca Rozelle-Stone and Lucian Stone (New
    York: Continuum, 2010), 139–58.
68 Hannah Arendt, *On Violence* (New York: Harvest, 1970), 65.
69 GG 53.
70 Ibid. 115.
71 Ibid. 114. At the age of twenty-one, Weil wrote a dissertation
    titled, "Science and Perception in Descartes," under the direction
    of the influential French philosopher and educator Émile Chartier
    (1868–1951) in which she performs her own version of the Cartesian
    meditations. See FW 31–88.
72 See especially, Jean-Luc Marion, *Being Given: Toward a
    Phenomenology of Givenness*, trans. Jeffrey L. Kosky (Stanford, CA:
    Stanford University Press, 2002).
73 See: Anthony J. Steinbock, *Phenomenology & Mysticism: The
    Verticality of Religious Experience* (Bloomington: Indiana University
    Press, 2007).
74 LP 62.
75 Ibid.

76 WG 22.

77 Ibid. 28.

78 Simone Weil, "A Few Reflections on the Notion of Value," trans. E. Jane Doering in *Cahiers Simone Weil* XXXIV(4) (December) 2011, 459–60.

79 GG 60.

80 Cf. n. 16.

81 WG 13. She writes elsewhere: "I am afraid of the Church patriotism existing in Catholic circles" (WG 12).

82 See Bernard McGinn, *The Foundations of Mysticism: Origins to the Fifth Century*, vol. 2 of *The Presence of God* (New York: Crossroad, 2005), Chapter 5.

83 WG 34.

84 Ibid. 34–5.

85 Ibid.

86 Ibid.

87 Ibid.

88 Steinbock, *Phenomenology & Mysticism*, 6.

89 "The metaphor of the 'veil' or the 'reflection' applied by the mystics to faith enables them to escape from this suffocating atmosphere. They accept the Church's teaching, not as the truth, but as something behind which the truth is to be found" (LP 39).

90 Steinbock, *Phenomenology & Mysticism*, 1.

91 Ibid. 4.

92 WG 22.

93 Ibid. 27.

94 Weil, "A Few Reflections on the Notion of Value," 461.

95 "I wish and implore that my imperfection may be wholly revealed to me in so far as human thought is capable of grasping it. Not in order that it may be cured but, even if it should not be cured, in order that I may know the truth" (GG 58).

96 A contemporary cynic might "diagnose" her psychologically as a masochist. But if we are to believe her own account, then we must dismiss this type of speculation. As she writes, "I do not mean, of course, that I have a preference for orders of this [hellish] nature. I am not perverse like that" (WG 31).

97 Ibid. 25.

98 Ibid. 26.

99 Ibid.

100 Ibid.

101 Ibid.

102 Ibid.

103 Ibid.

104 Ibid. 27.
105 Ibid. 27.
106 Weil, "A Few Reflections on the Notion of Value," 462. The French
     philosopher Pierre Hadot has lamented the historical shift in how
     philosophers have come to perceive and practice philosophy in con-
     temporary time. See: *Philosophy as a Way of Life*, ed. Arnold I.
     Davidson (Oxford: Blackwell, 1995) and *What is Ancient Philoso-
     phy?*, trans. Michael Chase (Cambridge, MA: Belknap Press of
     Harvard University Press, 2002).
107 Plato, *Phaedrus*, 249d, in *Complete Works*, 527.
108 WG 27.
109 Ibid. 28.

Chapter 2

1 Martin Buber, *I and Thou*, trans. Walter Kaufmann (New York:
   Touchstone Books, 1996), 123.
2 LP 9.
3 Ibid. 9–10. Emphasis added.
4 Ibid. 55.
5 GG 19.
6 Ibid. 89.
7 Ibid. 20. She also writes, "Deprivation of the future—void, loss of
   equilibrium. That is why 'to philosophise is to learn to die.' That is
   why 'to pray is like a death'" (Ibid.).
8 Ibid. 91. Similarly she writes, "When the whole universe weighs
   upon us there is no other counterweight possible but God himself—
   the true God, for in this case false gods cannot do anything, not even
   under the name of the true one. Evil is infinite in the sense of being
   indefinite: matter, space, time. Nothing can overcome this kind of
   infinity except true infinity. That is why on the balance of the cross
   a body which is frail and light which was God, lifted up the whole
   world. 'Give me a point of leverage and I will lift up the whole
   world.' This point of leverage is the cross. There can be no other. It
   has to be at the intersection of the world and that which is not the
   world. The cross is this intersection" (Ibid. 93).
9 Weil writes, "To be just it is necessary to be naked and dead—
   without imagination," and "[t]hat is why the model of justice has
   to be naked and dead. The cross alone is not open to imaginary
   imitation" (Ibid. 88).
10 Ibid. 90.
11 Ibid. 87.

12 Ibid. 88.
13 Ibid. 87.
14 Ibid.
15 In the following passage she emphasizes the correlation between God and necessity: "From human misery to God. But not as a compensation or consolation. As a correlation" (Ibid. 91).
16 Ibid. 90.
17 Ibid. 88–9.
18 Ibid. 88. Emphasis added.
19 Ibid. 89.
20 "Christ is the proportional mean between God and the Saints. The very word mediation indicates this" (LP 24).
21 GG 90.
22 LP 70.
23 Perhaps not coincidentally, of late there has been a surge of interest in political theology. See, for example: Giorgio Agamben, *The Kingdom and the Glory: For a Theological Genealogy of Economy and Government*, trans. Lorenzo Chiesa (Stanford, CA: Stanford University Press, 2011); Simon Critchley, *The Faith of the Faithless: Experiments in Political Theology* (London: Verso, 2012); and Clayton Crockett, *Radical Political Theology: Religion and Politics After Liberalism* (New York: Columbia University Press, 2011). For a comprehensive overview of Weil's ideas concerning colonialism see the wonderful collection of letters and essays translated and edited by J. P. Little, *Simone Weil on Colonialism: An Ethic of the Other* (New York: Rowman and Littlefield, 2003). Arguably the colonial mindset persists. The occupation of sovereign nation states by Western powers (e.g., Iraq and Afghanistan), calls for regime change, and other aggressive steps pursuing Western hegemony have been accompanied by Christian missionary discourses. Beginning with former president George W. Bush's use of the term "crusade" to describe the American invasions of Afghanistan and Iraq, to the abundance of reports exposing the conjoining of evangelical Christianity with the US military's missions in these Islamic countries (including evidence of the spreading of anti-Islamic propaganda and Christian proselytizing), it is clear that the Western imagination remains wedded to what Weil diagnoses as an unholy alliance between religion and the state. For example, it has been reported that some US military personnel serving in Afghanistan and Iraq wear patches reading "Pork Eating Crusader" around a picture of a medieval knight with a red cross on his breastplate eating a leg of pork or a patch that reads "Infidel" in both Arabic and English (Eric German, "Sewing Discord: American Troops are in the Market for Patches that Mock the Muslim Faith," *The Daily*, March 18, 2012 (www.thedaily.com/page/2012/03/18/031812-news-infidel-gear-1–2/).

24 LP 31–2. Emphasis added.
25 Ibid. 30. Emphasis added.
26 SWC 108. Emphasis added. In her letter to Father Couturier she writes, "The missionaries—even the martyrs amongst them—are too closely accompanied by guns and battleships for them to be true witnesses of the Lamb" (LP 33).
27 GG 87.
28 In *The Need for Roots*, she writes, "Uprootedness occurs whenever there is a military conquest, and in this sense conquest is nearly always an evil" (NR 44).
29 LP 33.
30 Ibid. 30.
31 Ibid. 29. Emphasis added.
32 In 1995, Robin Wright wrote an article in *The Guardian* calling the Iranian philosopher Abdolkarim Soroush, "the Martin Luther of Islam." This and related sentiments have become a common refrain in the Western media, academic circles, and during ecumenical dialogues. See: Robin Wright, "An Iranian Luther Shakes the Foundations of Islam," *The Guardian*, February 1, 1995 (reprinted and retrieved from: www.drsoroush.com/English/News_ Archive/E-NWS-19950201–1.html). For a scholarly assessment of just how far Soroush's philosophy truly "shakes the foundations of Islam," see, Hamid Dabashi, "Blindness and Insight: The Predicament of a Muslim Intellectual," in *Iran: Between Tradition and Modernity*, ed. Ramin Jahanbegloo (New York: Lexington Books, 2004), 95–116.
33 LP 65. Statements like this have led some scholars to suggest that Weil was perhaps influenced by and, thus, numbered among the Perennial Philosophy movement (*Philosophia Perennis*, also commonly referred to as Traditionalist Philosophy). See, for example, Frithjof Schuon, *The Transcendent Unity of Religions*, with an Introduction by Huston Smith (Wheaton, IL: Quest, 1993). The direct link drawn between Weil and Perennial Philosophy is through her relationship with René Daumal (1908–44), who loaned her books on Sanskrit grammar, the *Bhagavad Gita*, and other works related to Hindu philosophy and who assisted her studies (See: Pétrement, *Simone Weil*, 394, and 421–2). Xavier Accart has made the connection between Weil and the influential Perennial Philosopher René Guénon. See: "*Simone Weil découvre l'œuvre de Guénon par l'intermédiaire de Daumal*," in Xavier Accart, *Guénon ou le renversement des clartés: Influence d'un métaphysicien sur la vie littéraire et intellectuelle française (1920– 1970)* (Paris: Edidit – Milan: Archè, 2005), 607ff.
34 WG 118.

35 Ibid. 118–19.

36 LP 33–4. Emphasis added.

37 WG 136.

38 For a thorough and insightful account of Weil's reading of the *Bhagavad Gita*, see: "Simone Weil and the *Bhagavad-Gita*," Chapter 6 of Doering, *Simone Weil*, 151–82.

39 In the letter to Father Couturier she writes, "Zeus, in the *Iliad*, orders no cruelty whatever" (LP 13). Posthumously, two collections of her essays were published, which elaborate her readings of ancient Greek texts and teachings ranging from the *Iliad*, *Antigone*, various writings of Plato, and Pythagoreanism: *Le Source Grecque* and *Les Intuitions Pré-chrétiennes*. A collection of representative writings from these sources has been translated into English as *Intimations of Christianity among the Ancient Greeks*, trans. E. C. Geissbuhler (London: Routledge, 1988), as well as *On Science, Necessity, and the Love of God*, trans. Richard Rees (London: Oxford University Press, 1968).

40 She revered the ancient Egyptian sacred writings; for example, she writes, "The Egyptian *Book of the Dead*, at least three thousand years old, and doubtless very much older, is filled with evangelic charity" (LP 13). Or, later in her letter, she elaborates extensively: "His words: 'I am the Way' should be compared with the Chinese 'Tao,' a word signifying literally 'the way' and metaphorically, on the one hand the method of salvation, and on the other hand the impersonal God who is the God of Chinese spirituality, but who, although impersonal, is the model for the wise and acts continually. His words: 'I am the Truth' call to mind Osiris, Lord of Truth. When in one of his most important teachings he says: 'They which do the truth,' he uses an expression which is not a Greek one, and which, as far as I know, is not a Hebrew one (must verify this). On the other hand, it is an Egyptian one. *Maât* means at the same time justice and truth. That is significant. No doubt it is not for nothing that the Holy family went down into Egypt" (Ibid. 27–8).

41 Weil writes, "Greek mythology is full of prophecies; so are the stories drawn from European folklore, what are known as fairy tales" (Ibid. 20), and elsewhere she adds, "Any number of accounts drawn from mythology and folklore could be translated into Christian truths without forcing or deforming anything in them, but rather, on the contrary, thus throwing a vivid light upon them. And these truths, would in their turn, thereby take on new clarity" (Ibid. 28–9).

42 Ibid. 37.

43 This is the basic logic of Perennial philosophy, Cf. fn. 32. See, Schuon, *The Transcendent Unity of Religions*.

44 LP 47.

45 Ibid. 17–18. Emphasis added.
46 Cf. fn. 37 (IC).
47 Cf. fn. 30.
48 LP 16.
49 Ibid. 19.
50 Part of her letter to Thibon has been reproduced in his introduction to *Gravity and Grace* (GG xiii–xv). Particularly noteworthy is the following passage: "I do not know whether I have already said it to you, but as to my notebooks, you can read whatever passages you like from them to whomever you like, but you must leave none of them in the hands of anyone else" (Ibid. xiv).
51 Thomas Nevin argues that "nothing Weil wrote can safely be extracted as though it had attained resolution" in *Simone Weil: Portrait of a Self-exiled Jew*, 454. Nevin's "Bibliographical Essay" in his volume, pages 453–78, is an extremely useful reference for those interested in Weil studies.
52 Nevin, *Simone Weil: Portrait of a Self-exiled Jew*, 454.
53 Lawrence E. Schmidt, "Simone Weil's Understanding of Judaism Considered in the Context of Eric Voegelin's *Israel and Revelation*, A Reflection Inspired by Palle Yourgrau," unpublished essay presented at the 32nd Annual Colloquy of the American Weil Society held at the University of Notre Dame, March 22–5, 2012.
54 David Tracy, "Simone Weil: The Impossible," in *The Christian Platonism of Simone Weil*, ed. E. Jane Doering and Eric O. Springsted (Notre Dame, IN: University of Notre Dame Press, 2004), 231.
55 Lawrence E. Schmidt, "Simone Weil's Understanding of Judaism Considered in the Context of Eric Voegelin's *Israel and Revelation*, A Reflection Inspired by Palle Yourgrau."
56 Levinas, "Simone Weil against the Bible," 133. Emphasis added.
57 GG 77.
58 One exception to this observation is found in her *Notebooks*. There she acknowledges that, "there is a Mohammedan esotericism [Sufism]." However, she goes on to claim, "There must also be a Christian influence by way of Byzantium" (NB 102). In other words, the one positive light in Islam—its mystical tradition—she reckoned must be due to the external influence of Christianity.
59 Levinas, "Simone Weil against the Bible," 135. Levinas also writes, "She contrasts the Bible, which she knows poorly, with 'chosen bits' of civilizations foreign to Europe. Although 'digestible' texts fill the Old Testament, she treats them as exceptions and attributes them to strangers, but with a disconcerting generosity goes into ecstasies over the slightest trace of the Divine, which crosses distant worlds like the Moon" (136).

60 LP 16.
61 Although she found sections and some figures within Jewish sacred literature redeemable—Abel, Enoch, Noah, Melchisedek (GG 159), as well as "Isaiah, Job, the Song of Solomon, Daniel, Tobias, part of Ezekiel, part of the Psalms, part of the Books of Wisdom, the beginning of Genesis . . ." (LP 64)—she concludes, "The rest is indigestible, because it is lacking in an essential truth which lies at the heart of Christianity and which the Greeks understood perfectly well—namely, the possibility of the innocent suffering affliction. In the eyes of the Hebrews. . .sin and affliction, virtue and prosperity go hand-in-hand, which turns Jehovah into an earthly not a heavenly Father, visible and not invisible. He is thus a false god" (Ibid.). But as Levinas rightly notes, "she treats [the Scriptures] as historical books whenever they support her thesis, and false whenever they disturb it" (Levinas, "Simone Weil against the Bible," 135).
62 GG 161. Similarly she writes, "Israel was an attempt at supernatural social life" (Ibid. 160).
63 "Israel stood up to Rome because its God, even though immaterial, was a temporal sovereign on par with the Emperor . . ." (Ibid. 161).
64 FLN 214.
65 Ibid.
66 Ibid.
67 NB 102.
68 LP 14–15.
69 Levinas, "Simone Weil against the Bible," 134.
70 GG 160.
71 Abraham Joshua Heschel, *The Prophets* (Peabody, MA: Hendrickson Publishers, 2009), viii.
72 Gil Anidjar, *The Jew, the Arab: A History of the Enemy* (Stanford, CA: Stanford University Press, 2003).
73 Matthew 10:36. Anidjar discusses the particular use Augustine makes of this biblical verse in *City of God*; see, Anidjar, *The Jew, the Arab*, 20ff.
74 Anidjar, *The Jew, the Arab*, 38. The quote from Aquinas in this passage is from St. Thomas Aquinas, *Summa contra Gentiles*, trans. A. C. Pegis et al. (Notre Dame, IN: University of Notre Dame Press, 1975), I.2 as quoted in Anidjar.
75 GG 161.
76 Levinas, "Simone Weil against the Bible," 140.
77 Doering, *Simone Weil*, 73.
78 Ibid. 78. Emphasis added.
79 GG 167.
80 Doering, *Simone Weil*, 78–9. Emphasis added.

81 GG 172.

82 WG 94.

83 Ibid. 95. Emphasis added.

84 LP 38, 39–40. Emphasis added.

85 Ibid. 40.

86 Gerhard Kittel, ed., *Theological Dictionary of the New Testament*, ed. and trans. Geoffrey W. Bromiley (Grand Rapids, MI: WM. B. Eerdmans Publishing, 1964), 354. It is also interesting to note that the Hebrew term *herem* (related to the Arabic word *haram*) is translated as *anathema* in Greek; see, G. Johannes Botterweck and Helmer Ringgren, *Theological Dictionary of the Old Testament*, vol. V, trans. David E. Green (Grand Rapids, MI: WM. B. Eerdmans Publishing, 1986), 182. We are thankful to our colleague Charles Miller for his assistance in clarifying these points.

87 Here there is an important distinction between Weil's treatment of Islam and Judaism. She spares Islam any blameworthiness for the corruptions of Christianity, in particular, and even to modernity to a large extent. Because Christianity has inherited much of its civilization from the Roman Empire and Judaism, however, the latter receives the majority of her attention and the full brunt of her critique.

88 In her *Notebooks* she writes, "[Jesus] came into Israel—and his disciples were spread abroad in the Roman world—because up to then Israel and Rome had been denied any veritable revelation" (NB 103).

89 GG 162.

90 Ibid. 160. "Christendom has become totalitarian, conquering, and exterminating, because it has not developed the idea of God's absence and non-activity here below. It has attached itself to Jehovah no less than to Christ, and conceived of Providence in the manner of the Old Testament" (Ibid. 159).

91 Ibid. 162.

92 Weil contends that a prevalent yet mistaken theology of Christianity can be attributed to the fact that it worships YHWH, not Christ. She writes, "Christendom has become totalitarian, conquering, and exterminating, because *it has not developed the idea of God's absence and non-activity here below. It has attached itself to Jehovah* no less than to Christ, and conceived of Providence in the manner of the Old Testament. Only Israel could stand up to Rome, because it resembled it; and this is how the birth of Christianity was marked with the Roman stain before it became the official religion of the Empire" (Ibid. 159; emphasis added).

93 Pétrement, *Simone Weil*, 390.

94 SWR 79.

95 Ibid. 80.

96 Ibid.
97 Ibid.
98 Ibid.
99 Ibid.
100 Ibid. 81.
101 Pétrement, *Simone Weil*, 392.
102 Ibid.
103 Levinas, "Simone Weil against the Bible," 133.
104 Ibid. 140.
105 Ibid. 135.
106 WG 118–19. Emphasis added.
107 Levinas, "Simone Weil against the Bible," 134.
108 The lectures as well as transcripts from the ensuing discussions between these figures have since been published: Eduardo Mendieta and Jonathan Vanantwerpen, eds, *The Power of Religion in the Public Sphere* (New York: Columbia University Press, 2011).
109 Judith Butler, "Is Judaism Zionism?" in Eduardo Mendieta and Jonathan Vanantwerpen, eds, *The Power of Religion in the Public Sphere* (New York: Columbia University Press, 2011), 70–91.
110 Jewish authored literature on these issues is growing exponentially. See for examples: Peter Beinart, *The Crisis of Zionism* (New York: Times Books, 2012); Ilan Pappe, *The Ethnic Cleansing of Palestine* (Oxford: Oneworld, 2006); Gabriel Piterberg, *The Returns of Zionism: Myths, Politics and Scholarship in Israel* (London: Verso, 2008); and Shlomo Sand, *The Invention of the Jewish People* (London: Verso, 2009).
111 Butler, "Is Judaism Zionism?" 73.
112 Ibid. 77.
113 Ibid. 83.
114 Ibid. 74.
115 Levinas, "Simone Weil against the Bible," 139.
116 Butler, "Is Judaism Zionism?" 84.
117 Ibid. 88.

Chapter 3

1 Blaise Pascal, *Pensées*, trans. A. J. Krailsheimer (London: Penguin Books, 1995), 212–13.
2 WG 88.
3 GG 32.
4 WG 89.
5 NB 234.

6 GG 32–3.
7 Ibid. 64.
8 WG 89.
9 NB 236.
10 GG 10. Emphasis added.
11 Cf. Guignon, *On Being Authentic*.
12 NB 421. See also NB 471–2. Freud wrote, for example: "The erotic instincts appear to be altogether more plastic, more readily diverted and displaced than the destructive instincts." He later described erotic cathexes as having "a peculiar indifference in regard to the object." Sigmund Freud, "The Ego and the Id," in *The Freud Reader*, 649.
13 See, for example: Ibid. 639, 649–50.
14 Ibid. 649. Weil is unequivocal in her views of Freud's theory: "Only in the stupidity of the present day could the idea of sublimation arise" (GG 63).
15 Freud, "Civilization and Its Discontents," *The Freud Reader*, 728.
16 Freud, "Beyond the Pleasure Principle," *The Freud Reader*, 622.
17 Plato, *Symposium*, 189e–92e.
18 Anne Carson, *Eros: The Bittersweet* (Champaign, IL: Dalkey Archive, 2000), 68.
19 Plato, *Symposium*, 205e–6a, in *Complete Works*, 488–9. Emphasis added.
20 Iris Murdoch, *Metaphysics as a Guide to Morals* (New York: Penguin Books, 1992), 502.
21 NB 236.
22 GG 7.
23 SWR 90.
24 GG 16.
25 Pascal, *Pensées*, 37–8.
26 GG 16.
27 Ibid. 3.
28 Ibid. 2–3.
29 Rainer Maria Rilke, "Imaginary Career," *The Selected Poetry of Rainer Maria Rilke* (New York: Vintage International, 1989), 259.
30 GG 7.
31 Murdoch, *Metaphysics as a Guide to Morals*, 502–3.
32 GG 61.
33 Pascal, *Pensées*, 38–9. Emphasis added.
34 SWA 52.
35 Ibid.
36 GG 6.
37 Ibid. 712.
38 Ibid. 73, 72.

39 Ibid. 73.
40 On this point, a useful comparison may be made to Hannah Arendt's notion of "the banality of evil." See Hannah Arendt, *Eichmann in Jerusalem: A Report on the Banality of Evil* (New York: Penguin, 1964).
41 GG 69.
42 Ibid. For further discussion of false imitation of God (ersatz divinity), see Chapter 1.
43 Ibid. 70.
44 Ibid. 76–7.
45 Ibid. 77.
46 In an unpublished article titled "Gravity and Grace as 'Trends' of the Being and the Soul," presented at the 32nd Annual Colloquy of the American Weil Society, University of Notre Dame, March 23, 2012, Emmanuel Gabellieri has convincingly argued that rather than being identified with good and evil respectively, grace and gravity appear in Weil's works as "*conditions* of existence and at some other times as *effects* of freedom" (2).
47 SWR 90.
48 GG 77.
49 Miklos Vetö, *The Religious Metaphysics of Simone Weil*, trans. Joan Dargan (Albany, NY: SUNY, 1994), 11.
50 GG 32.
51 Ibid.
52 NB 469.
53 WG 61. She writes, "Attention [one manifestation of decreation] is an effort, the greatest of all efforts perhaps, but it is a negative effort."
54 GG 26.
55 Ibid. 62.
56 Ibid. 33.
57 Ibid.
58 NB 82.
59 Ibid. 83.
60 GG 40.
61 NB 87.
62 GG 40.
63 SNL 160.
64 GG 70.
65 Ibid.
66 SNL 162.
67 Ibid. 160.
68 WG 77.
69 Ibid.

Chapter 4

1 Sophocles, *Antigone*, as seen in *Sophocles I: Oedipus the King, Oedipus at Colonus, Antigone*, 2nd edn, trans. David Grene (Chicago: University of Chicago Press, 1991), 192.
2 Irving Singer, *The Nature of Love 1: Plato to Luther* (Cambridge, MA: MIT Press, 2009), 47.
3 SNL 89.
4 Anne Carson notes that "in the popular moral thinking of the day [ancient Greece], self-control or *sophrosyne* [was] the rule of an enlightened life." She goes on to argue, as do we, that ultimately, Socrates subverts this norm, vindicating the takeover of eros as a divine mania. *Eros: The Bittersweet*, 154.
5 Weil writes, ". . . It is God alone who comes down and possesses the soul, but desire alone draws God down . . . . Attention is an effort, the greatest of all efforts perhaps, but it is a negative effort" (WG 61).
6 SWA 69.
7 SNL 105.
8 SWA 72.
9 Plato, *Phaedrus*, 244a, in *Complete Works*, 522.
10 SNL 106.
11 Singer, *The Nature of Love*, 84–5.
12 Rush Rhees, *Discussions of Simone Weil*, ed. D. Z. Phillips (Albany, NY: SUNY, 2000), 110.
13 Plato writes, "It follows that Love *must* be a lover of wisdom and, as such, is in between being wise and being ignorant," 204b, in *Complete Works*, 487.
14 Singer, *The Nature of Love*, 48–9.
15 Plato, *Phaedrus*, 257a, in *Complete Works*, 533.
16 Singer, *The Nature of Love*, 63.
17 Ibid.
18 Plato, *Phaedrus*, 251a–b, in *Complete Works*, 528.
19 SNL 118.
20 Plato, *Symposium*, 219a, in *Complete Works*, 500.
21 SNL 126.
22 Ibid. 126–7.
23 Ibid. 127.
24 Ibid.
25 GG 124.
26 Michel Foucault, *Discipline and Punish: The Birth of the Prison*, 2nd edn, trans. Alan Sheridan (New York: Vintage, 1995), 25.
27 Aristotle, *Nicomachean Ethics*, 2nd edn, trans. Terence Irwin (Indianapolis, IN: Hackett, 1999), 110–11.

28 Susan Peake, Lenore Manderson, and Helen Potts, "'Part and Parcel of Being a Woman': Female Urinary Incontinence and Constructions of Control," *Medical Anthropology Quarterly* 13(3), 279.
29 Ibid. 276. Emphasis added.
30 Susan Bordo, *Unbearable Weight* (Berkeley: University of California Press, 1995), 147–8.
31 Ibid. 148.
32 Elizabeth Grosz, "Sexed Bodies," in *Continental Feminism Reader*, ed. Ann Cahill and Jennifer Hansen (New York: Rowman and Littlefield, 2003), 299.
33 Carson, *Eros: The Bittersweet*, 36.
34 NB 483.
35 GG 33.
36 NB 483.
37 bell hooks, "Choosing the Margin as a Space of Radical Openness," in *Women, Knowledge, and Reality: Explorations in Feminist Philosophy*, 2nd edn, ed. Ann Garry and Marilyn Pearsall (New York: Routledge, 1997), 51.
38 NB 23.
39 SNL 106.
40 Refer to our discussion of Rilke's notion of "blood-remembering" in the Introduction.
41 GG 125.
42 Ibid. 87.
43 Ibid. 88.
44 SNL 127.
45 GG 123.
46 WG 79.
47 Ibid.
48 Weil, "A Few Reflections on the Notion of Value," 459.
49 WG 79.
50 Weil, "A Few Reflections on the Notion of Value," 459.
51 WG 78.
52 GG 91.
53 Carson, *Eros: The Bittersweet*, 155.
54 Ibid.
55 Carson tells us: "Change of self is loss of self, according to the traditional Greek attitude. Categorized as madness, it is held to be an unquestionable evil . . . Wings, in traditional poetry, are the mechanism by which Eros swoops upon the unsuspecting lover to wrest control of his person and personality. Wings are an instrument of damage and a symbol of irresistible power. When you fall in love, change sweeps through you on wings and you cannot help but lose your grip on that cherished entity, your self" (*Eros: The Bittersweet*, 154, 155–6).

56 GG 63.
57 Weil, "A Few Reflections on the Notion of Value," 459.
58 bell hooks, "Choosing the Margin as a Space of Radical Openness," 49.
59 GG 126–7.
60 WG 61, 62.
61 SNL 121.
62 GG 120.
63 Huston Smith, *The World's Religions* (New York: HarperCollins, 1991), 339.
64 GG 55. This statement also implies a critique of Pascal's Wager. While Pascal admits that we are "incapable of knowing either what [God] is or whether he is," he argues that we must *wager* that God exists because this choice aligns most with our interests and has the most potential for increasing (and not decreasing) our future happiness. Pascal, *Pensées*, 122. Thus, such an orientation to God, for Weil, would be purely based on self-interest and hence "greedy."
65 GG 149.
66 Ibid. 53.
67 Weil, "A Few Reflections on the Notion of Value," 460.
68 Sara Ruddick, "Injustice in Families: Assault and Domination," in *Justice and Care: Essential Readings in Feminist Ethics*, ed. Virginia Held (Boulder, CO: Westview, 1995), 212.
69 Ibid. 212–13.
70 We will explain the relationship between beauty and Weilienne attention in more detail in the next chapter.
71 Peggy McIntosh, "White Privilege, Male Privilege," in *Applied Ethics: A Multicultural Approach*, 4th edn, ed. Larry May, Shari Collins-Chobanian, and Kai Wong (Alexandria, VA: Prentice Hall, 2005), 454.
72 Ibid. 456.
73 Sara Ruddick, *Maternal Thinking: Toward a Politics of Peace* (Boston: Beacon, 1995), 122.
74 SNL 109.
75 WG 100.
76 Ibid.
77 SWA 52. Emphasis added.
78 GG 105.
79 WG 86–7.
80 Ruddick, "Injustice in Families," 204.
81 WG 85.
82 See Guy Debord's *Society of the Spectacle*, trans. Donald Nicholson-Smith (New York: Zone Books, 1995).
83 SNL 109.

84 For instance, Theodor Adorno writes, "The masochistic mass culture is the necessary manifestation of almighty production itself. When the feelings seize on exchange value it is no mystical transubstantiation. It corresponds to the behavior of the prisoner who loves his cell because he has been left nothing else to love." Theodor Adorno, *The Culture Industry* (New York: Routledge, 2001), 40.

85 GG 63.

86 Steven J. Sandage, T. W. Wiens, and C. M. Dahl, "Humility and Attention: The Contemplative Psychology of Simone Weil," *Journal of Psychology and Christianity* 20(4) (2001), 364.

87 FLN 260. Emphasis added.

88 Ibid. 141.

89 It is important to note, as Emma Craufurd points out, that the English word "affliction" is somewhat insufficient to express the French meaning of *malheur*. "Our word *unhappiness* is a negative term and far too weak. Affliction is the nearest equivalent but not quite satisfactory. *Malheur* has in it a sense of inevitability and doom" (Emma Craufurd, WG 67).

90 GG 150.

91 Ibid. 80.

92 SWA 203.

93 WG 50.

94 SWA 203.

95 GG 65.

96 SWA 201.

97 Ibid. 54.

98 Ibid. 55.

99 WG 73.

100 SWA 203.

101 SNL 106.

102 WG 83.

103 Weil contends that the implicit love of God can have only three objects, or things, "here below in which God is really though secretly present": love of religious ceremonies, the beauty of the world, and our neighbor, and also perhaps friendship, which Weil thinks distinct from love of neighbor (Ibid.).

104 Ibid. 101.

105 SWA 65.

106 GG 11. Elsewhere, Weil writes, "It was perhaps better not to be a martyr. The God from whom the martyrs drew joy in torture or death is close to him who was officially adopted by the Empire and afterward imposed by means of exterminations" (Ibid. 84).

107 WG 67.

108 Ibid. 68.
109 Consider Richard Kearney's illuminating discussion of monsters in *Strangers, Gods and Monsters* (New York: Routledge, 2003).
110 WG 67.
111 Ibid. 69.
112 Ibid.
113 GG 123.
114 WG 70.
115 GG 81.
116 WG 72.
117 For more on the disturbing popularity of websites that post videos of real-life sadism and human suffering, and the subsequent trend of videotaping oneself watching such images and then posting *those* videos on the Internet, see Tracy Clark-Flory's "Let's Watch a Murder," *Salon*, June 9, 2012 (www.salon.com/2012/06/10/lets_watch_a_murder/singleton/).
118 WG 73.
119 Ibid. 75.
120 Ibid. 90.
121 Ibid. 64.
122 Ibid. 138.
123 FLN 286.
124 SWA 77.
125 J. M. Perrin and G. Thibon, *Simone Weil as We Knew Her*, trans. Emma Craufurd (London: Routledge, 2003), 23, 30.
126 Ibid. 114.
127 SL 13.
128 E. W. F. Tomlin, *Simone Weil* (Cambridge: Bowes & Bowes, 1954), 12–13.
129 SWA 77.
130 Ibid. 78.
131 Ibid. 76–7, 78.
132 GG 14.
133 D. Z. Phillips in "Editor's Preface" to Rush Rhees, *Discussions of Simone Weil*, ed. D. Z. Phillips (Albany: State University of New York Press, 2000), viii.
134 Rhees, *Discussions of Simone Weil*, 110.
135 Phillips, "Editor's Preface," in *Discussions of Simone Weil*, ix.
136 Rhees, *Discussions of Simone Weil*, 106, 107.
137 Ibid. 107.
138 Ibid. 108, 121.
139 Ibid. 110.
140 Ibid. 112, 113, 120.

141 Jean-Luc Marion's account of "the gift" will be useful in clarifying why Weil's notion of charity, in fact, requires *detachment*, not *attachment*. Jean-Luc Marion, *Being Given: Toward a Phenomenology of Givenness*, trans. Jeffrey L. Kosky, (Stanford, CA: Stanford University Press, 2002).

142 GG 65–6.

143 Rhees, *Discussions of Simone Weil*, 106.

144 GG 19.

145 Anthony Steinbock, in his phenomenological study of hope, writes: "I describe hope as directed principally toward the future, as engaged and sustainable, and as oriented to what is beyond myself. As such the experience of hope is essentially distinct from other experiences such as expectation, probability, wishing, longing, and denial, and is foundational for the experience of hopelessness" ("Hoping against Hope," in *Essays in Celebration of the Founding of the Organization of Phenomenological Organizations*, ed. Cheung, Chan-Fai, Ivan Chvatik, Ion Copoeru, Lester Embree, Julia Iribarne, and Hans Rainer Sepp. Web-published at www.o-p-o.net, 2003, 2). Although he affirms hope as a phenomenon that is futurally oriented, as a kind of engagement, hope is distinct from imagining or wishing, for Steinbock. Yet the way in which Rhees uses the word "hope"—to hope that things will go one way for the beloved and not another means "that I ought to hope he has not died and that he will not die"— indicates an equivocation with a void (future)-filling imagination, in our view (Rhees, *Discussions of Simone Weil*, 107).

146 Vance G. Morgan, *Weaving the World* (Notre Dame, IN: University of Notre Dame Press, 2005), 87.

147 SWA 202.

148 GG 18.

149 Rhees, *Discussions of Simone Weil*, 107.

150 Marion, *Being Given*, 86.

151 Matthew 25:37–9. Weil herself writes: "'I was an hungered, and ye gave me meat.' When was that, Lord? They did not know. We must not know when we do such acts" (GG 45).

152 Ibid.

153 Ibid.

154 Ibid. 46.

155 WG 91.

156 GG 68.

157 Ibid.

158 Rhees, *Discussions of Simone Weil*, 108.

159 Ibid.

160 GG 149.

161 Ibid. 23. In this respect, see also Anne Carson's discussion of Sappho's poetry in "What Does the Lover Want from Love?" in *Eros: The Bittersweet*, 62–3.
162 Emily Dickinson, *Selected Poems*, ed. Christopher Moore (New York: Gramercy Books, 1993), 26.
163 Rhees, *Discussions of Simone Weil*, 113.
164 Nel Noddings, "Caring," in *Justice and Care*, ed. Virginia Held (Boulder, CO: Westview Press, 1995), 18.
165 Jane Addams, *Democracy and Social Ethics* (Chicago: University of Illinois Press, 2002), 6. Emphasis added.
166 Ibid.
167 GG 64.
168 WG 114.
169 Matthew 19:24–6.
170 WG 119.
171 Ibid. 135–6.
172 Ibid. 142.
173 Ibid.
174 Rhees, *Discussions of Simone Weil*, 110.
175 GG 14.
176 Ibid. 30.
177 Emmanuel Levinas, *Totality and Infinity*, trans. Alphonso Lingis (Pittsburgh: Duquesne University Press, 2000), 201.
178 Ibid. 73.
179 Ibid. 75.
180 Ibid. 78.
181 Ibid. 254.
182 GG 65.
183 WG 135.
184 Levinas, *Totality and Infinity*, 263.
185 Ibid. 266.
186 GG 67.
187 Ibid. 38.
188 Ibid.
189 Ibid. 144.
190 Ibid. 95.

Chapter 5

1 Rainer Maria Rilke, "What Birds Dive through Is Not That Intimate Space," in *The Poetry of Rilke*, trans. Edward Snow (New York: North Point, 2009), 583.
2 GG 149.

3 Sushil Kumar Saxena, "The Aesthetic Attitude," *Philosophy East and West* 28(1) (January 1978), 81.

4 Ibid.

5 GG 149.

6 WG 105.

7 Andrew McGhie, *Pathology of Attention* (Middlesex, England: Penguin Books, 1969), 28.

8 Michael and Abigail Lipson, "Psychotherapy and the Ethics of Attention," *Hastings Center Report*, January–February 1996, 18. Weil may disagree with the moral equivalency of "I have done well" and "I have done badly." In "Reflections on the Right Use of School Studies with a View to the Love of God," she writes that one condition of putting studies to the right use is the attentive and slow contemplation of "each school task in which we have failed, seeing how unpleasing and second rate it is, without seeking any excuse of overlooking any mistake or any of our tutor's corrections, trying to get down to the origin of each fault" (WG 59–60). The point would be to recognize one's inherent mediocrity and thus humility, which would be entirely different from being conscious of one's sinful nature, in that the latter may give us a sense of pride.

9 NB 179.

10 Pascal, *Pensées*, 39.

11 GG 164.

12 FLN 146.

13 SNL 133.

14 Salomé Voegelin, *Listening to Noise and Silence: Towards a Philosophy of Sound Art* (New York: Continuum, 2010), 83.

15 GG 69–70.

16 Weil writes, "When . . . a man turns away from God, he simply gives himself up to the law of gravity. Then he thinks that he can decide and choose, but he is only a thing, a stone that falls" (WG 75).

17 FLN 286.

18 SNL 149.

19 Ibid. 149–50.

20 LOP 184.

21 Ibid. 189.

22 Vetö, *The Religious Metaphysics of Simone Weil*, 90.

23 GG 43.

24 Ann Pirruccello, "Interpreting Simone Weil: Presence and Absence in Attention," *Philosophy East and West* 45(1) (January 1995), 67.

25 WG 105.

26 SNL 133.

27 WG 105.

28 Pirruccello, "Interpreting Simone Weil," 67.
29 SNL 164.
30 T. S. Eliot, "Religion and Literature," in *Religion and Modern Literature: Essays in Theory and Criticism*, ed., G. B. Tennyson and Edward E. Ericson, Jr (Grand Rapids, MI: Eerdmans, 1975), 21.
31 GG 151.
32 Richard Kearney, *The Wake of Imagination* (Minneapolis: University of Minnesota Press, 1988), 8–9.
33 Ibid. 9.
34 Ibid. 12.
35 SNL 167.
36 Ibid.
37 Ibid.
38 Adorno, *The Culture Industry*, 49.
39 Ibid. 49–50. Emphasis added.
40 Actually, Adorno says that "their primitivism is not that of the undeveloped, but that of the forcibly retarded" (Ibid. 47).
41 Ibid. 51.
42 Ibid. 52.
43 Ibid. 48.
44 Ibid.
45 Ibid. 50.
46 Ibid. 49.
47 Ibid. 41.
48 Paula Varsano, translator, in the Preface to François Jullien, *In Praise of Blandness* (New York: Zone Books, 2004), 12.
49 GG 1.
50 Ibid. 130.
51 Ibid. 4.
52 LOP 184. All five traits—duration, purity, infinity, no flattery, and universality—are listed in this text, pp. 184–5.
53 GG 149.
54 Ibid. 148.
55 Ibid. 149. However, Michel Sourisse contends, "In music . . . this distance is abolished. That is why it envelops us on all sides. Space limitations being lifted, we abandon ourselves to the bewitching power of sounds that subjugate us like a magical charm." Michel Sourisse, "Simone Weil and Music," in *The Beauty that Saves: Essays on Aesthetics and Language in Simone Weil*, ed., John M. Dunaway and Eric O. Springsted (Macon, GA: Mercer University Press, 1996), 123–4.
56 Ibid. 131–2.
57 Ibid. 131.

58 SWA 73.
59 Ibid. 55.
60 Ibid. 57.
61 SNL 165.
62 SWA 67.
63 Ibid. 69.
64 SNL 162.
65 SWA 55.
66 SNL 161.
67 Ibid. 162.
68 Ibid. 160.
69 WG 77.
70 Ibid. 126.
71 SWA 72.
72 Wang Shizhen, as cited by François Jullien, in *In Praise of Blandness*, 116.
73 Ibid. 44.
74 WG 77.
75 SWA 78.
76 Jullien, *In Praise of Blandness*, 45.
77 Ibid.
78 Ibid.
79 Ibid.
80 Ibid. 66–7.
81 Ibid. 67.
82 Ibid.
83 Ibid. 104.
84 Ibid. 70.
85 Ibid.
86 GG 151.
87 Katherine T. Brueck, "The Tragic Poetics of Simone Weil," in *The Beauty That Saves: Essays on Aesthetics and Language in Simone Weil*, ed., John M. Dunaway and Eric O. Springsted (Macon, GA: Mercer University Press, 1996), 109. For an insightful and extended discussion of Weil's tragic, Christian conception of poetic beauty, see Katherine T. Brueck, *The Redemption of Tragedy: The Literary Vision of Simone Weil* (Albany, NY: SUNY, 1995).
88 Murdoch, *Metaphysics as a Guide to Morals*, 90.
89 Ibid. 104.
90 SL 104.
91 Cornel West, *Democracy Matters* (New York: Penguin Books, 2004), 20. For instance, West describes, "For too many in white America the blues remains a kind of exotic source of amusement, a kind of primitivistic

occasion for entertainment only. The blues is not simply a music to titillate; it is a hard-fought way of life, and as such it should unsettle and unnerve whites about the legacy of white supremacy" (20).

92 IC 18–23.

93 IC 20.

94 Sophocles, *Antigone*, 178.

95 IC 21.

96 Ibid. 23.

97 SWA 63.

98 William Robert, *Trials: Of Antigone and Jesus* (New York: Fordham University Press, 2010), 6.

99 Ibid.

100 Jacques Derrida, *Apories: Mourir—s'attendre aux "limites de la vérité"* (Paris: Galilée, 1996), 25; trans. by Thomas Dutoit as *Aporias: Dying—Awaiting (One Another at) the "Limits of Truth"* (Stanford: Stanford University Press, 1993), 8, as quoted in Robert, *Trials: Of Antigone and Jesus*, 6.

101 Sophocles, *Antigone*, 164.

102 Robert, *Trials: Of Antigone and Jesus*, 36.

103 Sophocles, *Antigone*, 164.

104 GG 122.

105 Ibid.

106 Ibid. 148.

107 Diotima reminds us of this character of Beauty in Plato's *Symposium*. When we are in the presence of the beautiful, we are impregnated with inspiration and give birth to more beauty.

108 GG 151.

109 Ibid.

110 In Martin Buber's words, an "ordered world" is erected and "does not give itself to you," while the "world order" cannot be fabricated, it "comes even when not called and vanishes even when you cling to it" (*I and Thou*, 83).

111 WG 107. Emphasis added.

112 Ibid. Moreover, Weil tells us, "Luxury itself represents beauty for a whole class of men. It provides surroundings through which they can feel in a vague fashion that the universe is beautiful" (Ibid. 106).

113 Chris Hedges, *War is a Force that Gives us Meaning* (New York: Anchor Books, 2003), 6–7. It is no accident that Hedges employs a term—"void"—so familiar to Weil, for he is deeply influenced by her thought and references her in his book.

114 SNL 149.

115 Tom Gjelten, "Karadzic Was Once Considered a Moderate by Many," *NPR* (July 24, 2008) (www.npr.org/templates/story/story. php?storyId=92878854).

116 WG 116–17.
117 Murdoch, *Metaphysics as a Guide to Morals*, 90.
118 SNL 165.

Chapter 6

1 Simon Critchley, *Infinitely Demanding: Ethics of Commitment, Politics of Resistance* (New York: Verso, 2008), 38.
2 See for example, Thomas Rogers' "Our Kids' Glorious New Age of Distraction," *Salon*, August 21, 2011 (www.salon.com/2011/08/21/now_you_see_it_interview/).
3 GG 4.
4 In employing the terms "event" and "subjectivating," we are intentionally invoking the philosophy of Alain Badiou, whose ideas on grace, event, and love will help to systematize and clarify Weil's notion of the double movement of grace.
5 GG 4.
6 Ibid. 10.
7 Ibid. 10–11.
8 Ibid. 10.
9 Ibid. 11.
10 Badiou, *Ethics*, 41.
11 Vetö, *The Religious Metaphysics of Simone Weil*, 42.
12 GG 16.
13 Ibid. 33.
14 Ibid. 88.
15 Alain Badiou, *Saint Paul: The Foundation of Universalism*, trans. Ray Brassier (Stanford, CA: Stanford University Press, 2003), 91–2.
16 GG 18.
17 Badiou, *Ethics*, 47.
18 GG 3.
19 Ibid. 8.
20 Badiou, *Saint Paul*, 77.
21 GG 22.
22 Badiou, *Ethics*, 46.
23 WG 147.
24 GG 13. Emphasis added.
25 WG 93.
26 Ibid. 147.
27 GG 3.
28 WG 138.
29 GG 99.

30 Ibid.
31 Ibid.
32 Ibid. Emphasis added.
33 Ibid. 99–100.
34 Ibid. 101.
35 Ibid.
36 SNL 159.
37 Ibid.
38 Ibid.
39 Ibid. 151.
40 Ibid.
41 Ibid. 157. In this vein, Huxley writes, "Probably all persons, even the most saintly, suffer to some extent from distractions . . . [But] some of the most profitable spiritual exercises actually make use of distractions, in such a way that these impediments to self-abandonment, mental silence and passivity in relation to God are transformed into means of progress." The "lumps of sugar" in Weil's passage above may be analogous to the making "use" of distractions, here. Interestingly, Huxley argues, "We must give up the attempt to fight distractions and find ways either of circumventing them, or of somehow making use of them," for (alluding to Benet of Canfield in his *Rule of Perfection*) "the more a man operates, the more he is and exists. And the more he is and exists, the less of God is and exists within him" (Aldous Huxley, *The Perennial Philosophy*, [New York: Harper Perennial, 2009], 284).
42 SNL 157. Weil also said, in a letter to Father Perrin: "I may say that never at any moment in my life have I 'sought for God.' For this reason, which is probably too subjective, I do not like this expression and it strikes me as false. As soon as I reached adolescence, I saw the problem of God as a problem the data of which could not be obtained here below, and I decided that the only way of being sure not to reach a wrong solution, which seemed to me the greatest possible evil, was to leave it alone. So I left it alone" (WG 22).
43 GG 149.
44 FLN 141.
45 WG 93.
46 Ibid.
47 GG 23.
48 Ibid. 24. Matthew 6:2.
49 Ibid. 112.
50 Ibid. 112–13.
51 WG 100.
52 Ibid. 76.

53 Ibid.
54 Ibid. 77.
55 Alain Badiou, "Thinking the Event," in *Philosophy in the Present* (Malden, MA: Polity, 2009), 2.
56 Ibid. 5. Emphasis added.
57 Ibid. 4.
58 Ibid. 24.
59 Ibid. 23–4.
60 GG 44.
61 WG 75.
62 Ibid. 80.
63 GG 95.
64 Ibid. 46. Emmanuel Gabellieri offers an elucidating discussion of the "refusal of the gift" in Chapter 8, "*Décréation et Donation,*" of his book *Être et Don: Simone Weil et la Philosophie* (Paris: Éditions Peeters, 2003).
65 GG 94.
66 Ibid. 130.
67 SWA 71.
68 Slavoj Žižek, "Slavoj Žižek speaks at Occupy Wall Street: Transcript," *The Parallax/Impose Magazine*, October 25, 2011 (www.imposemagazine.com/bytes/slavoj-zizek-at-occupy-wall-stree t-transcript).
69 GG 95.
70 Judith Butler, "Judith Butler at Occupy Wall Street," *Salon*, October 24, 2011(http://www.salon.com/2011/10/24/judith_butler_at_occupy_ wall_street/).
71 SWA 66.
72 GG 132.

Conclusion

1 Paul J. Griffiths, *Religious Reading* (New York: Oxford University Press, 1999), ix.
2 Don Ihde, *Experimental Phenomenology: An Introduction* (Albany, NY: SUNY, 1986), 31.
3 WG 61.
4 GG 42. Emphasis added.
5 WG 58.
6 GG 99. Eric Springsted helpfully distinguishes three ways in which thoughts can be in opposition to each other for Weil: as paradox, as incommensuration, and as mystery. Paradox is the simple "opposition

between perceptions, thoughts, ideas or the predication of terms
that we need to solve in order to contemplate their truth." What
Weil means by "contradiction" is really a "method of investigation"
that "occurs whenever our intellect comes up against an unforeseen
obstacle that forces us to recast our thoughts in order to
accommodate it. In this sense," Springsted continues, "'contradiction'
is the sort of thing we set in front of our students' minds in order to
get them to think on their own by considering problems they have
not previously seen." Eric O. Springsted, "Contradiction, Mystery, and
the Use of Words in Simone Weil," in *The Beauty that Saves: Essays
on Aesthetics and Language in Simone Weil*, ed. John M. Dunaway
and Eric O. Springsted (Macon, GA: Mercer University Press, 1996),
14–15.

7 Weil, "A Few Reflections on the Notion of Value," 461–2, 461.
8 GG 98.
9 Ibid. 180, 181.
10 WG 59–60.
11 GG 40–1.
12 Anthony Steinbock, "Interpersonal Attention Through Exemplarity,"
Journal of Consciousness Studies 8(5–7) (2001), 187.
13 GG 83. Emphases added.
14 Weil, "A Few Reflections on the Notion of Value," 461.
15 WG 63.
16 GG 180.
17 WG 64.
18 NR 216. Emphasis added.
19 Ibid. 232.
20 Steinbock, "Interpersonal Attention Through Exemplarity," 188.
21 Ibid. 190.
22 GG 60–1.
23 Eliot, "Preface," viii.

BIBLIOGRAPHY

Accart, Xavier. *Guénon ou le renversement des clartés: Influence d'un métaphysicien sur la vie littéraire et intellectuelle française (1920– 1970)*. Paris: Edidit – Milan: Archè, 2005.

Addams, Jane. *Democracy and Social Ethics*. Chicago: University of Illinois Press, 2002.

Adorno, Theodor. *The Culture Industry*. New York: Routledge, 2001.

Agamben, Giorgio. *The Kingdom and the Glory: For a Theological Genealogy of Economy and Government*, trans. Lorenzo Chiesa. Stanford, CA: Stanford University Press, 2011.

Anidjar, Gil. *The Jew, the Arab: A History of the Enemy*. Stanford, CA: Stanford University Press, 2003.

Aquinas, St. Thomas. *Summa contra Gentiles*, trans. A. C. Pegis et al. Notre Dame, IN: University of Notre Dame Press, 1975.

Arendt, Hannah. *Eichmann in Jerusalem: A Report on the Banality of Evil*. New York: Penguin, 1964.

— *On Violence*. New York: Harvest, 1970.

Aristotle. *Nicomachean Ethics*, 2nd edn, trans. Terence Irwin. Indianapolis, IN: Hackett, 1999.

Badiou, Alain. *Ethics*, trans. Peter Hallward. New York: Verso, 2001.

— *Saint Paul: The Foundation of Universalism*, trans. Ray Brassier. Stanford, CA: Stanford University Press, 2003.

— "Language, Thought, Poetry." In *Theoretical Writings*, ed. and trans. Ray Brassier and Alberto Toscano. London and New York: Continuum, 2006.

Badiou, Alain and Slavoj Žižek. *Philosophy in the Present*, ed. Peter Engelmann, trans. Peter Thomas and Alberto Toscano. Cambridge: Polity, 2005.

Beinart, Peter. *The Crisis of Zionism*. New York: Times Books, 2012.

bell hooks. "Choosing the Margin as a Space of Radical Openness." In *Women, Knowledge, and Reality: Explorations in Feminist Philosophy*, 2nd edn, ed. Ann Garry and Marilyn Pearsall. New York: Routledge, 1997.

Bell, Richard H. *Simone Weil: The Way of Justice as Compassion*. New York: Rowan & Littlefield, 1998.

Blanchot, Maurice. *The Infinite Conversation*, trans. Susan Hanson. Minneapolis and London: University of Minnesota Press, 1993.

Bordo, Susan. *Unbearable Weight*. Berkeley: University of California Press, 1995.

Botterweck, G. Johannes and Helmer Ringgren. *Theological Dictionary of the Old Testament*, vol. V, trans. David E. Green. Grand Rapids, MI: WM. B. Eerdmans, 1986.

Brueck, Katherine T. *The Redemption of Tragedy: The Literary Vision of Simone Weil*. Albany, NY: SUNY, 1995.

— "The Tragic Poetics of Simone Weil." In *The Beauty That Saves: Essays on Aesthetics and Language in Simone Weil*, ed. John M. Dunaway and Eric O. Springsted. Macon, GA: Mercer University Press, 1996.

Buber, Martin. *I and Thou*, trans. Walter Kaufmann. New York: Touchstone Books, 1996.

Butler, Judith. "Is Judaism Zionism?" In *The Power of Religion in the Public Sphere*, ed. Eduardo Mendieta and Jonathan Vanantwerpen. New York: Columbia University Press, 2011.

— "Judith Butler at Occupy Wall Street," *Salon*, October 24, 2011. www.salon.com/2011/10/24/judith_butler_at_occupy_wall_street/ (retrieved January 10, 2012).

Camus, Albert. "Letters to a German." In *Resistance, Rebellion, and Death*, trans. Justin O'Brien. New York: Vintage, 1974.

Carson, Anne. *Eros: The Bittersweet*. Champaign, IL: Dalkey Archive, 2000.

Clark-Flory, Tracy. "Let's Watch a Murder," *Salon*, June 9, 2012. www.salon.com/2012/06/10/lets_watch_a_murder/singleton/ (retrieved June 10, 2012).

Coles, Robert, *Simone Weil: A Modern Pilgrimage*. Woodstock, VT: Skylight Paths, 2001.

Courtine-Denamy, Sylvie. *Three Women in Dark Times: Edith Stein, Hannah Arendt, and Simone Weil*, trans. G. M. Goshgarian. Ithaca, NY: Cornell University Press, 2000.

Critchley, Simon. *Infinitely Demanding: Ethics of Commitment, Politics of Resistance*. London: Verso, 2008.

— *The Faith of the Faithless: Experiments in Political Theology*. London: Verso, 2012.

Crockett, Clayton. *Radical Political Theology: Religion and Politics After Liberalism*. New York: Columbia University Press, 2011.

Dabashi, Hamid. "Blindness and Insight: The Predicament of a Muslim Intellectual." In *Iran: Between Tradition and Modernity*, ed. Ramin Jahanbegloo. New York: Lexington Books, 2004.

Debord, Guy. *Society of the Spectacle*, trans. Donald Nicholson-Smith. New York: Zone Books, 1995.

Derrida, Jacques. *Aporias: Dying – Awaiting (One Another at) the "Limits of Truth,"* trans. Thomas Dutoit. Stanford: Stanford University Press, 1993.

Dickinson, Emily. *Selected Poems*, ed. Christopher Moore. New York: Gramercy Books, 1993.

Doering, E. Jane. *Simone Weil and the Specter of Self-Perpetuating Force.* Notre Dame, IN: University of Notre Dame Press, 2010.

Doering, E. Jane and Eric O. Springsted, eds. *The Christian Platonism of Simone Weil.* Notre Dame, IN: University of Notre Dame Press, 2004.

Eliot, T. S. "Religion and Literature." In *Religion and Modern Literature: Essays in Theory and Criticism*, ed. G. B. Tennyson and Edward E. Ericson, Jr. Grand Rapids, MI: Eerdmans, 1975.

— "Preface." In *The Need for Roots*, trans. Arthur Wills. London: Routledge, 2002.

Estelrich, Bartomeu. "Simone Weil on Modern Disequilibrium." In *The Relevance of the Radical: Simone Weil 100 Years Later*, ed. A. Rebecca Rozelle-Stone and Lucian Stone. New York: Continuum, 2010.

Fiedler, Leslie. "Introduction." In Simone Weil, *Waiting for God*, trans. Emma Craufurd. New York: HarperCollins, 2001.

Fiori, Gabriella. *Simone Weil: An Intellectual Biography*, trans. Joseph R. Berrigan. Athens, GA: University of Georgia Press, 1989.

Foucault, Michel. *Discipline and Punish: The Birth of the Prison*, 2nd edn, trans. Alan Sheridan. New York: Vintage, 1995.

Freud, Sigmund. *The Freud Reader*, ed. Peter Gay. New York: W.W. Norton & Company, 1989.

Gabellieri, Emmanuel. *Être et Don: Simone Weil et la Philosophie.* Paris: Éditions Peeters, 2003.

— "Gravity and Grace as 'Trends' of the Being and the Soul," unpublished essay presented at the 32nd Annual Colloquy of the American Weil Society, University of Notre Dame, March 23, 2012.

German, Eric. "Sewing Discord: American Troops are in the Market for Patches that Mock the Muslim Faith," *The Daily*, March 18, 2012. www.thedaily.com/page/2012/03/18/031812-news-infidel-gear-1–2/ (retrieved June 10, 2012).

Gjelten, Tom. "Karadzic Was Once Considered a Moderate by Many," *NPR*, July 24, 2008. www.npr.org/templates/story/story.php?storyId=92878854 (retrieved June 10, 2012).

Griffiths, Paul J. *Religious Reading.* New York: Oxford University Press, 1999.

Grosz, Elizabeth. "Sexed Bodies." In *Continental Feminism Reader*, ed. Ann Cahill and Jennifer Hansen. New York: Rowman and Littlefield, 2003.

Guignon, Charles. *On Being Authentic.* New York: Routledge, 2004.

Hadot, Pierre. *Philosophy as a Way of Life*, ed. Arnold I. Davidson. Oxford: Blackwell, 1995.

— *What is Ancient Philosophy?* trans. Michael Chase. Cambridge, MA: Belknap Press of Harvard University Press, 2002.

Hedges, Chris. *War is a Force that Gives us Meaning.* New York: Anchor Books, 2003.

Heschel, Abraham Joshua. *The Prophets.* Peabody, MA: Hendrickson, 2009.

Huxley, Aldous. *The Perennial Philosophy.* New York: Harper Perennial, 2009.

Ihde, Don. *Experimental Phenomenology: An Introduction.* Albany, NY: SUNY, 1986.

Jullien, François. *In Praise of Blandness*, trans. Paula Varsano. New York: Zone Books, 2004.

Kearney, Richard. *The Wake of Imagination.* Minneapolis: University of Minnesota Press, 1988.

— *Strangers, Gods and Monsters.* New York: Routledge, 2003.

Kierkegaard, Søren. *The Point of View for my Work as an Author: A Report to History and Related Writings*, trans. Walter Lowrie. New York: Harper & Brothers, 1962.

Kittel, Gerhard, ed. *Theological Dictionary of the New Testament*, ed. and trans. Geoffrey W. Bromiley. Grand Rapids, MI: WM. B. Eerdmans Publishing, 1964.

Levinas, Emmanuel. "Simone Weil against the Bible." In *Difficult Freedom: Essays on Judaism*, trans. Seán Hand. Baltimore, MD: Johns Hopkins University Press, 1990.

— *Totality and Infinity*, trans. Alphonso Lingis. Pittsburgh, PA: Duquesne University Press, 2000.

Lipson, Michael and Abigail Lipson. "Psychotherapy and the Ethics of Attention," *Hastings Center Report* (January–February 1996).

McGhie, Andrew. *Pathology of Attention.* Middlesex, England: Penguin Books, 1969.

McGinn, Bernard. *The Foundations of Mysticism: Origins to the Fifth Century*, vol. 2 of *The Presence of God.* New York: Crossroad, 2005.

McIntosh, Peggy. "White Privilege, Male Privilege." In *Applied Ethics: A Multicultural Approach*, 4th edn, ed. Larry May, Shari Collins-Chobanian, and Kai Wong. Alexandria, VA: Prentice Hall, 2005.

Marion, Jean-Luc. *Being Given: Toward a Phenomenology of Givenness*, trans. Jeffrey L. Kosky. Stanford, CA: Stanford University Press, 2002.

Mendieta, Eduardo and Jonathan Vanantwerpen, eds. *The Power of Religion in the Public Sphere.* New York: Columbia University Press, 2011.

Morgan, Vance G. *Weaving the World.* Notre Dame, IN: University of Notre Dame Press, 2005.

Murdoch, Iris. *Metaphysics as a Guide to Morals.* New York: Penguin Books, 1992.

Nevin, Thomas R. *Simone Weil: Portrait of a Self-exiled Jew*. Chapel Hill: University of North Carolina Press, 1991.

Noddings, Nel. "Caring." In *Justice and Care*, ed. Virginia Held. Boulder, CO: Westview, 1995.

Pappe, Ilan. *The Ethnic Cleansing of Palestine*. Oxford: Oneworld, 2006.

Pascal, Blaise. *Pensées*, trans. A. J. Krailsheimer. London: Penguin Books, 1995.

Peake, Susan, Lenore Manderson, and Helen Potts. "'Part and Parcel of Being a Woman': Female Urinary Incontinence and Constructions of Control," *Medical Anthropology Quarterly* 13(3) (September 1999).

Perrin, J. M. and G. Thibon. *Simone Weil as We Knew Her*, trans. Emma Craufurd. London: Routledge, 2003.

Pétrement, Simone. *Simone Weil: A Life*, trans. Raymond Rosenthal. New York: Pantheon Books, 1976.

Phillips, D. Z. "Editor's Preface." In Rush Rhees, *Discussions of Simone Weil*, ed. D. Z. Phillips. Albany: State University of New York Press, 2000.

Pirruccello, Ann. "Interpreting Simone Weil: Presence and Absence in Attention," *Philosophy East and West* 45(1) (January 1995).

Piterberg, Gabriel. *The Returns of Zionism: Myths, Politics and Scholarship in Israel*. London: Verso, 2008.

Plato. *The Complete Works of Plato*, ed. John M. Cooper. Indianapolis, IN: Hackett, 1997.

Postman, Neil. *Amusing Ourselves to Death: Public Discourse in the Age of Show Business*. New York:, Penguin, 1985.

Rhees, Rush. *Discussions of Simone Weil*, ed. D. Z. Phillips. Albany, NY: SUNY, 2000.

Rilke, Rainer Maria. *The Notebooks of Malte Laurids Brigge*, trans. Stephen Mitchell. New York: Vintage International, 1990.

— *Rilke on Love and Other Difficulties*, trans. with commentary by John J. L. Mood. New York: W.W. Norton & Company, 2004.

Robert, William. *Trials: Of Antigone and Jesus*. New York: Fordham University Press, 2010.

Rogers, Thomas. "Our Kids' Glorious New Age of Distraction," *Salon*, August 21, 2011. www.salon.com/2011/08/21/now_you_see_it_interview/ (retrieved June 10, 2012).

Rozelle-Stone, A. Rebecca and Lucian Stone. "The 'War' on Error? Violent Metaphor and Words with Capital Letters." In *The Relevance of the Radical: Simone Weil 100 Years Later*, ed. A. Rebecca Rozelle-Stone and Lucian Stone. New York: Continuum, 2010.

Ruddick, Sara. *Maternal Thinking: Toward a Politics of Peace*. Boston: Beacon, 1995.

— "Injustice in Families: Assault and Domination." In *Justice and Care: Essential Readings in Feminist Ethics*, ed. Virginia Held. Boulder, CO: Westview, 1995.

Sand, Shlomo. *The Invention of the Jewish People*. London: Verso, 2009.

Sandage, Steven J., T. W. Wiens, and C. M. Dahl. "Humility and Attention: The Contemplative Psychology of Simone Weil," *Journal of Psychology and Christianity* 20(4) (2001).

Sappho. *The Poems*, trans. Sasha Newborn. Santa Barbara, CA: Bandana Books, 2000.

Saxena, Sushil Kumar. "The Aesthetic Attitude," *Philosophy East and West* 28(1) (January 1978).

Schmidt, Lawrence E. "Simone Weil's Understanding of Judaism Considered in the Context of Eric Voegelin's *Israel and Revelation*, A Reflection Inspired by Palle Yourgrau," unpublished essay presented at the 32nd Annual Colloquy of the American Weil Society, University of Notre Dame, March 22–25, 2012.

Scholem, Gershom. *On the Kabbalah and Its Symbolism*, trans. Ralph Manheim. New York: Schocken Books, 1996.

Schuon, Frithjof. *The Transcendent Unity of Religions*, with an Introduction by Huston Smith. Wheaton, IL: Quest, 1993.

Singer, Irving. *The Nature of Love 1: Plato to Luther*. Cambridge, MA: MIT Press, 2009.

Smith, Huston. *The World's Religions*. New York: HarperCollins, 1991.

Sophocles. *Antigone*, in *Sophocles I: Oedipus the King, Oedipus at Colonus, Antigone*, 2nd edn, trans. David Grene. Chicago: University of Chicago Press, 1991.

Sourisse, Michel. "Simone Weil and Music." In *The Beauty that Saves: Essays on Aesthetics and Language in Simone Weil*, ed. John M. Dunaway and Eric O. Springsted. Macon, GA: Mercer University Press, 1996.

Springsted, Eric O. "The Baptism of Simone Weil." In Diogenes Allen and Eric. O. Springsted, *Spirit, Nature, and Community: Issues in the Thought of Simone Weil*. Albany: State University of New York Press, 1994.

— "Contradiction, Mystery, and the Use of Words in Simone Weil." In *The Beauty that Saves: Essays on Aesthetics and Language in Simone Weil*, ed. John M. Dunaway and Eric O. Springsted. Macon, GA: Mercer University Press, 1996.

Steinbock, Anthony. "Interpersonal Attention Through Exemplarity," *Journal of Consciousness Studies* 8(5–7) (2001).

— "Hoping against Hope." In *Essays in Celebration of the Founding of the Organization of Phenomenological Organizations*, ed. Cheung, Chan-Fai, Ivan Chvatik, Ion Copoeru, Lester Embree, Julia Iribarne,

and Hans Rainer Sepp. Web-published at www.o-p-o.net, 2003
(retrieved June 10, 2012).

— *Phenomenology & Mysticism: The Verticality of Religious Experience.*
Bloomington: Indiana University Press, 2007.

Tomlin, E. W. F. *Simone Weil.* Cambridge: Bowes & Bowes, 1954.

Tracy, David. "Simone Weil: The Impossible." In *The Christian Platonism
of Simone Weil*, ed. E. Jane Doering and Eric O. Springsted. Notre
Dame, IN: University of Notre Dame Press, 2004.

Varsano, Paula. "Preface." In François Jullien, *In Praise of Blandness.*
New York: Zone Books, 2004.

Vetö, Miklos. *The Religious Metaphysics of Simone Weil*, trans. Joan
Dargan. Albany, NY: SUNY, 1994.

Voegelin, Salomé. *Listening to Noise and Silence: Towards a Philosophy
of Sound Art.* New York: Continuum, 2010.

Weil, Simone. *Seventy Letters*, trans. Richard Rees. New York: Oxford
University Press, 1965.

— *On Science, Necessity, and the Love of God*, trans. Richard Rees.
London: Oxford University Press, 1968.

— *First and Last Notebooks*, trans. Richard Rees. London: Oxford
University Press, 1970.

— *Oppression and Liberty*, trans. Arthur Wills and John Petrie. Amherst:
University of Massachusetts Press, 1973.

— *Simone Weil Reader*, ed. George A. Panichas. Wakefield, RI and
London: Moyer Bell, 1977.

— *Lectures on Philosophy*, trans. Hugh Price. Cambridge: Cambridge
University Press, 1978.

— *Simone Weil: An Anthology*, ed. Siân Miles. New York: Weidenfeld and
Nicolson, 1986.

— *Formative Writings 1929–1941,* trans. Dorothy Tuck McFarland and
Wilhelmina van Ness. Amherst: University of Massachusetts Press,
1987.

— *Intimations of Christianity among the Ancient Greeks*, trans. E. C.
Geissbuhler. London: Routledge, 1988.

— *Waiting for God*, trans. Emma Craufurd. New York: HarperCollins,
2001.

— *Gravity and Grace*, trans. Emma Crawford and Mario von der Ruhr.
London: Routledge, 2002.

— *Letter to a Priest*, trans. Arthur Wills. London: Routledge, 2002.

— *The Need for Roots*, trans. Arthur Wills. London: Routledge, 2002.

— *Simone Weil on Colonialism*, ed. and trans. J. P. Little. New York:
Rowman and Littlefield, 2003.

— *The Notebooks of Simone Weil*, trans. Arthur Wills. London:
Routledge & Kegan Paul, 2004.

— "A Few Reflections on the Notion of Value," trans. E. Jane Doering, in *Cahiers Simone Weil* XXXIV(4) (December 2011).

Weil, Sylvie. *At Home with André and Simone Weil*, trans. Benjamin Ivry. Evanston, IL: Northwestern University Press, 2010.

West, Cornel. *Democracy Matters*. New York: Penguin Books, 2004.

Wright, Robin. "An Iranian Luther Shakes the Foundations of Islam," *The Guardian*, February 1, 1995. Reprinted and retrieved from: www. drsoroush.com/English/News_Archive/E-NWS-19950201–1.html (retrieved June 10, 2012).

Yourgrau, Palle. *Simone Weil*. London: Reaktion Books, 2011.

Žižek, Slavoj. "Slavoj Žižek speaks at Occupy Wall Street: Transcript," *The Parallax/Impose Magazine*, October 25, 2011. www. imposemagazine.com/bytes/slavoj-zizek-at-occupy-wall-street-transcript (retrieved January 10, 2012).

INDEX